The Case for
Regional Reform

The Case for Regional Reform

Extracts from Essential Documents
Edited and Introduced by

W. Thornhill

Nelson

Thomas Nelson and Sons Ltd
36 Park Street London W1Y 4DE
PO Box 18123 Nairobi Kenya
Thomas Nelson (Australia) Ltd
597 Little Collins Street Melbourne 3000
Thomas Nelson and Sons (Canada) Ltd
81 Curlew Drive Don Mills Ontario
Thomas Nelson (Nigeria) Ltd
PO Box 336 Apapa Lagos
Thomas Nelson and Sons (South Africa) (Proprietary) Ltd
51 Commissioner Street Johannesburg

First published 1972

SBN 0 17 138041 X

Printed in Great Britain by Hazell Watson & Viney Ltd, Aylesbury, Bucks

Acknowledgements

The author and publishers would like to thank the following who kindly allowed extracts to be included from their publications:

Hutchinson University Library: C. B. Fawcett, *Provinces of England*. Clarendon Press, Oxford: R. J. Lawrence, *The Government of Northern Ireland*. Edinburgh University Press: J. N. Wolfe (ed), *Government and Nationalism in Scotland*. The Liberal Party Organisation: *Parliaments for the Future*. George Allen & Unwin Ltd: Sir David Milne, *The Scottish Office*; and W. A. Robson, *Local Government in Crisis* and *The Development of Local Government*. The Political Quarterly: P. A. Jones, *Post-War Machinery of Government*; 'Regionaliter', *The Regional Commissioners*; and D. Senior, *The City Region as an Administrative Unit*. Royal Institute of Public Administration: A. W. Peterson, *The Machinery for Economic Planning III*, from 'Public Administration' Spring 1966. BBC Publications: Patrick Beech, *New Dimensions in Regional Broadcasting* (BBC Lunchtime Lecture, March 1970). Architectural Press Ltd: Association for Planning and Regional Reconstruction, *A Preliminary Analysis of 42 Maps of Regional Boundaries*, (Report No. 42). Routledge and Kegan Paul Ltd: R. E. Dickinson, *City, Region and Regionalism*. 'Architect and Building News': E. G. R. Taylor: *Land and Plan*. R. D. P. Smith, *The Changing Urban Hierarchy*. Fabian Society: W. Sanders, *Municipalization by Provinces* (Fabian Tract No. 125). The Labour Party: *The Future of Local Government*. National and Local Government Officers Association: *Reform of Local Government*. Cassell and Co. Ltd: G. D. H. Cole, *The Future of Local Government*. 'The Economist': *Federal Britain's New Frontiers*. Her Majesty's Stationery Office: House of Commons Paper 233 (1953–4); Command Papers Nos. 692, 6502, 6153, 6579, 4040, 4040–1. 'The Times': Ronald Butt,

A Basis for Reform. County Councils Association: *Memorandum on the Report of the Royal Commission on Local Government in England.* Association of Municipal Corporations: *Reorganisation of Local Government: Proposals for a Dual System.* The Urban District Councils Association: *Evidence to the Commission on the Constitution.*

Contents

Preface

Interest in regionalism has ebbed and flowed in the years since 1945, sometimes as a kind of gravitational response to proposals for local government reform, sometimes for a variety of other reasons. Each new flow of interest seems to have caught popular opinion unawares; yet the ideas, if not the particular propositions put forward from time to time, are by no means new. Concern with regionalism can arise from such diverse causes as the desire to reform local government, the arguments for the devolution of power from central government, the work of a number of geographers, and a large number of *ad hoc* solutions to particular problems. This book aims to bring together for the convenience of the student and the general reader extracts from works which illustrate each of these major contributory sources.

My thanks are due to my colleague, Dr K. W. Watkins, for his editorial help and guidance, and to the staff of the Sheffield University Library, especially Mrs J. Crane, for willing and unstinted assistance in copying the extracts from books, journals and other sources.

W. Thornhill.
Sheffield,
October, 1970.

1

Introduction

The resurgence of interest in regionalism in the late nineteen-sixties, for the second time in a generation, can be explained in immediate terms by the creation of the economic planning boards and councils in 1965, by the electoral successes of the Scottish and Welsh Nationalists, and by the creation of the Commission on the Constitution at the beginning of 1969. In addition to all this, many of the proposals for local government reform extended to the idea of regional territories. What is the argument all about? Why has regionalism been resurrected so soon after its interment at the end of World War II? Why, in spite of the lack of interest by practising politicians, has the subject once more been brought to the stage of public discussion?

Notwithstanding the lack of political interest, during the period since the end of World War I a succession of administrative units have been organized on a regional base. All too often the regional solution has been an escape from existing unsatisfactory arrangements, particularly when local government units have been recognized as too small for the efficient performance of functions, whether existing functions as in the case of the management of police forces or proposed ones as in the case of hospitals in the national health service in 1948. Yet it would be wrong to assume that the movement for regionalism was solely, or even largely, based on arguments about the size of operating units. There were other equally significant factors at work.

Firstly, there is the desire of some people to encourage regional differences of culture, society, language and customs. This is usually assumed to be one of the important bases of Scottish and Welsh nationalism, and it has been apparent in parts of England too, for example in Cornwall and in East Anglia. It is not, of course, easy to equate cultural differences with the need for separate political or administrative institutions. Scotland has been able to retain its separate principles of law and justice without a separate parliament, but this has not prevented the development of Scottish nationalist movements from time to time. It is obvious that many people place great faith in the capacity of separate institutions to provide for their needs in their own way, yet there are many cases where this has not happened. Northern Ireland is an example; much of the legislation and administrative actions which have emanated from the Ulster institutions have slavishly followed the British precedents.

Secondly, there are some people who argue that the centralizing tendencies of the unitary state have gone too far and that it is necessary to weaken the power of the national institutions of government by reducing their functions and creating competing foci of power. This is another basis for nationalist movements, and it is also one of the arguments used to support the case for provincial parliaments. Those who put forward this case are not so much interested in fostering cultural diversity as in attacking the power of the central institutions. They are concerned about the great power of the central government and the consequent loss to the individual which arises from the impossibility of his seeking support in other institutions.

Thirdly, there is the argument that a highly centralized state is inefficient and that central government should be made more responsive to localized needs by some decentralization both of decision-taking and administration. The case for provincial parliaments often includes this assertion that the centralized institutions are inefficient. Apart from this, the continuing concern with the efficiency of government has led in recent years to suggestions that devolution or decentralization might help, for example, the proposals of the Fulton Committee on the Civil Service for 'hiving off' some activities from the central departments.

Finally, there is the argument that larger areas of administration are necessary to provide more efficient services. Changes in techniques of operation and of management have the double effect of requiring larger units of organization in order to yield their benefits, and also of facilitating the working of those larger units. This argument has been used to justify both the creation of *ad hoc* regional authorities and the reform of local government.

Though these arguments point in the same direction, they do not lead to a common solution. The different people who are concerned with these causes aim at different objectives. There is a wide gulf, for example, between the Scottish Nationalists and the regionalists in the local government reform movement. Even with a single problem there are different views on how to handle it. Thus, a variety of solutions have been put forward and though most have been described as 'regionalism' they exhibit wide divergencies. Some differences are due to the long time span over which the ideas have been put forward. Others reflect the pressures which have helped to determine the particular regional solutions which have been advocated for individual problems.

Such common factor as there is in all the diverse ideas which have been put forward lies in the general definition given to the term 'regionalism'. For the sake of brevity, we are not concerned with any semantic or philosophical problems about the relative merits of the terms 'regional' and 'regionalism' as against those of 'provincial' and 'provincialism'. For our purposes they are synonymous, and imply a system of political or administrative units intermediate between the state—the United Kingdom of Great Britain and Northern Ireland to give it its formal title—and the traditional local units of borough and county and their nineteenth-century manifestations. We are, then, concerned with a level of organization which is in limited use in our existing system of government.

The regional institutions already in existence are all administrative bodies; there are no *political* institutions organized on this level. The one possible exception is the Parliament of Northern Ireland, but the precise nature of this institution, whether it is a federal or a regional institution, is a matter upon which there is scope for argument. The regional organizations of central departments; the area boards in the nationalized industries; the regional hospital boards; the joint boards of local authorities; and the new combined police authorities, indicate the spread. The contemporary interest in regionalism arises partly from a desire to systematize this large number and variety of organizations, and also partly from the arguments put forward by those who wish to establish major political institutions on the regional base.

The number of the latter was boosted by various political events, of which the most dramatic, if not the most significant, were the campaigns of the Scottish and Welsh Nationalists which resulted in each getting a member elected to Parliament. At about the same time, the Isle of Man and Jersey showed signs of restiveness with their relationships with the United Kingdom. The Liberal Party, after only a minute increase in its parliamentary strength, saw its future lying in the creation of provincial parliaments; but its proposals, in spite of their concern for the party's self-preservation, were also an expression of popular rumblings of discontent at the increasing tendency towards the centralization of power in Westminster and Whitehall. Indeed, that centralization finds an expression in the one common feature of most of our present range of regional bodies: the absence of control by any group of directly-elected representatives.

Whether or not this lack of direct citizen control is undemocratic, it would be placing too great a strain on our electoral processes to provide popular elections to secure the membership of each of the governing boards of this vast number of organizations. The best practical way to bring most of them within the orbit of direct representative control would be to put them into the hands of a single directly-elected authority for each regional area. This would involve both the initial problem of compressing the separate organizations into uniform regional areas, and the continuing problem of creating and maintaining a representational system at the regional level. It is hardly likely, however, that all of these different organizations could be satisfactorily compressed into a single territorial mould, even though most of the differences can be traced to the separate development of the services involved, rather than to specific technical requirements.

On the other hand, the creation of a representative political body is probably the most contentious aspect of the concept of regionalism. The idea encounters opposition from the present political members at both the central and local levels. In the first place, regional politicians, almost certainly paid, directing vast enterprises which would affect the daily lives and environment of the people, would compete with national politicians for power and influence, or for prestige and loyalty. The idea of preserving the power of the central government over the direction and progress of the national economy, based on the argument that our state is too small and compact to require or permit of major provincial division, has already been used a number of times as a defence against the regional arguments. Yet whatever the merits of such a case, and there are merits, it is a convenient cloak for hiding the real argument which is basically the reluctance of the national politicians, especially those who enjoy or are likely to enjoy Government office, to share their power and prestige with other political groups.

Secondly, the opposition from local councillors to the creation of a regional political activity is equally motivated by self-interest. Regional politicians would take over some of the services now carried out by local authorities, leaving less for the local councillors. One of the arguments for reform in local government, both of structure and of management, is that a reformed system will attract a different type of person to the representative office. One of the avowed aims of the Redcliffe-Maud proposals was to reduce the total number of elective offices from about thirty thousand to about six thousand, a fact which has not been lost on the local party activists, who object to such a reduction of their influence. The creation of political representation at the regional level would undoubtedly strike a further blow at the position of a large number of contemporary office-holders.

The main difficulty is that we cannot predict with any certainty what the consequences would be if a political function were to be created at the regional level. Quite apart from the question of the kind of institutional relationships which would be created, partly by statute and partly by normal intercourse, between the central government and the regional authorities, we cannot even speculate about the type of people from whom the regional politicians would be drawn. The regional politicians might well be more akin to our Members of Parliament than to our local councillors. There would certainly be more scope for the full-time politician and less for the part-time volunteer, and there would also be considerable consequences for the internal structure of the political parties.

Whilst it may well be the case that there is little love for the regional idea amongst the politicians, there is no doubt that changes in communications, technology and in social life, have repeatedly forced regional solutions at the administrative level. Here lies a crucial question. The notion of the region is often dismissed as being arbitrary: useful, perhaps, from an administrative point of view, but politically impossible. Representation, it is argued, is a collective and participatory activity and politicians are elected to represent not individuals but groups of individuals, in the parliamentary constituency or the local government ward, to which electors have a sense of belonging. And, so it is argued, whilst people have a sense of belonging to the nation or to their local community, in the management of whose affairs they desire to participate, there is no regional focus which generates similar feelings. In this argument that there is no such thing as a regional community, lies the third source of objection to political regionalism.

The denial of the sense of community at the regional level has not gone unchallenged. Certain elements of regional foci have been developed, and these have sometimes found expression in *ad hoc* regional institutions, such as the North Eastern Development Council. The concept of the city-region which had been developed by the geographers long before it became an object of contention before the Royal Commission on Local Government, is essentially based on the recognition that there are social and economic factors which unify and bring a sense of common purpose to areas much greater than the basic local government units of the nineteenth century. There may not be the old sense of community—the evidence put before the Royal

Commission on Local Government showed that the sense of belonging which was implied by this emotive word was, in fact, of far more limited application in existing society than most people had supposed —but there is undoubtedly a complex mass of economic and social relationships underlying the 'city-region' which makes it reasonable for one to infer some element of common purpose and common interest amongst its inhabitants.

'Regionalism' thus embraces a number of different approaches to the concept of an intermediate level of government. The question is whether this intermediate tier is capable of absorbing the diverse institutions, political and administrative, which are put forward by the different protagonists. An effective and acceptable form of regional government would bring some order out of chaos and reduce most of this diversity to a clear, understandable system. The problem is whether the undoubted pressures for regional organization for administrative purposes are to be accompanied by a regional political movement. The documents which are brought together in the following chapters illustrate the various strands of controversy which comprise this problem.

Chapter
2
Regional Devolution

The devolution of central government activities is a key factor in the creation of effective regional government. Whether the aim is to reduce or offset the political power of highly centralized institutions, or simply to provide more effective and responsive administrative machinery, little progress has been made in this country. Devolution has found little favour, amongst either Members of Parliament or civil servants. The national interest and the need for effective economic planning have been plausible excuses behind which to hide the real reason: a reluctance to lose any of the strings of power.

Nevertheless, the British political system is littered with a large number of *ad hoc* examples or 'experiments' in devolution and/or decentralization from the central government. These have been responses to particular circumstances, and to this extent have not contributed to any systematic development of regional institutions. The apparent success of most of these arrangements in dealing with the problems for which they were originally established has made it easy for central politicians and officials to deny the need for more effective and unified regional institutions. Yet the very proliferation of these *ad hoc* devices is both an indication of the gap which exists in the regular structure of government and a factor which militates against the citizen's understanding of government and his ability to maintain effective relations with state agencies. The latter defect arises because most of the organs concerned are not directly controlled by elected representatives, so that democratic control is remote and sometimes ineffective.

This situation has arisen because the arguments for political and administrative devolution have developed separately, and little consideration has been given to the creation of regional governments with directly elected members controlling and supervising the work of regional officials. There are two reasons for this. One is the haphazard and partial nature of the developments which have taken place, and the other is the peculiar British refusal to countenance any movement which smacks of federalism. For instance, the institutions of government in Northern Ireland, which do not conform to any general classification, were not devised but were an historical accident: the residue of a larger system which never got off the ground. The contemporary movements of Scottish and Welsh nationalism only just, by their relatively minor successes in the late nineteen-sixties, brought tentative thoughts of federalism into the ambit of contemplation.

A regionalist development is probably more likely than a federalist one, if only because true federalism involves characteristics which are not under discussion. In a federal system, the powers of the state are shared by co-ordinate institutions, each of which is supreme in its own sphere. The usual pattern is a central or federal government exercising functions over the whole area of the state, and a series of regional or provincial governments carrying out other functions in their territories. The essence of federalism is a written constitution which defines the respective powers of the two levels of government, and a supreme judicial authority which can adjudicate on alleged contraventions of the division of power. None of the 'neo-federalist' suggestions for the United Kingdom have gone as far as this. They may produce something which looks like the pattern of federalism, a central government and regional or provincial assemblies, but they lack the essential constitutional and judicial safeguards of true federalism. The 'experiment' of Northern Ireland is not true federalism, and it seems unlikely that any true system would be established in the United Kingdom except under the threat of some kind of revolution.

The readings which are brought together in this chapter illustrate the partial character of the objectives with which they are concerned. All involve some form of devolution or decentralization from the central government to regional bodies, but they are grouped according to their broad objectives.

(a) Political Decentralization

Political devolution implies a sub-national level of political activity, such as the creation of provincial parliaments for the various parts of the United Kingdom, but that is the only common feature of the various proposals that have been put forward. The readings which follow show the variety of arguments which have been used.

Firstly let us take the simple idea of C. B. Fawcett that Parliament was overworked and must shed some of its functions to provincial assemblies to avoid breakdown. More than fifty years have elapsed since Fawcett put forward this view, but Parliament has shed nothing to other kinds of assemblies (apart from a small range of activities to the Ulster Parliament) and yet it is still in operation. In so far as parliamentary work has been reduced, this has been achieved by devices such as delegated legislation, not by devolution to other assemblies. Moreover, the span of activities comprehended by Parliament is now vastly greater than it was at the time that Fawcett wrote.

Fawcett's proposals were sometimes linked with the cry of 'Home rule all round', a reaction to the struggles over Ireland. But the Conference on Devolution which was appointed by the House of Commons in October 1919, and which was chaired by Mr Speaker, was as much concerned with the problem of freeing the Imperial Parliament from domestic matters to enable it to give more attention to the more 'general interests of the United Kingdom' and to matters 'of common Imperial concern'. The conference was not concerned with the desirability of devolution, but with the most practicable way of putting it into operation. The proceedings of the conference were overtaken by the Government of Ireland Bill, which became law in 1920, and the report was for this reason confined to Great Britain, though it recognized that Ireland might eventually be brought into the scheme. This, on the face of it, meant that devolution in Britain had nothing to do with the separate arrangements for Ireland, yet we cannot escape the fact that as the Irish went their own way the British parliamentary interest in devolution fizzled out.

The conference agreed that Scotland and Wales should form separate and undivided areas, but was less sure whether England should be a single unit or should be subdivided (it eventually settled on the former for the initial stage). A large measure of agreement was reached on the powers which should be devolved, on the financial arrangements and on the system of judicial administration, but there was a division of opinion about the character and composition of the subordinate bodies which should be established. The two schemes, one prepared by Mr Speaker and the other by Mr Murray Macdonald, which were published in the conference's report, are reproduced below.

The Government of Ireland Act, 1920, authorized the creation of separate legislatures and governments for Southern Ireland and for the six counties of the north-east, and topped the system with a Council for All Ireland. The southerners, for a variety of reasons, refused to operate their side of the system, leaving the arrangements for the six counties to work as best as the Ulstermen could manage. As a consequence, the government of Northern Ireland has operated much more as an element of internal devolution within the United Kingdom than was ever intended when its powers and institutions were originally devised. Its congenital deformities have since been aggravated by the contagious effects of bigotry. The riots of 1968 and subsequent years may well lead to further constitutional developments, but until these mature the best assessment is that given in the middle nineteen-sixties by R. J. Lawrence, in spite of its apparent wishful thinking.

The Scottish scene has been rather different. The Act of Union in 1707 allowed the Scots to retain their own distinctive principles of law and justice, and in spite of the fact that a separate parliamentary institution was not provided for, these distinctive features have not been lost. They have, to some extent, been consolidated by the growth of a separate system of local government in Scotland. Yet the unification of the central administration, the monetary system and the economy, and the absence of restrictions on movement between Scotland and England, which has led to a loss of population in Scotland and to some run-down of the economy, have given rise to a resistance. It is not possible to summarize in a simple manner the doctrine and aims of the contemporary Scottish Nationalists, nor those of the less extreme but still patriotic Scotsmen. The extracts show how confused the Scottish claims are.

Whilst the Scottish Nationalists appear to thrive on a bed of confliction – they frequently ignore the maintenance of the Scottish principles of law and justice, refuse to believe the credibility of the official statistical comparisons of the English and Scottish finances, and maintain an idealistic vision of the possibilities of the Celtic language – their Welsh counterpart, Plaid Cymru, has more realistic objectives. These are: a well-defined administrative structure; some devolution of decision-taking; and more scope for the use of the Welsh language, which has a firmer foundation and is more widely used than Gaelic in Scotland. These all seem reasonable enough, and yet the Welsh nationalists are no more successful than their Scottish brethren. The fact is that the nationalists in Scotland and in Wales, though perhaps growing in numbers, are very much minority groups. This applies equally to the Liberals throughout Great Britain, who see their continued existence having a greater likelihood in a system of subordinate legislatures throughout England as well as in Scotland and Wales. The most advanced ideas of the Liberal Party appeared in their evidence to the Commission on the Constitution, from which an extract is included.

The sad fact is that the proponents of political devolution have all so far been crying in the wilderness. The members of the Parliament of the United Kingdom and the officials of the centralized administrative system are the two strongest pressure groups against change. It is their support which must be won to any proposals for regional assemblies. To their natural distaste for any proposals designed to reduce their power, it is easy to add the arguments against devolution which arise from the necessities of national economic planning, and from the centripetal forces of modern communications. No one has yet argued the case for political devolution on its own merits, as an integral element in a rationally organized political system. Maybe the Commission on the Constitution will fill this gap.

Fawcett's *Provinces*

From C. B. Fawcett, *Provinces of England,* Williams and Norgate, London, 1919. pp. 17–29.

This extract gives Fawcett's arguments for the devolution of power from Parliament to subordinate parliaments for provincial areas in England. The interesting point that he makes is that the existing system of local government was already inadequate and could not hope to handle any powers devolved from the centre.

Introductory

Many suggestions for the devolution of some of the powers and duties of the Parliament of the United Kingdom to subordinate parliaments have been made in recent years. The steady demand for Home Rule for Ireland, and the extent to which that country has a separate administration for its local government, have kept this topic in the forefront of public life. Scotland also has in many respects a different legal and administrative system from that of England. As yet there is no such separate administration for Wales in the British Government; and the educational and registration systems of that country, and its local government in general, unlike those of Scotland and Ireland, are controlled from London along with those of England. But there is now a strong tendency towards the development of a Welsh administration, especially in educational matters; and the co-operation of Welsh local authorities, together with a revival of Welsh nationalism and the study of the Welsh language, has paved the way for a Welsh demand for Home Rule, akin to that which has long been demanded by Irish Nationalists. This demand has become articulate within the last two years. A similar tendency is traceable in Scotland. The satisfaction of these several demands for 'Home Rule All Round' would obviously involve the transformation of the United Kingdom of Great Britain and Ireland from a unified to a federal state. If such a change was made merely by setting up four separate national parliaments – for England, Scotland, Ireland and Wales respectively – it would lead to many difficulties in working inherent in the fact that one of the four constituent countries would have more than three-fourths of the total population and wealth of the union.[1] Under these

[1] Populations in 1911, from the *Statesman's Year Book*:

United Kingdom	45,370,530
England	34,045,290
Scotland	4,760,904
Ireland	4,390,219 }11,176,325
Wales	2,025,202

conditions, the Parliament of England would inevitably be so power-ful in the union as to be co-ordinate with, rather than subordinate to, the British Parliament. The English and British parliaments would both sit in London, and there would probably be some rivalry between them and a strong tendency for the former to dominate the federation. If Ireland had 'Dominion' Home Rule apart from the divisions of the larger island, the predominance of England in Great Britain would be still greater. A corresponding state of affairs existed from 1871 to 1918 in the German Federal Empire, where the Prussian and the Imperial German Parliaments met in Berlin. Prussia had a little less than two-thirds of the population,[1] and so was less overwhelmingly dominant in the German Empire than England is in the United Kingdom, but none the less Prussia so effectively dominated the whole Empire that the other states had very little influence on its government and policy. And Prussian dominance was not materially lessened by the fact that many of the leading statesmen and thinkers of the Empire were natives of the minor states. In a federal state in which no one of the partners is dominant, as in Canada, Australia and the United States of America, the smaller states have relatively much greater influence on the federal government and its policies. The advantage to the smaller constituents clearly lies in not having a too predominant partner; and it is arguable that this is also much better for the federal state as a whole and all its citizens.

The powers and duties of the British Parliament in the last two or three generations have fallen into three chief classes:

1. Those concerned with the British Commonwealth as a whole, or with the relations between different constituents of that Common-wealth, such as the conduct of foreign affairs and of defence, and the control of those parts which have not self-government. These may be spoken of as its 'imperial' functions; and it is obvious that they should be discharged by a body representative of, and responsible to, at least all the self-governing States of the Commonwealth.

2. Those concerned with the British Isles, including such matters as the administration of justice, the control of communications, and most of the legislation referring to education and to social, industrial, and commercial life. These are obviously the true functions of a parliament for the British Isles.

3. Those concerned essentially with local government, such as legis-lation for tramways, gas and electric light undertakings, and the supervision of local governing bodies in their administrative work. This should be the work of provincial parliaments.

[1] Census of 1910: German Empire, 64,925,993 ; Prussia, 40,165,219.

This classification is necessarily a very rough one, and this is not the place in which to discuss it at any length. Hence we will only note here that in very many cases it may be difficult to place a particular Act of Parliament into one class only.

In the British Commonwealth as a whole there are already three ranks of parliaments, whose powers and functions correspond in some degree to those of the classes just set out, in spite of a high degree of confusion and overlapping. In the first rank is the British Parliament, in so far as it is the Parliament of the whole. In the second rank come the Parliaments of the Dominion of Canada and of the Common-wealth of Australia. And in the third rank are those of the several provinces of Canada and the several states of Australia. The Parlia-ments of the unified self-governing dominions of New Zealand and Newfoundland combine the functions of the second and third ranks. Yet all those we have just mentioned as primarily exercising functions of the second rank have some functions, such as the control of defence, tariff legislation and coinage, which would place them in the first rank.

All proposals for parliamentary devolution in the British Isles rest on one or both of two main grounds: first, the demand of the people of some parts of the United Kingdom for local autonomy; and second, the fact that the present British Parliament is, and has long been, so overburdened by its manifold duties that its business is hopelessly congested and many of its Acts receive very insufficient consideration. The tasks of governing the British Empire and the British Isles and of providing and controlling the machinery of local government for forty-five millions of people have jointly proved too great for the time and energy of one parliament. 'It has often been overburdened with a mass of parochial detail,'[1] a mass which might also overburden a parliament of England. And the devolution proposals all agree in planning to establish several parliaments, of what we have here called the third rank, to provide for and control local government within their areas.

The considerations so far mentioned point to the conclusion that what is now required is a division of England into a group of pro-vinces, or major local government areas. These should be comparable to the other divisions of the United Kingdom – Scotland, Ireland and Wales – in resources and population, and should have self-government of the same order as that of these divisions or of a province of Canada. If any such division of England is to be satisfactory, it must be based primarily on geographical considerations. Many other series of con-siderations are necessarily involved – historical, administrative, finan-

[1] *Times* leader of April 25, 1918.

cial, and so on – but the basis of any such division into provinces must be the geography of the country. The results of the division of Revolution France into a series of purely artificial departments, designed to secure as much uniformity as possible, irrespective of any natural geographical relationships, and the modern revolt against that division in the regionalist movement in that country, offer a warning that should not go unheeded. Any attempt to secure an artificial uniformity of area or population in our provinces would inevitably give rise to corresponding evils. And the weakness of a division based entirely on party interests has also been shown by the rapid and complete disappearance of Cromwell's divisions of England. A strong local patriotism is essential to good provincial government under democratic conditions; and this can only be developed if the provinces are closely related to natural divisions of the country. Hence the question to which this book attempts to give a tentative answer may be stated as 'What are the Major Natural Political Divisions of England ?'

The question will here be discussed in its geographical aspects only. This book is only incidentally concerned with any other aspect of the problems of division and devolution. Since we are considering divisions of one state for the sake of greater efficiency in its local government, it is clear that no strategic problems can arise in connection with any of the boundaries which may be suggested. Also any such province can only have those powers and duties which the British Parliament delegates to it; and there is no necessary reason why each provincial parliament should have precisely the same functions. The problem is one of devolution, not of federation. It is comparable to the establishment of the prairie provinces of Canada rather than to the formation of the Australian Commonwealth. In many respects the distinctive nationality of Scots and Welshmen might be held to justify the delegation to their parliaments of some powers which were not desired by East Anglians or Lancashiremen; even though the differences between East Anglia and Lancashire are in some ways greater than those between Wales and Scotland. The position of our suggested Province of Devon in reference to the railway system is so different from that of the Midland Provinces that its influence on that system within its bounds would probably be very different. But the railways, as a principal means of communication, are essentially a matter for the federal government. Free and abundant interchange of ideas and goods, and frequent direct intercourse of persons, among all its parts are among the most powerful factors making for the unity of any state or nation. Hence it is a prime duty of the government which represents the whole to facilitate such intercourse as much as possible.

This implies that the federal government should control posts and telegraphs, railways, roads and waterways, and any other means of communication, either directly or indirectly, and employ its powers to facilitate all communications.

Our discussion of this problem of division into provinces is here limited to England. Scotland and Ireland are not considered, and Wales is referred to only in so far as the principles applied to the delimitation of our suggested English provinces would affect the Anglo-Welsh boundary.

The essential assumption which underlies all the criticism and suggestion with regard to the areas and boundaries of our local government divisions in this volume is that such divisions exist only in order to facilitate good government. In a country which is occupied by a united nation and is governed on democratic principles, that assumption is fundamental for all its internal divisions. Boundaries between separate sovereign states have often been drawn with reference to the strategic and tactical considerations of one party, to the control of important military and economic roadways, access to seaports or mining areas, and so on. No such considerations can enter into a discussion of these suggested Provinces of England.

The division must also be affected by the nature and extent of the powers and duties to be allotted to the provincial parliaments. Here the dominant fact is that these parliaments can have only such powers as may be conferred on them by the British Parliament, and no others. The British Parliament is supreme in these islands, and it can confer, or withhold, or withdraw, any such powers at its own discretion. And it is evidently not essential that each provincial parliament should possess exactly the same powers. There is no more reason to require absolute uniformity in this respect than in relation to area or population. It is quite sufficient that the several provinces should be fairly comparable to each other.

The precedent set by the many Public Acts which have already been based on Private Acts obtained by a progressive local authority will probably be of great value in actually determining the powers and functions of provincial parliaments; since a provincial parliament could at any time ask the British Parliament to confer on it any additional powers which it desired. In England the first suggestion is that the functions of the provincial parliaments would be primarily administrative rather than legislative; though they would necessarily have much more power of initiative than any present local authorities. They should at once take over all the 'county' powers of local government, i.e. they would directly supersede and absorb the county councils. In most cases they would probably consist very largely of the persons who were formerly members of the councils of counties and cities: the first parliament in each province might well be to some extent an amalgamation of some few county and city councils. This control of 'county' powers should also extend over the county boroughs in each province. In this way the establishment of the provinces would do something to reverse the disastrous separation of town and country in local government which has grown up in this country, a separation which was largely due in the first instance to the different relations of the boroughs and manors to the feudal lords. All the lesser local authorities in each province, such as the councils of towns, of urban and rural districts, and of parishes, should derive their authority from, and be directly subordinated to and under the control of, the provincial parliament, since that body is to be fully responsible for all local administration within its area. Indeed, the numbers and powers of these subordinate councils is a matter which should be left entirely to the provincial parliament; since the conditions affecting these matters differ considerably in the different provinces.

In many departments of local government, especially in regard to its provision for the future, we have been compelled to realize of late that the areas and powers allotted to many local authorities in this country are inadequate to the efficient performance of the duties laid on them. Hence many of them have been compelled to obtain special authority from Parliament by Private Acts and go outside their own areas in making provision for the health of their people by sanatoria and cottage homes, for the supply of water or the disposal of sewage, the regulation of flooded streams, and so on. We have covered the land with a needlessly large number of small, and therefore relatively costly and inefficient, electric generating stations and gasworks. And our planning for the betterment of our towns and villages and the improved housing and other accommodation of our people is hampered on every hand by obsolescent local boundaries. Our local government garb is inherited from the days of the small self-contained borough, jealous of its independence of the feudal lord, and the isolated village, which was under his control. It has been strained and torn in innumerable places by the growth and shifting of our population and the changes in our modes of life and association. And to meet these difficulties it has been darned and patched at frequent intervals, without any system or regularity. The problem of adjusting the local government divisions to the needs of the people has never been viewed as a whole; but until it is so considered there can be no hope of any real solution of it.

Subordinate Legislatures

From Conference on Devolution, *Letter from Mr Speaker to the Prime Minister*, 27 April 1920. Cmd. 692, 1920, pp. 9–15.

Though the conference came to a substantial measure of agreement on the powers which could be devolved to local legislatures, on the areas to be used, the financial and judicial arrangements, it could not agree on the character and composition of the legislative bodies themselves. The following two schemes were accordingly put forward.

Transitional Scheme proposed by Mr. Speaker (as modified in the Course of Discussion in the Conference).

Explanatory Note

This Scheme is devised to give a practical trial of the working of devolution by responsible persons with political experience.

It devolves specified powers on subordinate legislative bodies for England, Scotland, and Wales (including Monmouthshire) respectively, and constitutes these bodies not by special election, but of persons who are members of the United Kingdom Parliament.

After a limited period of trial it lays upon each of these bodies the duty of deciding, in the light of practical experience, the permanent constitution of the legislative bodies for their respective areas.

It ensures the determination of this matter by each of the three areas through its representatives without outside interference.

It leaves the choice open to each of these areas either to adopt a constitution involving separate elections, or to revert to the position prior to devolution, or to continue as constituted, just as experience may dictate.

I. Composition of the Local Legislatures

1. There shall be established local subordinate legislatures for England, Scotland, and Wales (including Monmouthshire) severally, to which shall be devolved the powers and duties stated below.

2. These legislatures shall be styled 'Grand Councils'.

3. A 'Grand Council' shall consist of two Chambers.

4. The first Chamber shall be called 'The Council of Commons,' and

shall consist, for each of the three areas, of all the Members returned to the House of Commons to sit for constituencies in that area.

5. The second Chamber shall be called 'The Council of Peers,' and shall consist, for each area, of a number of Members of the House of Lords equal to half the number of Members of the House of Commons for that area, and chosen for the duration of each Parliament by the Committee of Selection of the House of Lords. Any vacancies that may from time to time arise in a Council of Peers shall be filled by the Committee of Selection of the House of Lords.

Time and Place of Meetings

6. The Home Secretary shall fix the time and place of the first meeting of the first Session of each of the several Grand Councils. He shall also fix the date of the termination of their first session.

7. Thereafter the Home Secretary shall, after consultation with the Chairman of the Executive Committee of each Grand Council (see Section III below), fix the date of the commencement and the termination of the session of each Grand Council.

8. It is suggested that the spring and summer months be reserved for the ordinary session of Parliament, and the autumn for the ordinary sessions of the Grand Councils.

9. Each Grand Council shall be free to decide whether it shall sit in London or elsewhere.

10. If Parliament is summoned at a time when a Grand Council is in session, the session of that Grand Council shall be suspended.

11. If a Grand Council desires to hold a session during the session of Parliament, the Home Secretary shall, on application being made to him by the Chairman of the Executive Committee of that Grand Council, fix a date for the commencement of such session of that Grand Council, and from that date that Grand Council shall have leave to sit on any day or at any hour when Parliament is not sitting, and may so continue in session until any date which the Home Secretary, after consultation with the Chairman of the Executive Committee, shall fix as the date of the termination of such session.

12. It is suggested that, when Parliament is not sitting, the Palace of Westminster, and the staff employed there, shall (so far as is convenient to Parliament) be at the disposal of the Grand Councils for the purpose of holding their sessions.

Procedure

13. The Council of Commons and the Council of Peers shall at their first meeting proceed to elect severally, for the duration of the Parliament, a President, and, if desired, a Vice-President, who shall preside over their debates.

14. Each Grand Council shall have complete control of its own internal organisation, but at the outset they shall adopt the procedure of the House of Commons (with power to alter it subsequently).

II. Legislative Powers

15. The powers devolved on Grand Councils shall be those specified in Appendix III, List A. All powers not so devolved shall be reserved for the United Kingdom Parliament.

16. If it be desired to allot further powers to Grand Councils beyond those allotted by this scheme, this result would be attained by an Act of Parliament originating either in a request from a Grand Council or on the initiative of Parliament.

17. The powers granted to all Grand Councils shall be identical.

18. In order to prevent a Grand Council dealing in its legislative proposals with matters not within its competence, the following recommendations are made:

(a) The Home Secretary shall watch Bills of a Grand Council, and satisfy himself that they are not *ultra vires*.

(b) The Home Secretary may (following Clause 49 of the Government of Ireland Bill, 1920) refer a Bill at any stage or an Act of a Grand Council to the Judicial Committee of the Privy Council, who shall decide upon its validity or otherwise.

(c) The Crown, on the advice of the United Kingdom Cabinet, may withhold its assent to Grand Council legislation, pending such inquiry.

In the event of a Grand Council Act not having been submitted, as above mentioned, the right of a private individual, who questions its validity, of resorting to the Courts of Law remains unaffected.

19. The United Kingdom Parliament is not debarred from legislating on devolved subjects and may pass an Act over-riding a Grand Council Act.

20. The Royal Assent may, on the advice of the United Kingdom

Cabinet, be withheld from a Grand Council Act – on the ground not only of invalidity but also of policy.

21. For the purpose of dealing with Private Bill legislation the dates for the preliminary deposits for Private Bills shall be altered so as to be suitable to the time at which a Grand Council sits, and any private business not disposed of before the end of a session may be carried over to the next session of the Grand Council. The principle of the Scottish Private Bill procedure may be extended so as to be made applicable to English and Welsh Private Bill Legislation.

22. The name 'Grand Council Bills (and Acts)' shall be used to distinguish them from Bills and Acts of the United Kingdom Parliament.

23. The Council of Commons shall retain (within its sphere) the privileges in respect of finance possessed by the House of Commons. The Speaker of the House of Commons shall, after consultation with the President of the Council of Commons and the President of the Council of Peers, decide in each case whether a Grand Council Bill is, or is not, a Money Bill in the sense defined in the Parliament Act, and shall give his certificate accordingly in the manner prescribed by the Parliament Act.

24. With regard to other Bills, disagreement between the two Houses shall be referred to a Free Conference between the two Houses, and if an agreement is not reached in the Free Conference, shall be settled by a joint session of a Grand Council consisting of the Council of Commons and the Council of Peers, who shall sit and vote, and may debate, together.

III. Organisation of the Executive of a Grand Council
Administration

25. All powers in respect of the devolved matters, which are exercised under any Act of Parliament, shall be transferred to each Grand Council.

26. Each Grand Council shall exercise the powers and discharge the duties so transferred, through the departments transferred, or the parts of departments transferred.

27. There shall be an Executive Committee for each Grand Council who shall be responsible to the Grand Council.

28. The Executive Committee shall consist of a Chairman appointed by the Grand Council and heads of Departments appointed by the Chairman as his colleagues.

29. No person may be a member of the Executive Committee for more than six months without being a member of the Grand Council (*see* Government of Ireland Bill, 1920, Clause 8 (4) (*b*)).

30. The existing practice with regard to the vacation of seats shall not apply to members of the Executive Committee as and when appointed.

31. At least one member of the Executive Committee must be a member of the Council of Peers.

32. The channel of communication between an Executive Committee and the Imperial Government shall be through the Home Secretary.

Civil Servants

33. The interests of transferred Civil Servants shall be safeguarded (on the model of clause 52 in the Government of Ireland Bill, 1920).

34. Appointments of Civil Servants shall be made in accordance with the existing practice regulating appointments in the Home Civil Service.

IV. Provisions for Transitional Period

35. The transitional period shall consist of:

(*a*) A period of three years after the coming into operation of the Act embodying this scheme during which the duties of the Grand Councils shall be confined to exercising the powers (both legislative and administrative) devolved upon them.

(*b*) A further period of two years during which it shall be incumbent on each Grand Council to consider its future constitution.

(*c*) A final period of one year during which any schemes devised by the Grand Councils shall be submitted to Parliament.

36. During the first period of three years above-mentioned each Grand Council shall transact its business as a body consisting of two Chambers sitting separately.

37. During the second period of two years above-mentioned each Grand Council shall, in addition to discharging the duties devolved upon it (as above organised bicamerally) also sit as a constituent council, consisting of the Council of Commons and the Council of Peers in joint session. The President of the Council of Commons shall be *ex-officio* President of the joint session of the Grand Council. The duties of each Grand Council, acting as a constituent council, shall be to submit to Parliament, within the prescribed

period, resolutions or schemes devised to give effect to one of the following conclusions:

(a) To substitute for itself a separately elected legislature of one or two Chambers, or

(b) To continue as at the time constituted, or

(c) To revert to the *status quo ante*, or

(d) To continue as at the time constituted for a further limited period (subject to obtaining for any scheme subsequently submitted to Parliament the benefit of the procedure set out in paragraph 40), or

(e) To make any other proposals it chooses, dealing exclusively with the composition and organisation of the body or bodies to which it proposes to entrust the functions then discharged by itself.

38. Schemes submitted by this body to Parliament shall deal only with its own constitution, and shall not contain proposals for the devolution of further powers.

39. It is not necessary that such schemes should be uniform with one another.

40. Any such scheme shall be submitted by a Grand Council to Parliament in the shape of a schedule to a Bill, which shall be presented to Parliament by the Home Secretary, and shall be accepted or rejected by Parliament without any amendment. If, within one year after it has been so submitted, no adverse action shall have been taken by either House of Parliament, the Bill shall be deemed to have been passed by both Houses and shall be submitted for the Royal Assent.

V. Financial Powers

41. In order to meet the expenditure on the transferred Services (including those covered by Local Taxation Grants) there shall be handed over annually for a period of five years to the Grand Councils in Great Britain with power to vary those particular duties the following sources of revenue:

(a) Liquor Licences (Dealers and Retailers but not Producers).

(b) Establishment Licences.

(c) Traders' Licences.

(d) Entertainments Duty.

(e) Inhabited House Duty.

(f) Land Values Duties.

together with the equivalent of the nett yield of so many pence in the pound of the annual Income Tax (excluding Super Tax) as will, at

C.R.R.—2

the outset, balance the account. After the end of five years the whole situation with regard to allocated funds and allocated taxes shall be reviewed.

42. All Money Bills must originate in the Council of Commons, and must, following Parliamentary practice, receive the recommendation of the Crown.

43. The Home Secretary shall, on the application of the Financial Member of the Executive Committee of a Grand Council, signify the recommendation of the Crown to proposals for creating charges upon the public.

44. In order to provide for the current expenditure of the Department during the period of the ensuing financial year it is recommended that the Grand Councils should meet before the end of March in order to pass a Vote on account.

45. The taxes imposed by the Grand Councils shall be assessed and collected through the existing United Kingdom machinery, so far as that machinery is capable of being employed for that purpose.

46. The Grand Councils shall be given powers of borrowing upon their own credit under similar conditions to those observed by the United Kingdom Parliament.

47. The auditing of the accounts of the local administrations shall be referred to the Comptroller and Auditor-General, who shall report to the Grand Councils separately.

Mr Murray Macdonald's Scheme

PREFATORY NOTE

This scheme is recommended as the only possible scheme of devolution which would secure:

(a) effective relief of the present Parliamentary congestion

(b) the strengthening of the control of electors over their representatives

(c) effective control of the representative bodies over their executives; and

(d) the avoidance of that hopeless confusion of political issues and responsibilities inseparable from a scheme which charges the same representatives, acting in separate and independent legislatures, with the control and management both of local and central interests.

I. Constitution of the Subordinate Legislatures

1. There shall be established legislatures subordinate to, but separate from, the Parliament of the United Kingdom for England, Scotland, and Wales (including Monmouthshire), respectively, to which shall be devolved the powers and duties stated below.

2. Each subordinate legislature shall have a directly elected chamber.

3. Each chamber shall consist respectively of the same number of members as now represent England, Scotland, and Wales (including Monmouthshire) in the United Kingdom Parliament.

4. The members of each chamber shall be elected for the same constituencies and by the same electors, within the several countries, as now return members to the United Kingdom Parliament.

5. In view of the fact that the Conference has had no information before it upon which to form a judgment regarding the opinion prevailing in the several countries in respect to the question whether the subordinate legislatures should have one or two chambers, nor has had any means of obtaining such information, this question is left to the Government to determine. But if, in any or all cases, the Government should determine that the subordinate legislatures shall be bicameral, it be suggested with respect to the composition and powers of the Second Chambers and to the relations between them and the First Chambers, that the proposals of Lord Bryce's Conference on the Reform of the Second Chamber shall be taken into consideration.

6. Whether the subordinate legislature be unicameral or bicameral, peers shall not be disqualified for election to the popularly elected Chambers.

7. The subordinate legislatures shall determine the question of the payment of their members.

8. The subordinate legislatures shall sit for five years unless sooner dissolved.

II. Legislative Powers

9. The inherent and supreme rights and powers of the Parliament of the United Kingdom shall remain absolutely unimpaired.

10. The powers devolved on the subordinate legislatures shall be those specified in Appendix III, List A.

11. If it be desired to allot further powers to subordinate legislatures beyond those allotted by this scheme, this result would be attained by

an Act of Parliament originating either in a request from a subordinate legislature or on the initiative of Parliament.

12. The powers granted to all subordinate legislatures shall be identical.

13. In order to prevent a subordinate legislature dealing in its legislative proposals with matters not within its competence, the following recommendations are made:

(a) The Secretary of State shall watch Bills of a subordinate legislature, and satisfy himself as to whether they are *ultra vires*.

(b) The Secretary of State may (following Section 49 of the Government of Ireland Bill, 1920), refer a Bill at any stage or an Act of a subordinate legislature to the Judicial Committee of the Privy Council, who shall decide upon its validity or otherwise.

(c) The Crown, on the advice of the United Kingdom Cabinet, may withhold its assent to a Bill pending such inquiry.

In the event of an Act of a subordinate legislature not having been submitted, as above mentioned, the right of a private individual, who questions its validity, of resorting to the Courts of Law, shall remain unaffected.

14. The United Kingdom Parliament shall not be debarred from legislating on devolved subjects, and may pass an Act overriding an Act of a subordinate legislature.

15. The Royal Assent may, on the advice of the United Kingdom Cabinet, be withheld from an Act of a subordinate legislature on the ground not only of invalidity, but also of policy.

16. A distinctive name shall be used to mark Bills and Acts of the subordinate legislatures from Bills and Acts of the Imperial Parliament.

III Organisation of the Executive of a Subordinate Legislature
Administration

17. All powers in respect of the devolved matters, which are exercised under any Act of Parliament, shall be transferred to each subordinate legislature.

18. Each subordinate legislature shall exercise the powers and discharge the duties so transferred, through the departments transferred, or the parts of departments transferred.

19. So far as is necessary, separate administrative departments shall be established in England, Scotland, and Wales respectively.

20. Each subordinate legislature shall have an Executive Committee responsible to it.

21. The members of each Executive Committee shall be appointed by His Majesty the King in accordance with the existing constitutional practice.

22. No person may be a member of the Executive for more than six months without being a member of the Subordinate Legislature (see Government of Ireland Bill, Clause 8 (4) (b)).

23. The existing practice with regard to the vacation of seats shall not apply to members of the Executive Committee as and when appointed.

24. All powers vested in the Crown shall, so far as they affect the powers of the subordinate legislatures, be exercised through a Secretary of State, who shall act on instructions issued to him by His Majesty the King in Council.

Civil Servants

25. The interests of transferred Civil Servants shall be safeguarded (on the model of clause 52 in the Government of Ireland Bill).

26. Appointments to the Civil Service shall be made in accordance with the existing practice.

IV. Financial Powers

27. In order to meet the expenditure on the transferred Services (including those covered by Local Taxation Grants), there shall be handed over annually for a period of five years to the subordinate legislatures, with power to vary those particular duties, the following sources of revenue:

(a) Liquor Licences (Dealers and Retailers, but not Producers)

(b) Establishment Licences

(c) Traders' Licences

(d) Entertainments Duty

(e) Inhabited House Duty

(f) Land Values Duties

together with the equivalent of the net yield of so many pence in the pound of the annual Income Tax (excluding Super Tax) as will, at the outset, balance the account. After the end of five years the whole situation with regard to allocated funds and allocated taxes shall be reviewed.

28. If the subordinate legislatures are to be bicameral, all Money Bills must originate in the popularly elected Chamber.

29. The Secretary of State shall, on the application of the Finance Minister of a subordinate legislature, signify the recommendation of the Crown to proposals for creating charges upon the public.

30. The taxes imposed by the subordinate legislatures shall be assessed and collected through the existing United Kingdom machinery so far as that machinery is at present employed.

31. The subordinate legislatures shall be given powers of borrowing upon their own credit under similar conditions to those observed by the Imperial Parliament.

32. The auditing of the accounts of the local administrations shall be referred to the Comptroller and Auditor-General.

Appendix III. Allocation of Powers
List A. Powers Devolved on Local Legislatures

1. Regulation of Internal Commercial Undertakings, Professions and Societies
Advertisements
Amusement Places and Theatres
Auctioneers
Building Societies and Loan Societies
Licensing (Liquor)
Markets and Fairs

2. Order and Good Government
Cruelty to Animals
Betting and Gaming
Charities and Charitable Trust Acts
Inebriates
Police (other than Metropolitan Police)
Poor Law and Vagrancy
Prisons
Reformatories

3. Ecclesiastical Matters
Burial Law
Matters affecting religious denominations

4. Agriculture and Land
Commons and Enclosures
Game Laws

Land:
(a) Drainage
(b) Improvements
(c) Settled Land Acts
(d) Distress and Tenure

5. Judiciary and Minor Legal Matters
Coroners
County Courts
Criminal Law, Minor Offences (procedure, definition, and punishment)
Law of Inheritance
Intestates' Estates
Conveyancing and Registration of Land
Minor Torts
Trustees, guardians and wards

6. Education
Education:
Primary
Secondary
University (except Oxford, Cambridge, and London)

7. Local Government and Municipal Undertakings
County Council and Municipal Bills
Fire Brigades
Local Legislation:
(Private Bills, Gas, Water, and Electricity undertakings)
Municipal Government:
(including Local Franchise)

8. Public Health
Public Health Matters :
(a) Preventive measures
(b) Contagious diseases
Hospitals
Housing
National Health Insurance
Lunacy and Mental Deficiency

List B. Powers Reserved for the United Kingdom Parliament

1. Crown and Matters relating thereto
(a) Succession to the Crown

(*b*) Regency
(*c*) Civil List
(*d*) Crown Properties
(*e*) Treasure Trove

2. Peace and War

3. Navy, Army, and Air Services

4. Foreign Affairs and Extradition

5. Dominions, Colonies, and Overseas Possessions

6. Dignities and Titles

7. Treason and Alienage

8. Postal, Telegraph, and Telephone Services

9. Submarine Cables

10. Wireless Telegraphy

11. Aerial Navigation (Civil)

12. Lighthouses, Buoys, and Beacons

13. Currency, Coinage, Legal Tender, and Weights and Measures

14. Trade Marks, Patents, and Copyrights

15. Regulation of Trade, Banking, and Commercial Law
Law of Agency
Banking
Census of Production
Internal Commerce
Company Law
Bills of Exchange and Negotiable Instruments
Insurance Companies
Sale of Poisons
Bankruptcy
Bills of Sale
Sale of Goods
Shipping and Pilotage
Quarantine

16. Fisheries, Forestry, and certain Agricultural Services
Forestry Commission
Ordnance Survey
Animals, Import and Diseases of

Fisheries:
(a) Inland
(b) Sea
Wild Birds' Protection

17. *Industrial Legislation*
Employers' Liability and Workmen's Compensation
Factories and Workshops
Industrial Disputes
Regulation of Hours and Wages
Truck Acts
Law of Master and Servant
Unemployment Insurance
Mines and Quarries
Trades Unions
Friendly Societies
Old Age Pensions
Development Commission

18. *Railways and Canals*

19. *Registration and Census*

20. *Food Regulations*

21. *Marriage Law and Divorce*

22. *Vivisection*

23. *Criminal Law*
Major Offences (Procedure, Definition and Punishment)

24. *Civil Torts*
Major Torts

25. *Education*
University (Oxford, Cambridge, and London)

26. *Metropolitan Police*

**List C. Powers to be partly exercised by the United Kingdom
Parliament and partly by Local Legislatures**

1. *Corrupt Practices*

2. *Explosives*

3. *Harbours*

C.R.R.—2*

4. Land – *Acquisition for Public Purposes*
5. Transport – *Roads and Highways*

All other matters not expressly enumerated in the above lists are reserved to the United Kingdom Parliament.

Government in Northern Ireland

From R. J. Lawrence, The Government of Northern Ireland, 1921–1964,
Clarendon Press, Oxford, 1965, pp. 166–76.

There are very few assessments of the experience of devolution in
Northern Ireland. Lawrence's account, though the most
comprehensive and up-to-date has been overtaken by the strife of
the late 'sixties and early 'seventies and this must inevitably require
a further assessment in due course, even if the existing institutions
manage to survive

Today Lord Carson's statue stands at the approach to the Parliament
Buildings at Stormont. And Ulster has not merely survived as a
political unit. Her relations with Britain have been singularly free
from friction. Whether we can conclude from this that devolution
would be equally practicable in Scotland and Wales, where there is
still some demand for it, is a question that must be examined in this
chapter.

It will, however, be better to begin by considering the value of
Home Rule in Ulster; for what is practicable in politics depends in
large part on the value people attach to the courses that are open to
them. We have seen that in 1921 Northern Ireland was given the
choice of accepting Home Rule (and, with it, partition) or of joining
a united Ireland; and in later years she could have pressed for independence within the Commonwealth or for reversion to direct
government from London. Of these, only the first and last are relevant
to our theme. Is devolution preferable to government from Whitehall?

Now, in Ulster's case it seems that Home Rule has two special
advantages. Since distance and expense separate her from the mainland, she probably gains more from local institutions than would small
areas in Britain. Ministers and M.P.s are easily accessible to constituents; businessmen and interest groups of all kinds can press their
cases on the spot; witnesses can appear before parliamentary committees with little inconvenience; and members and officials of local
authorities have developed close and easy relations with government
departments. As the Nugent Committee on the Finances of Local
Authorities observed in 1957:

This interaction between the government on the one hand and the
local authorities on the other has led naturally to the formation of
close personal relationships. Local councils look to central departments for help and guidance on points of difficulty, whilst the departments in their turn seek advice in local government circles as to the

probable effect of new proposals. Local government deputations to Ministries are a common occurrence, readily sought and readily received; sometimes they are undertaken to settle a disagreement or to ventilate a grievance, but more often to plan together for the attainment of some common aim. Again, it is by no means unusual for a Ministry official to attend a council or committee meeting. Council members and officers of central and local government are generally known to one another, so that negotiations within the strictest official setting are conducted as between persons with official responsibilities rather than between impersonal offices. Thus it is that we may well be witnessing the evolution of a new pattern of relationships between the local bodies and government departments peculiar perhaps to Northern Ireland, but none the less adapted to our special needs.[1]

Intimacy & Impartiality

In general the whole political and administrative process is more intimate than it would be if control were remote. Against this it can be urged that intimacy may not be of equal value in all fields of public activity. Impartiality, the greatest political virtue, tends to increase with distance. So while the point must not be overlooked, in the final reckoning we must not put too much weight on it.

The second special advantage is related to Ulster's social divisions. Intolerance and hatred were once endemic, not only or even mainly because of tension between Protestants and Catholics, but because Nationalists hoped and Unionists feared that violence would break the British connexion. Today these emotions have lost their edge. A spirit of indifference, if not yet of toleration, is abroad.

This transformation is attributable, not merely to the passage of time (which may inflict new wounds as fast as old ones heal), but to growing consciousness among Irishmen of the fact that force is neither necessary to maintain the *status quo* nor likely to end it. Parliament at Stormont has always reflected the determination of most people to stay in the United Kingdom. Any lingering fears that a bargain struck in London might lead to their incorporation in a Roman Catholic republic were laid to rest by the Ireland Act, 1949. As long as that Act remains on the statute book and the electorate continues to return a majority pledged to maintain the Union, Ulster can count with absolute confidence on remaining part of the United Kingdom. To supporters of the régime, therefore, it gradually became obvious that reprisals against sporadic outrages were pointless. To its opponents, who profess to desire the unity of Ireland and the co-operation of all her people, it became equally obvious that bloodshed must frustrate

[1] *Report of the Committee on the Finances of Local Authorities*, Cmd. 369 (1957), p. 73.

their own purposes. Home Rule at least enabled both sides to live together in peace, and without that there can be no progress of any kind.

The merits of parliamentary devolution as a general reform have always turned mainly on two points. First, it would relieve congestion at Westminster. This was a live question a generation and more ago, but it has lost much of its urgency because the House of Commons has transformed its procedure. Governments have taken most of the time of the House, debate is frequently cut short, the committee system has been extended, questions to Ministers are rationed, and delegated legislation is more common. True, time is still a scarce commodity, and it would be somewhat less scarce if purely regional affairs were hived off, but the gain would be trivial compared with that which followed the exclusion of Irish business.

The second point is that devolution is a method of securing regional self-government without fundamental reconstruction of the constitution. With the passage of time, it can fairly be argued, this has become more rather than less urgent. The vast expansion of centralized State activity has weakened local initiative, and the very effectiveness of procedural reforms has left the House of Commons with limited opportunities for reviewing matters of special concern to particular areas. Regional government, together with regional elections and political parties, would help to reverse these trends and give local people greater freedom and independence in the management of their own affairs.

This, then, is the crux of the matter, and we must not lose sight of it. For if we are to draw useful conclusions from Northern Ireland's experience, we must begin with a clear idea of what to look for. Proponents of Home Rule are apt to point to the extent to which Ulster differs from Britain in policy and administration and to conclude that devolution is justified on this ground. Diversity rather than independence is made the touchstone. This is to confuse the accidental with the essential. Although Ireland had no parliament in the nineteenth century, she probably differed from Britain to a greater extent than Northern Ireland does now. Besides, the example of Scotland (to which we shall presently turn) shows that even today a local legislature is not necessary to secure variety. Parliamentary devolution is to be distinguished from other forms of decentralization because it provides for a regional executive which is accountable, not to some outside body, but to a regionally elected legislature whose discretion within a defined field is unlimited.

The Government of Ireland Act was obviously intended to secure this. Ministers in Northern Ireland were to be responsible to a

Parliament that was free to legislate on all matters not withheld from it. Subject only to this (and to the United Kingdom's overriding supremacy), Ulstermen through their representatives had complete liberty to make whatever changes they desired, whereas the people of Ireland before 1920 could do no more than try to influence Westminster, Whitehall and Dublin Castle. We have seen, however, that regional autonomy has in part become a fiction. The problem is, therefore, to try to determine how much of the substance, as distinct from the trappings, of independence still remains.

In forming a judgment on this point it must be noted in the first place that Ulster need not seek Britain's agreement in matters that are free from financial implications. Many of these are far from trivial. By a free vote in October 1962 the Commons at Stormont retained capital punishment and did not adopt the distinction between capital and non-capital murder which Westminster embodied in the Homicide Act, 1957. The system and procedure of the inferior courts in Northern Ireland are unique in material respects. Legislation to improve the standard of agricultural produce is distinctive. Such highly controversial questions as the management of schools, religious instruction and methods of appointing teachers have been resolved by local debate. There is plural voting in elections; the local government franchise, tied for the most part to ownership or occupancy of property, is more restricted than in England; and constituency boundaries are not subject to adjustment by an impartial body. In these and other respects Northern Ireland differs from any part of Great Britain. But (to repeat) it is not the differences that are relevant; if it were, their value would come into question. Our concern is with self-government, not good government, and there can be no doubt that Stormont has been wholly free to go its own way.

In the second place, however, governments can do relatively few things without money. 'Finance', as Mr J. M. Andrews once observed, 'governs nearly everything we do.' Financial relations have certainly developed in a manner that has greatly diminished Stormont's autonomy. Its powers in taxation are now very slight indeed. We have seen that transferred taxes as a proportion of tax revenue have fallen from an average of 17·9 per cent. in the ten years 1929–38 to 5·9 per cent. in 1962–63, and even in this limited field Ulster is bound to observe parity. While this does not mean that every local tax must be levied at the same rate as in Britain, free trade with the more prosperous mainland sets sharp limits to divergence. On the revenue side the local Budget is now so dominated by decisions taken in London that few people in Northern Ireland would notice any difference if all taxes were imposed there.

In expenditure, however, Ulster's leaders have more freedom. They must 'clear the rails with the Treasury', but Treasury control appears to be applied with every consideration – and it is essentially negative. Local institutions provide seedbeds for initiative which may be pruned but is never stifled. Nor do Ministers need to rely solely on the Treasury's goodwill. The Home Secretary, always a member of the British Cabinet, watches Ulster's interests. The Joint Exchequer Board, composed of a chairman appointed by the Crown and one member each from the Treasury and the Ministry of Finance, can be a buffer between London and Belfast. The Ministry of Finance itself stands between the Treasury and the spending departments in Ulster, so that the latter are probably not conscious of Treasury control at all. The terms inserted in the post-war financial agreements – parity, general parity and general conformity – give deliberate scope for variation because they prescribe general standards for comparing the services to which they apply with similar services in Britain; and when submitting Budget proposals for discussion with the Treasury, it is open to the Ministry of Finance to make proposals for diverging from parity.

The trouble with these arrangements is that they appear to give more freedom to the provincial Government than to local people. Knowledge of what can be done is essential to liberty of action; but nobody, it seems, outside a narrow circle of Ministers and civil servants can forecast whether departures from British practice are likely to be feasible in any particular case. Discussions between the Treasury and the Ministry of Finance, like the proceedings of the Cabinet and the Joint Exchequer Board, are shielded from public scrutiny. This situation is in sharp contrast to that provided for by the constitution, whose published rules were designed to give freedom to the provincial Parliament by enabling its members to know in advance what they were and were not permitted to do. Judged by the intentions of its creators, it seems clear that devolution has failed.

The failure would be more obvious, and more serious, if Stormont were to insist on some innovation which the Treasury (or the Joint Exchequer Board) were not prepared to sanction. That, however, has never occurred. On the one hand, party ties are tightly drawn. No party with policies different from those of Ulster Unionism stands any chance of victory at the polls, and though Ministers are sensitive to back-bench parliamentary opinion, there is little danger of radical changes being pressed against their advice. On the other hand, financial arrangements are flexible. Ulster is neither expected nor obliged to imitate England exactly, and her leaders have been able to devise methods of overcoming problems that reflect the needs and desires of local people. What this means in concrete terms is sufficiently illustrated in earlier chapters. The Housing Trust was the outcome of the failure of local authorities to build houses on the necessary scale before the war and of the need to provide them quickly and in large numbers after it. The Tuberculosis Authority, though transient, was a unique device to meet a special problem. The health service is modelled on, but is by no means an exact replica of, the British service. Educational policy is the product of compromises arrived at by debate at Stormont and by consultations between Ministers and interested bodies. Agriculture, land drainage, the fire service, public transport and other services have been shaped by local conditions.

While, therefore, Ulstermen do not in practice enjoy the freedom to control their own affairs that is still enshrined in the constitution, they do have a government which they can influence. And their government can not only initiate proposals and amend them in the light of local discussion; it can concentrate its whole attention on them and if necessary exert pressure to obtain Treasury approval. In these respects it seems clear that Ulster is at least better off than any part of England.

To sum up so far, We have suggested that Home Rule in Ulster has special merits which are the product, not of devolution as such, but of its application to a geographically remote and politically abnormal area. Whether it would be of much value as a general reform is by no means certain. Regional institutions have made it possible for people in Northern Ireland to escape complete centralization and uniformity and to exert more influence on their affairs than they would secure as members of a wholly undifferentiated political unit, but there are other ways of securing these benefits. What is certain is that Ulster's experience does little to encourage the belief that the creation of regional parliaments will safeguard that measure of independence which parliamentary devolution is designed to secure.

Scottish Nationalism

From J. N. Wolfe (ed), *Government and Nationalism in Scotland*, Edinburgh University Press, Edinburgh, 1969. Gordon Donaldson and others, 'Scottish Devolution: The Historical Background', pp. 12–16.

This is one of the best accounts we have of the course of Scottish Nationalism in the period since 1920, and this extract ends with the interesting suggestion that devolution to Scotland is unlikely to arise from the influence exerted by the nationalists.

Part of the explanation of the cessation of Home Rule bills after the 1920s is, of course, that the party which had come nearest to being seriously committed to Scottish Home Rule – the Liberal party – was now an almost negligible political force. And, despite the favourable attitude of individual Scottish socialists, the cause of Home Rule seems to have made little appeal to the central organization of the Labour party. In any event, the Labour government of 1929, like that of 1924, was weak and short-lived, the Unionists were in office from 1931 to 1945, and, when Labour came to effective power in 1945, other issues predominated.

Failure to gain effective support from any existing party had led in 1928 to the formation of the National Party of Scotland, formed from an amalgamation of some existing small bodies, possessing a left-wing bias and aiming at complete separation from England. Among its leaders were notable and picturesque figures like R. B. Cunninghame Graham and Sir Compton Mackenzie, but its hard-working secretary, John MacCormick, deserves more than almost anyone else to be remembered as a founder of the modern Home Rule movement. It contested seats in the elections of 1929 and 1931 but made a very poor showing at the polls. A separate Scottish party, with a more moderate political tone, was formed in 1932. It was supported by Sir Alexander McEwen, Professor Dewar Gibb and the Duke of Montrose. McEwen wrote an interesting little book, *The Thistle and the Rose* (1932), which can still be read with profit, and in 1933, at a by-election, the Scottish party's candidate polled 6,000 votes. In 1934 the two groups amalgamated to form the Scottish National party, but tensions between moderate and extreme elements continued and in 1942 the party split again. MacCormick, who had been secretary of the combined party, was the moving spirit behind the withdrawal of the moderates to form a body called Scottish Convention, aiming at a federal system within the United Kingdom. Until 1939 there had been no indications that either an organized party or the body of opinion in favour of Home Rule was going to be anything like a real force in politics, and the 1930s, despite these minority activities, look on the whole like one of the troughs between two waves of interest in Home Rule.

The next wave of activity came after the Second World War, and it can be argued that a sufficient number of novel features have affected the situation in the last twenty years to make it almost a new phase, though, as we shall see, much was unchanged. Among the novelties has been the vast extension of the scope of governmental activity and the tendency to centralization at the expense of local government. This has made the whole question of the repository of real power a critical one for all thinking men, and the most casual glance at the dictatorial attitude sometimes adopted by the Secretary of State and the permanent officials who advise him has made it seriously debateable whether the government of Scotland is in any real sense of the term democratic. Secondly, the economic distress of the inter-war period left bitter memories, and even in the improved conditions since World War II the contrast between the unemployment figures in Scotland and those in south-east England inevitably raised questionings as to whether an autonomous Scotland might fare better. Thirdly, what can be called something of a literary renaissance has taken place, in the work, for example, of Hugh MacDiarmid. Not one person in a hundred may read the verses of MacDiarmid or of any other Scottish poet, but the fact that they write and gain recognition is of some importance and may contribute to a conscious reaction against the prevailing tendency towards assimilation to England. Fourthly, Scotland is in some ways a more united society than it was in the nineteenth century. The division between Lowland and Highland is far less marked than it was – mainly, of course, because of the predominance of Lowland culture in the mass media and because of the decline of Gaelic until it is now spoken by only about 1·5 per cent. of the population. Equally, religious divisions are on the whole less marked. The Protestant *versus* Roman Catholic issue, which at one time seriously complicated thinking on the question of Home Rule, seems less often to enter into calculations nowadays. The Church of Scotland has, on the whole, taken a more nationalistic line than it did before World War II.

All these factors have influenced the events which have taken place since 1947. In that year Scottish Convention called a Scottish National Assembly and demanded parliamentary devolution. After the government refused even to hold an enquiry into the case – though the Scottish Grand Committee was strengthened in 1948 – the convention brought forward a National Covenant, which pledged its signatories 'within the framework of the United Kingdom to do everything in our power to secure for Scotland a parliament with adequate legislative authority in Scottish affairs'. Ultimately this pledge was signed by 2 million persons – or, to be more precise, had 2 million names appended to it, some of them said to be of children, some said to be actually forged. But, with all qualifications, this did indicate a substantial body of opinion, perhaps not very well considered opinion, in favour of legislative devolution of some kind. Interest in the cause of Home Rule was maintained by a series of incidents which followed shortly afterwards. There was the removal of the Coronation Stone from Westminster Abbey at Christmas 1950: many Scots who did not approve of the exploit itself were shocked when this ancient relic of Scottish kingship was ignominiously taken back to London in the boot of a police car. There was agitation against the numeral II in the title of the present queen; and the Lord President gave a solemn and considered ruling against its propriety. There was a somewhat dubious plot to blow up St Andrew's House, and there was the actual blowing up of one or two pillar-boxes carrying the obnoxious numeral in the royal monogram.

Once again there was something of a lull, in the later 1950s and early 1960s. But once again the agitation had produced certain concessions in various fields. Tom Johnston, as a forceful Secretary of State during the war, had been able to use the strength of Scottish sentiment as a lever to obtain concessions in the administrative sphere, especially in the setting up of separate Scottish organizations for certain functions. Succeeding Secretaries of State have not followed his example, but it seems that the idea he put forward has remained at the back of the minds of successive governments, and there is no doubt that all the manifestations of national feeling in the post-war era had some effect. It was significant, for example, that the Forth Road Bridge, denied again and again in the 1930s, was at last authorized in the late 1950s. Some impression was made, too, in matters like the stay of the execution of the Beeching axe on certain railway lines and the retention of the North of Scotland Hydro-Electric Board's identity. It was obviously as a sop to Scottish opinion that Queen Elizabeth, after her coronation, came to Edinburgh for a ceremony which involved conveying the Honours of Scotland through the streets of the city for the first time since the Union. The effect was rather spoiled by the fact that Her Majesty had been advised not to wear ceremonial dress for the occasion, and there was something like disgust when she turned up in the church of St Giles to receive the ancient symbols of Scottish sovereignty dressed in everyday costume and with a handbag slung over her arm.

In the political scene, however, all the agitation and incident of the post-war period amounted to very little. It remained true, on the whole, that Scotland shared its policies with England, and when Scottish voters went to the polling booths they voted for a party policy or programme covering the whole range of British political issues. People might sign the Covenant, but they did not allow their pledge to effect their voting habits. This explains the fate of Scottish Nationalist candidates at parliamentary elections. Until 1967, once only had a Scottish Nationalist candidate, Dr Robert McIntyre, been returned to Westminster, and that at a by-election at Motherwell in 1945, only to be promptly unseated at the next general election. The second victory, that of Mrs Ewing at Hamilton in November 1967, was again at a by-election, and the general election has not yet followed. However strong the sentiment, and even considered opinion, in favour of some kind of Home Rule, it seemed unlikely that Home Rule could become practicable until one of two things should happen: either Scots, at general elections, should abandon the habits of generations and put Scottish issues before British issues; or that a major party should commit itself to the Home Rule cause.

Some novel features have, indeed, again emerged in the present situation. One is the remarkable successes of Nationalists in local authority elections. Another is the phenomenal growth of the membership of the National party, which now claims to have the highest paid-up membership of any party in Scotland. The latter fact suggests a growing sense of frustration with both the major parties, and a feeling that neither will do much for Scotland, especially its more outlying areas. Unquestionably it was this attitude of 'a plague on both your houses' which has led in recent elections to the capture of all the northern seats, and one Border seat, by the Liberals – who were, and are, of course, still in favour of a policy of federal devolution. It is true, too, that the 1966 general election represented far and away the largest Nationalist vote to date. But it is too soon to say that a revolution has taken place, or is taking place, in the Scottish political outlook and that this is going to have a substantial effect in parliamentary elections. It may be that one of the major parties will attempt to make capital out of the situation and adopt Home Rule as part of its programme. But it is barely conceivable that the Unionist party should do so – even though, paradoxically, that party no less than the Labour party has 'presided over the dissolution of the British Empire', to use Mr Churchill's words. The Labour party, on its side, is pledged in theory to an emphasis on class rather than on nation, and, besides, finds itself in the same situation as the Liberals were in before 1914 – with a strong disincentive to permit the withdrawal from Westminster of the phalanx of Scottish socialists to whom, on at least one occasion in the past, they owed their majority. It seems much more likely that both the major parties will launch out with further instalments of appeasement of the traditional kind. The authors of this paper are not disposed to indulge in prophecy. But to anyone who reviews the past the question must arise whether or not Scotland is at the moment any nearer to the realization of Home Rule than it was in 1913.

Provincial Assemblies, Liberal Style

From Liberal Party Organization, *Parliaments for the Future,*
Liberal Research Department, London, 1970, pp. 1–5.

**This is the evidence of the Liberal Party Organization in London to
the Commission on the Constitution, and it follows the trend set by
a previous Liberal pamphlet *Power to the Provinces* in arguing for
provincial assemblies to relieve an overworked central Parliament
and to provide more freedom for the determination of many aspects
of home affairs at the provincial as distinct from the central level.**

'This Joint Assembly, convinced that democracy in the United Kingdom is being stifled by the over-centralisation of government in
London, calls for a Federal system of government to be established to
bring power to the people. It urges that Parliaments be established in
Scotland and Wales, that the Northern Ireland constitution be so
reformed as to provide safeguards for minority rights and fair elections, that Provincial Assemblies be established in the regions of
England, and that effective executive, financial and legislative powers
be transferred from London.' 1968

This resolution, passed by a joint Liberal Assembly at Edinburgh in
September 1968, brings up-to-date the development of Liberal policy
on Home Rule, which has its origins in the stormy debates on Ireland
in the nineteenth century. The resolution forms the basis for our
evidence to the Commission which is enquiring into the functions of
government in the latter half of the twentieth century.

The present scale of local government is too small for many services
today; that of the national government too large and remote. So, as a
typically British compromise, there has grown up a network of
regional bodies, charged with a variety of functions Regional Economic Planning Councils, Regional Hospital Boards, Regional Sports
Councils, Regional Crime Squads, Electricity Boards, Gas Boards and
many others. Linked with this has been the re-establishment of
regional offices of the central Ministries, and devolution of administrative functions to Edinburgh and, more recently and less completely, to Cardiff. In other words, we already have a system of regional
government, if it can be called a system. It is rather a jumble of
assorted bodies, with varying functions, varying areas and varying
compositions. The ruling bodies are nominated, not elected, and there
is no co-ordinating body to make sense of their divergent plans and

interests. It is reminiscent of the chaos of local government in the nineteenth century with its countless highway boards, sanitary boards, poor law guardians, lighting inspectors, drainage boards, school boards, burial boards, etc. These were finally brought together into a coherent pattern by Liberal legislation in 1894. Now a similar process is called for at a higher level – the regional level.

The problem is not one of Scotland and Wales alone. In England there are regional differences and regional points of view. The needs of the Black Country are not the same as those of Devon; Tyneside's problems are not those of East Anglia. There is not the same passionate demand for independence, but for a less remote central government; for participation.

Much of the force behind the new interest in regionalism in England stems from the spread of government and the effective centralisation to which this leads. Fifty years ago Manchester *was* a regional capital in many senses; it was the centre of the cotton industry and it had to bow to London for fewer decisions about the North-West – about transport, industrial and commercial finance, health services, etc. Many of these remained in either private, charitable or municipal hands. The effect of nationalisation, the expansion of government social security provision, and economic and land-use planning, as well as the decline of the old regionally-based industries, has been to take effective power away from the regions. Similarly with the West Riding of Yorkshire and the woollen industry. The effect of their greater dependence upon consultations with, for example, the Board of Trade, is to make regional leaders feel more provincial.

The need for change arises also in another quarter. The House of Commons today is hopelessly entangled in a mass of detail and procedure. There is little time for major debates on matters of national importance, while the day-to-day business of amendments to legislation is very ill done . . . The House of Commons remains immersed in the mass of minor questions, while it fails to perform its major function. It even spends its limited time discussing local Bills referring only to the affairs of a single town, while national issues are crowded out of the Parliamentary programme.

Our objective is to find the means of giving to the nations and regions or Provinces a feeling of identity; and the power to make this identity a reality will only be brought into being when the limiting hand of Whitehall is removed.

The objective could be achieved in several ways. The most obvious is by Parliament establishing Regional Councils in Scotland and Wales and in the Provinces of England. It could then assign (as it does to the existing local authorities) a list of functions to be carried out by the Councils under the general direction of the central government. This need not entail detailed supervision, and the Councils could be given wide discretion in how they do their work and in how they raise their money (though some Grants-in-Aid might be necessary). Thus such matters as education, town and country planning, health services, police, fire services, hospitals, etc., could be devolved upon the Regional Councils. The Scottish and Welsh Councils could be given somewhat wider powers over, for example, the Scottish legal system, law courts, prisons, all Home Office functions except immigration and passport control.

But it does not really go far enough. The central government could still control the finances, and thus the policies of the Regional Councils, as it now controls the county councils and county borough councils. Parliament is sovereign. Parliament is constantly stretching out its controls into the fields previously regarded as the preserves of local discretion. It can, by statute, abolish county councils, or strip them of their powers or restrict their discretion. It is constantly tempted to intervene in local problems or to give orders to local authorities.

If we are to take the demand for self-government and liberty seriously we must think in far bolder terms. We must search for a system which keeps the essential services such as defence and the national economy in the hands of a British Parliament but gives to the constituent parts (Scotland, Wales, which for convenience we may call States, and the Provinces of England) real liberty to control affairs in their own spheres. This means that power should be granted out-and-out for the States to make their own decisions; in our opinion, such a purpose can only be achieved by a form of federalism.

(b) Administrative Decentralization

The prototype of administrative decentralization is the Scottish Office, which dates from the latter part of the nineteenth century. Sir David Milne's account of the Office produced for the New Whitehall Series of the Royal Institute of Public Administration is the standard account of the history and organization of the Department. Apart from the decentralization of army administration through the Command organization in 1916, and the special case of Northern Ireland (which was part of a process of political devolution and has already been dealt with in the preceding section), no systematic attempt to create a regional organization of government departments was made until just before the outbreak of war in 1939. The regions used by most of the departments (the Post Office was a major exception) followed a standard pattern in order to facilitate the arrangements for civil defence in the event of invasion (see the next following section). Though these regional arrangements were continued after the end of the war, from the early nineteen-fifties some departments began to depart from the standard pattern, partly owing to demands for economy in governmental expenditure and partly because the standard pattern was not entirely suitable for the requirements of departmental activities.

The regional organizations were not completely abandoned, however, and it is possible to see that they fulfilled three different kinds of functions in departmental organization. First, and of major importance with the great extension of public social services in the period after 1946, was the use of regional offices by departments with a large chain of local offices: the Ministry of Labour, the Ministry of Pensions and National Insurance and the National Assistance Board. In these departments, or their successors, the regional offices, lying at an intermediate level between headquarters and local offices, carry out certain 'housekeeping' activities in relation to the local office network and also handle some of the more specialized problems of the department, for example, the administration of the appellate tribunals and advisory committees and dealing with cases of fraud. Secondly, in some other departments such as the Department of Trade and Industry, customer relations can be handled directly from the regional offices or sub-offices. In these cases the number of clients dealt with by the department is far fewer than is the case with the social service departments. The third function is in departments, such as the Department of the Environment, the Department of Health and Social Security and the Department of Education and Science, where the regional office is the base for large numbers of operating staffs: chiefly those exercising professional or technical skills.

Apart from the concentration on the standard regions during the 1939–45 war, there has been no overall reason compelling the different departments to follow a uniform pattern of decentralization. Customer and service needs have varied from one department to another. The problems of providing office buildings and facilities in different parts of the country have provided arguments both for maximum dispersal, so that all parts of the country get the benefits to be derived from an influx of government workers; and for concentration, so that ancillary facilities can be provided on a more economic basis and also for the convenience of clients whose business may involve more than one department. There is now the further possibility that if local government reorganization should result in fewer but larger units of local government, such a concentration might well encourage the central departments to return to a more co-ordinated development of decentralized offices bearing some relationship on the territorial plane to the new units of local government. This kind of development might be further encouraged by the possible devolution of activities from government departments to regional or local authorities, and by the likelihood of the extension of the notion of 'partnership' between the central government and other authorities in the administration of many services.

The experience of the regional economic planning boards and advisory councils since they were set up in 1965 lends weight to these arguments. In the first place, the regional areas which were used for these bodies show marked variations from both the 'standard' regions of war-time and the regions which were in use in 1965 by government departments: for example, the Yorkshire and Humberside region had no antecedent. Secondly, the economic planning activities of these bodies could not be effective whilst divorced from other planning activities, particularly the land-use planning of local authorities. In the long run, planning in the country will remain ineffective until there is close co-operation between all levels of planning activity, national, regional and local. So far from the separate authorities endeavouring to maintain their own separate spheres of influence, active co-operation or 'partnership' is essential to the planning activity. This, of course, is equally true in many other spheres of public activity. For instance, the attempts introduced in 1968/9 to give more effective control of public expenditure, which will give Parliament an opportunity to range over the entire extent of public spending, and not just that of the central government, will mean that the activities of the subordinate bodies are increasingly brought within some kind of national review. There is an organizational consequence, in that sub-units of the central government will be able to perform their work more effectively if the subordinate authorities with whom they have contact are organized territorially in a similar pattern. But also, co-operation between the individual sub-units of the government will be the more effective if they can be brought together in a rational pattern. This, at least, was one of the attainments of the regional economic planning boards when they were established in 1965.

The brief selection of extracts which follows attempts to give ex-amples of the developments which have been outlined in this section.

Scottish Administration

From Sir David Milne, *The Scottish Office*, Allen and Unwin, London, 1957, pp. 4–7, 15–17, 18–19 and 210–11.

These extracts which follow are from the volume on the Scottish Office in the New Whitehall Series promoted by the Royal Institute of Public Administration. The author has had distinguished service in the Department whose history and organization is described, and this is one of the best accounts we have of the organization of the Scottish Office.

The Scottish Office, in one sense, denotes the headquarters of the Secretary of State. It includes, on the Ministerial side, a Minister of State and three Parliamentary Under-Secretaries of State, and on the official side, the Secretary of State's chief permanent adviser (the Permanent Under-Secretary of State), the Assistant Under-Secretary of State, and of course the various private secretaries. All these lead a nomadic life between Edinburgh and London, but the majority of them will be for the most part in London while Parliament is sitting and in Scotland when it is not. (The two Scottish law officers, the Lord Advocate and the Solicitor-General for Scotland, are *not* part of the Scottish Office, but have their own departments – the Lord Advocate's Department in London and the Crown Office in Edinburgh. Although these departments are entirely separate and independent, their contacts with the Scottish Office are necessarily close and frequent and no account of Scottish administration would be complete that did not deal with them. See therefore Part VII of this book.)

In the more general sense with which this book is concerned, the Scottish Office includes four separate departments, each located in Scotland with its headquarters at St Andrew's House, Edinburgh, and each with only a small liaison staff in London. These departments – Agriculture, Education, Health and Home – are the instruments with which the Secretary of State administers in Scotland, matters which in England are the concern of eight separate Ministers. The main functions of the departments are summarised on page 51.

The four Scottish departments have no legal existence independent of the Secretary of State, for whom they act, although the Secretary of each, like the head of an English department, is responsible to Parliament as Accounting Officer for the money spent by his department. Therefore when the functions of the Department of Agriculture for Scotland, for example, are discussed later in this book, they are

Function	Scottish Department	Corresponding English Minister
Agriculture	Department of Agriculture for Scotland	Minister of Agriculture, Fisheries and Food
Food	Primarily Department of Agriculture for Scotland but also	Minister of Agriculture, Fisheries and Food
	Department of Health for Scotland and Scottish Home Department	Minister of Health
Education	Scottish Education Department	Minister of Education
Health and Welfare Services		Minister of Health
Housing and General Sanitation	Department of Health for Scotland	Minister of Housing and Local Government
Town and Country Planning		
Public Order (Police, Fire, Prisons, Civil Defence), Criminal Justice and Miscellaneous Social Services		Home Secretary
Local Government	Scottish Home Department	Minister of Housing and Local Government
Fisheries		Minister of Agriculture, Fisheries and Food
Electricity		Minister of Power
Roads		Minister of Transport and Civil Aviation
Legal Services		Lord Chancellor

simply the functions of the Secretary of State wearing his agricultural hat. Indeed it would be more helpful to an understanding of Scottish administration if the six symbolic figures which decorate the outside of St Andrew's House could be replaced by statues showing the same man clad symbolically in different ways.

The identity of the Secretary of State with his department is perhaps not yet fully understood, although it has been a constitutional fact since 1939. There is still prevalent in Scotland a vague belief that the departments can act on their own authority and make decisions against which there is an appeal to the Secretary of State.

The tendency to regard the Scottish departments as something separate from the Secretary of State is probably a survival of the days when a great deal of Scottish administration was carried on by Boards or departments with an independent legal existence. As the following chapters will show, once the office of Secretary for Scotland had been created in 1885, the new Minister was regarded as the natural spokesman of these Boards in Parliament. It was clearly an awkward arrangement for the Secretary for Scotland (or Secretary of State for Scotland, as he became in 1926) to have to answer in Parliament for Boards for which he had only partial responsibility as a Minister, and with whose actions he might not even agree. Gradually, therefore, the Boards were abolished and their functions were transferred to the Secretary of State.

Once the office of Secretary for Scotland had been created, it also tended to exercise a sort of magnetic attraction on other administrative organisations concerned with Scotland. Because a Minister existed who had very substantial responsibilities in Scotland and was indeed the chief representative of the Government in Scotland, it was a natural step for Parliament to give him other important duties. Some of these are discharged through the St Andrew's House departments, and others not through those departments at all but through such bodies as the Forestry Commission and the Office of the Crown Estate Commissioners. Thus, although the four Scottish departments have no existence independent of the Secretary of State, the reverse is not true.

It is curious to record that the general principle that there should be a Scottish Secretary, which had been generally regarded in 1853 as a romantic extravagance of Lord Eglinton's Society, was accepted in 1885 virtually without debate. Discussion centred mainly on whether education should be included among the new Secretary's manifold functions, and the view that it should not was expressed picturesquely by Sir Lyon Playfair:

'But Scotland alone, which above all other countries is essentially educational, is in future to have a Minister made up of a large variety of heterogeneous materials mixed up like a Scotch haggis and then salted with education to give it a flavour.'

CREATION OF THE SCOTTISH OFFICE

The Secretary for Scotland Act of 1885 transferred to the new Minister a list of duties in Scotland previously carried out under various statutory powers by the Home Secretary, the Privy Council, the Treasury and the Local Government Board. The list of functions transferred, which was so miscellaneous as to lead to some witticisms when the Bill was going through, ranged from police to fisheries, and from wild birds' protection to prisons. The Duke of Richmond and Gordon was immediately appointed as the new Minister and set up his office in Dover House, Whitehall, which continued to be the Scottish Ministerial headquarters until damaged by enemy action in 1941, and to which the Scottish Office has recently returned. The Duke's tenure of the newly created post was brief and that of his immediate successors briefer still. When the Secretary for Scotland Act of 1887 – which increased the powers and duties of the office – was before Parliament, Lord Rosebery complained that it was not so much new powers as continuity of administration that was required, and he pointed out that there had been five Secretaries for Scotland within 16 months. He was also insistent that the Minister responsible for Scottish administration should have the prestige conferred by membership of the Cabinet. In the Commons, Members complained of the inconvenience of having the Scottish Secretary in the Lords. Several more Peers were to hold the post but after 1892 the Scottish Secretary was always a member of the Cabinet, except during the periods of the War Cabinets.

The Secretary for Scotland remained in sole charge of Scottish affairs – with assistance of course from the two Law Officers, the Lord Advocate and the Solicitor-General for Scotland – until 1919, when the office of Parliamentary Under-Secretary for Health was created by the Scottish Board of Health Act. In 1926 the office of Secretary for Scotland was abolished by the Secretaries of State Act and the functions hitherto exercised by its holder were transferred to one of His Majesty's Principal Secretaries of State – the roundabout but constitutionally correct method of making the principal Scottish Minister a full Secretary of State. As a result of the change, the Parliamentary Under-Secretary for Health became a Parliamentary Under-Secretary of State. The increasing volume of work in the Scottish Office was reflected in the appointment of a second Parliamentary Under-Secretary of State in 1940, and of a third in 1952. A

Minister of State, Scottish Office, was also added, towards the end of 1951, to assist the Secretary of State.

To sum up the Ministerial story, from 1707 to 1725 and from 1741 to 1745 there was a Secretary of State mainly responsible for Scotland; from 1745 to 1885 there was no special Scottish Minister, other than the Lord Advocate, concerned with Scottish administration; from 1885 to 1926 there was an office of Secretary for Scotland; and from 1926 onwards the Ministerial responsibility for Scottish business has been carried by one of the Principal Secretaries of State, who is now assisted by a team of four Ministers – the Minister of State and three Parliamentary Under-Secretaries of State – and who also continues to rely on the advice and assistance of the Lord Advocate and the Solicitor-General for Scotland.

INCREASING RESPONSIBILITIES OF THE SECRETARY OF STATE

The tendency in the twentieth century had in fact been to increase the direct responsibility of the Scottish Secretary for Scottish administration and this culminated in the reorganisation of 1939. Up to that year there had been, since 1707, various separate Scottish Boards, Commissions and departments, established from time to time for varying purposes, modified or superseded as new needs arose and – after 1885 – responsible in varying degrees to the Secretary for Scotland or, from 1926, the Secretary of State. In 1939, as a result of a general review of Scottish administration by a Committee under the chairmanship of Sir John Gilmour, the Secretary of State's responsibility was made almost complete when the functions of the Departments of Agriculture, Education, Health and Prisons and the Fishery Board for Scotland were vested directly in the Secretary of State by the Reorganisation of Offices (Scotland) Act, 1939. Only the Trustees of the National Galleries, the Keeper of the Registers and Records, the Registrar General and the General Board of Control for Scotland remained separate entities after 1939 and the last two were brought into closer association with the Secretary of State's departments. Everything else of importance became the direct responsibility of the Secretary of State in the same way as the functions he had acquired by statute in and since 1885 and had hitherto administered through the Scottish Office in Dover House, Whitehall. Those functions, as well as those of the Prisons Department and the Fishery Board for Scotland, were allocated to a new department which was named the Scottish Home Department.

Since 1939 the Scottish Office has taken the form suggested by the Gilmour Committee and outlined in Chapter I. In London, there is the Ministerial and Parliamentary headquarters and a liaison office for each of the four departments. In Edinburgh, there are the departments themselves – no longer statutory bodies each with a separate legal identity but organisations existing to aid the Secretary of State in discharging his functions. There is in addition the Permanent Under-Secretary of State, who acts as a general adviser to the Secretary of State over the whole range of his duties. The Secretary of State can alter the allocation of functions between the departments as circumstances from time to time may require.

The concentration of powers in the hands of the Secretary of State in 1939 was symbolised by a physical change in the same year when the major departments – or as much of them as could be got in – were brought under one roof in a new Government building at St Andrew's House, Edinburgh.

CONCLUSION

Early in its Report, the Royal Commission on Scottish Affairs set out what it regarded as the principles that must be observed if Scotland was to be governed effectively and acceptably. The first principle was that 'the machinery of government should be designed to dispose of Scottish business in Scotland'. The Scottish Office is in itself a recognition of this principle, and this book, while we cannot describe every detail of the work of the departments for which Scottish Ministers are responsible, may at least demonstrate just how much Scottish business is in fact disposed of in Scotland.

There is, however, more than one way of observing the Royal Commission's principle, and Great Britain Departments such as the Board of Trade, the Ministry of Labour and National Service, the Ministry of Pensions and National Insurance, the Post Office, the Ministry of Power and the Ministry of Works, none of whose work could be described in this book, also dispose of much of their Scottish business in Scotland. All of them have Scottish headquarters under the charge of experienced senior officers to whom substantial responsibilities are devolved.

Another essential principle summarised by the Royal Commission was that Scottish needs and points of view should be kept in mind 'at all stages in the formulation and execution of policy'. The importance of this, particularly at the early stages when policy is being conceived, should hardly need emphasizing; a suit that is made to measure will always fit better than one originally designed for someone else and hastily altered at the last moment. To ensure that the measurements are correct when a policy is being cut out is one of the continuous preoccupations of Ministers and civil servants.

⌈All Government departments with business in Scotland must, of course, consider Scottish needs and points of view, but the Scottish Office is in a special position in that it alone has its administrative headquarters in Scotland and is concerned solely with Scotland. It has therefore acquired – or if it has not, it has been very much at fault – a specialised knowledge and experience of the country.⌋ This knowledge and experience are at the disposal of the Secretary of State, who is Scotland's representative in the Cabinet, and they make the Scottish Office something more than the sum of its component departments. Not only is it responsible for the central administration of agriculture, education, health and home affairs in Scotland, with the duty of helping to work out for all these a policy that will both meet Scottish requirements and be fundamentally consistent with what is proposed for England and Wales; it also has to keep an eye on what other departments are doing, and to be ready to bark, and if need be to bite, when it senses danger to Scottish interests.⌋

Departmental Decentralization

From Philip Asterley Jones, 'Post-war Machinery of Government, VI – Regional Administration', *The Political Quarterly*, Vol. 15, No. 3, 1944, pp. 196–7 and 204–5.

This is in the nature of an interim assessment of regional developments, made during the later stages of the war when there was some considerable concern about the possible adverse effects of this new level of administration.

The second tendency has been that of certain departments of the Central Government to decentralise their powers and responsibilities. It is important when considering this matter to differentiate between those departments which are concerned with matters of high national and international or imperial importance, those whose function is to supervise other bodies such as local authorities or public utilities, and those whose activities bring them into direct contact with the public and which are, in fact, carrying on a business with the public as the customers.

The pioneer in decentralisation was the Post Office. It is now over ten years since the Bridgeman Committee recommended, among other things, the devolution of many of the responsibilities of the Headquarters of the Post Office to Regional Directors. For some reason (probably the presence of a very active Postmaster-General) the proposals of this Committee, unlike those of most others, were put into practice in a remarkably short space of time. In 1935 a start was made in two regions as an experiment and the results were so successful that the scheme was extended to cover the whole country. Regional Directors are given a free hand within the broad lines of policy laid down by Headquarters: they co-ordinate at their level administrative, technical and financial functions.

Similarly, prior to and during 1936 the Ministry of Labour carried out a scheme of decentralisation on a considerable scale. According to the Report of the Ministry of Labour for 1936 the following departments had local organisations of their own in that year: Industrial Relations Department, Trade Boards Branch, Services and Establishments Department (which controls the employment exchanges) and Finance Department. Adjudication work was divided between the Chief Insurance Officer at headquarters, the divisional Insurance Officers at divisional offices and the local Insurance Officers at the exchanges. It is noteworthy, however, that even within one Ministry it was found convenient to divide the country in a different way for each department – the Industrial Relations Department into three divisions, the Trade Boards Branch into eight, the exchange service into nine.

The Factory Department of the Home Office (now transferred to the Ministry of Labour) has from its inception been decentralised. In 1833, for the purpose of factory inspection, the United Kingdom was divided into four divisions within which the inspectors possessed very great powers. They reported to the Home Secretary only twice a year and themselves met in London twice a year to discuss common policy. It appears that since that time central control has tightened while the necessity for specialised inspectors in small technical branches prevents full decentralisation. In spite of this the Superintending Inspector in each of the twelve divisions into which the country is now divided has considerable powers in his or her own hands.

The Unemployment Assistance Board (now the Assistance Board) was from the outset organised for decentralisation. The country was divided into seven regions which were further subdivided into twenty-seven districts. While the primary responsibility for control and co-ordination lies with the District Officers, the Regional Officers exercise general oversight and control. They must ensure that the work proceeds with due regard to the expressed views of the Board on matters of principle and policy and that any practical difficulties or doubts which come to light in the implementation of the Board's policy are effectively brought to the notice of the Board.

It is convenient at this stage to consider what are the factors which militate in favour of decentralisation in a government department and of the enlargement of areas or combination by local authorities. Many of the same arguments apply in the case of commercial organisations.

The prime fault of centralisation is that it begets rigidity and from this fault others follow. In all organisations of any size or complexity, problems and situations arise which cannot always be dealt with purely as a matter of routine. Again, local conditions may call for a modification in certain circumstances of the normal routine. There are two methods of dealing with such matters. Either each as it arises can be referred to the authority empowered to give a decision, or, alternatively, the rules and regulations governing the organisation can be so comprehensive and strictly drafted as to cover every contingency. The former alternative produces one answer which infuriates the public: 'I am sorry, but I cannot give a decision on this; I must refer it to higher authority,' while the latter produces another answer which also infuriates the public: 'I am sorry, but there are the regulations and I have to keep to them.' Admittedly, there must in a large organisation be consistency in dealing with the public: the problem is to decide to what level it is safe to delegate responsibility, while at the same time being able to ensure that a reasonable consistency is maintained.

Thus, on the one hand, central control, if exercised by means of sheaves of detailed regulations, breeds an exasperating rigidity, whereas, if it is exercised by means of reference of all difficult problems to one central authority, it breeds intolerable delay. Again, either method precludes the training of subordinate officials in the exercise of responsibility and discretion: they live their lives as rubber stamps, afraid and unable to exercise any initiative of their own. A high degree of centralisation, by the concentration of responsibility at the top, inevitably results in a lack of contact with the public. The Civil Service or any other organisation exists to serve the public and its members can only fully carry out their function if they are kept in touch with the public for whose good they exist and draw their pay. By spreading responsibility, officials at all levels are enabled to see more closely how their administration affects the consumer.

It is therefore evident that those departments referred to at the beginning of this article whose activities bring them into direct contact with the public should decentralise responsibility so far as possible in order to achieve flexibility, speed, initiative and knowledge of the needs and reactions of the public. It is not thought desirable, however, that those departments whose function consists of the exercise of administrative supervision should decentralise their responsibilities, at all events where the larger local authorities are concerned. It is not possible to discuss in the present article the methods whereby decentralisation may become effective: it is only necessary to emphasize that it must be complete, it must embrace all related functions, responsibility as well as power, it must be free from constant interference from the centre and, most important of all, it must be entrusted to carefully selected and trained officials who are capable of carrying it out.

Departmental Regional Organizations

From the Sixth Report of the Select Committee on Estimates:
'Regional Organisation of Government Departments'. H.C.P. No. 233, 1953/4,
pp. iv, 5, 118–19, 137–8, 153–4 and 217–18.

This is the report of a parliamentary review of the regional
organization of seventeen government departments, together with
the memoranda submitted to the Select Committee by three local
authority associations and by the Treasury. The restiveness of the
local authorities in having to handle some of their ministerial
transactions through the regional machinery is clearly apparent in
this inquiry.

2. It is inevitable that Government Departments, which must maintain
a series of local offices, should have a regional organisation of some
kind. This applies especially to the social service Departments: the
Post Office, the Ministry of Pensions and National Insurance, the
National Assistance Board and the Ministry of Labour and National
Service. In the case of such regional organisations, therefore, Your
Committee are only concerned to see that they are not unnecessarily
large or extravagant and that a constant effort is made to maintain
economy. No evidence has been adduced to show that they are
inefficient or extravagantly run, and it appears that efforts are being
made to maintain and increase their efficiency. Whenever possible
the local offices of the various social service Departments have been,
and are being, concentrated in single buildings in local centres, in
order to reduce overheads and economise in clerical and lower-grade
staff, and to avoid unnecessary travelling for the public served. This
arrangement appears to be working satisfactorily wherever it has been
made, and Your Committee hope that such arrangements will become
general in the near future.

3. The regional organisation of the other Departments was either
created during the last war, as a result of wartime conditions, or in the
case of Ministries such as Housing and Local Government, which
although new in form, are in fact portions of pre-war and war-time
Departments, has followed a similar pattern. The object of creating
the regional organisations set up during the late war was to provide an
alternative to the central Government if contact with headquarters in
Whitehall were interrupted by enemy action. Regional Commissioners
were appointed to co-ordinate the work of the Departments in the
various regions. The regional organisations thus constructed have
continued to function ever since. Their purpose was thus originally

strategic, and in the cases where the justification of the organisation is still largely strategic, such as that of the Home Office, there is little that can usefully be said by Your Committee.

4. The remaining Departments which maintain regional organisations do so either for the purpose of administering controls or for advisory purposes.

5. The principal Departments concerned in administering controls are the Ministry of Housing and Local Government, the Ministry of Supply, the Ministry of Food, the Ministry of Fuel and Power, and the Board of Trade. In the case of the Departments which have administered controls which either have been lifted, such as the Ministry of Food, or are being lifted, such as the Ministry of Supply, the staff of the regional organisations is being rapidly run down. Your Committee are aware that there is a danger that organisations which administer controls may continue by their own momentum after the reason for their existence has ceased, and although it appears from the evidence that the Departments are aware of this danger and are determined to guard against it, Your Committee recommend that the Treasury should keep this aspect under review.

6. The Ministry of Works and the Ministry of Transport and Civil Aviation come within this category to a certain extent. Although the greater part of the duties of the Ministry of Works consists in maintaining and erecting Government buildings, the Ministry were to a large extent and still are to a lesser extent concerned with the licensing of building. The regional organisation of the Ministry of Transport and Civil Aviation controls the building and maintenance of roads which receive a grant from the Exchequer, and the erecting and placing of highway signs and omnibus stops, functions which appertained to the Ministry of Transport before the war. The considerations mentioned in the preceding paragraph apply therefore to them.

7. Smaller undertakings and small local authorities appear to have benefited more than larger undertakings and larger local authorities from the regional organisations of the Departments mentioned in the last two paragraphs and from those Departments the functions of which are largely advisory. The evidence on the value of these regional organisations is conflicting. The majority of the County Councils and the larger local authorities appear to be rather critical of the regional organisations, but it is not clear that they have had very much contact with them. The opinion expressed by the County Councils Association, the Association of Municipal Corporations and the Association of British Chambers of Commerce was summed up in an appendix to the

Report of the Local Government Manpower Committee, quoted in a memorandum submitted to the Sub-Committee, where the general conclusion is reached that either more power should be given to the regional organisations, or that they should be abolished. The opinion of the Treasury is that the abolition of regional organisations would involve increases in staff and cost in the Departments. The evidence does not justify Your Committee in making any definite suggestions, except in the case of the Ministry of Agriculture and Fisheries.

8. Generally, the evidence seems to show that Departments are not maintaining regional organisations without good reason. The Departments appear to be alive to the dangers inherent in semi-independent organisations of this kind, and it is hoped that they will continue to remain on the alert.

9. The case of the regional organisation of the Ministry of Agriculture and Fisheries presents greater difficulties. It is so complicated that it may be called not one organisation but several. In the opinion of Your Committee this complexity may result in overlapping, inefficiency, and waste. Serious criticisms have been made, particularly by the County Councils Association, who suggest in their memorandum that there is here duplication of work and unnecessary interference with the work of the local authorities. Your Committee have not been able to come to any considered conclusion on the evidence given on this subject, but they suggest that the regional activities of the Ministry of Agriculture and Fisheries should be the subject of a special inquiry by the Committee of the next Session.

Memorandum 9
Regional Organisations of Government Departments

MEMORANDUM FROM THE COUNTY COUNCILS ASSOCIATION

1. The Departments with regional organisations with which county councils are mostly concerned appear to be as follows:

(a) Home Office – Civil Defence section.

(b) Ministry of Housing and Local Government – who have regional offices and whose central organisation includes the following divisions: local government organisation; housing; new towns; planning; water supply and sewerage; and minerals.

(c) Ministry of Agriculture and Fisheries – who have regional priority officers and an inspectorate and whose central organisation includes the following divisions: animal health; education and advisory services including National Agricultural Advisory Service; finance and accounts; horticulture and poultry; labour and machinery; land – agricultural land service; land drainage and water supply; land use; the Welsh Department.

(d) Ministry of Health – who have regional offices and whose central office deals with the local health service; nursing; national assistance; and the blind, deaf and dumb service.

(e) Ministry of Labour and National Service – who have inspectors and a regional organisation.

(f) Ministry of Works.

(g) Ministry of Fuel and Power.

(h) Ministry of Transport and Civil Aviation.

All county councils have been asked for their observations on the letter of the 25th March from Sub-Committee D and the replies received have been carefully considered.

2. It seems likely that the administrative and executive side of the present-day regional organisation of Government Departments was developed and extended in order to deal with day to day problems arising in the field of local government during the war when decentralisation, or provision for decentralisation, of detailed administrative control became a necessity. Such a method of administration, with the duplication of staff and overlapping of functions which it exhibits, is, however, no longer justifiable on such a ground and the necessity for the retention of the administrative and executive side of all regional organisations of Departments should be reconsidered.

Some Departments, for example, the Ministry of Education, operate without a regional organisation relying on an inspectorate. The Home Office, however, operate some of the services over which they exercise oversight, without a regional organisation – police, fire and children, relying in each case on an inspectorate – but have introduced a regional organisation for another service – civil defence.

Regional organisation should be maintained only if it can be demonstrated to be positively advantageous.

3. Regional government is sometimes criticised as an emanation from the national Government constituting either an unnecessary interpolation between the local authority and the central Government and Parliament or as a bureaucratic addition to the Government Departments' power of controlling the local authorities. While regional government cannot be thought to have been conceived for these purposes it is nevertheless true that the conclusion to be drawn from the evidence of experience is that the criticism is often justly founded on the result. The delegation of authority from the central Govern-

ment Department to their regional off-shoots is not generous and any tendency to empire building at regional level can be gratified only at the expense of the local authorities.

4. If the need for a regional organisation is established then it is important, first, that the scope of its authority should be known, and, second, that the authority given should be both sufficient and sufficiently exercised to justify the existence of the machine. All too often neither of these conditions is satisfied and the replies of county councils to questions addressed to them by the Association, variable though the replies are on other matters, are consistent in expressing the need for observance of these two conditions.

5. Furthermore, the existence of a regional office means that discussions often start at regional level but are ended at headquarters or, conversely, that communications sent to London are referred to the region either to be settled direct with the county council or for regional observations before a decision is communicated from the centre to the county council. On many occasions, therefore, the mere existence of a regional organisation will slow up procedure for it is often drawn into the maelstrom of administration whether or not communication with the Government Department is made through the regional office. The two following examples demonstrate not only what has just been said but also the need for observance of the two conditions mentioned in paragraph 4. In one county the council wished to lease land to a municipal authority for a children's recreation ground. The proposal was initiated at regional level but referred for settlement to London. The opposite case occurred when, in the same county, application was made direct to a Government Department for consent to the sale of surplus land. The application was referred to and settled by the regional office. The policy of Departments in referring to regional offices questions relating to the disposal of land should be consistent not only within a single Department but also as between Departments.

6. It is, perhaps, important to make clear before dealing with the Departments of Government individually that in discussing the regional organisation of Government Departments the Association have not in mind that there should be any interference with the existing arrangements for devolution to Wales. It is clear, however, that the Welsh county councils consider that Welsh regional officers have insufficient authority given to them.

7. It is quite obvious from the replies received from county councils that there are many occasions upon which the Regional Office is not

consulted. A system under which reference may be made either to regional headquarters or to London at the election of a county council hardly impresses on the score of efficiency, and if left with the choice of communication between either the regional organisation or the central department there is little doubt that county councils would elect as they now usually do for the latter. It is certain that so long as regional offices have the little authority they possess the two criticisms referred to in paragraph 3 of this memorandum will continue to be well-founded.

8. One of the further disadvantages of the regional organisation is that the regional officer, in fear of setting a precedent which may be quoted in other regions, refers to headquarters merely on that account and not necessarily because of the intrinsic importance of the matter dealt with. This is a delaying factor which should not operate. Additionally it is the experience of the Association that when regional officers, for example, of the Ministry of Transport, act upon instructions from headquarters, they do not always do so consistently with the result that the action which county councils are asked to take in some parts of the country is not the same as in others.

9. The county councils esteem greatly the personal contacts maintained between their senior officers and the senior civil servants who are associated with the creation of policy. The value attached to these is such that they would accept, and it is apparent that many county councils would welcome, severe contraction of the functions, and in some cases an abolition, of the regional office. The administrative arrangements in the case of Home Office and the Ministry of Education, where an advisory service and an inspectorate are preferred to a regional organisation, appear to work very satisfactorily and a change from regional organisation to such an inspectorate where it is necessary should be considered.

Memorandum 11

ASSOCIATION OF MUNICIPAL CORPORATIONS

1. The Association of Municipal Corporations represents all the county boroughs and non-county boroughs in England and Wales and all but two of the metropolitan boroughs.

2. The Association expressed its views on the regional organisations of Government Departments to the Local Government Manpower Committee and a paper on this subject is set out in Appendix VIII to the Second Report of that Committee (Cmd. 8421). It will be observed

that the general conclusion of the Local Government Side was that either more power should be given to the regional organisations or that they should be abolished.

3. Members of this Association prefer to deal with the headquarters of the Ministries direct but under war conditions and conditions of shortages in materials the necessity for some form of regional organisation has been accepted.

4. The regional organisations with which local authorities now have most contact are those set up by the Ministry of Housing and Local Government and the Ministry of Transport and Civil Aviation. In so far as technical matters or matters of detail are concerned, contact with the regional staff of these Ministries is still regarded as advantageous by some local authorities and such contact may still be necessary while the control of materials continues. In general, however, it can be said that this Association does not desire the continuance of regional organisations by Government Departments.

Appendix 1

MEMORANDUM BY THE TREASURY

1. Regional devolution, which developed in the '30s and was continued during and after the war, has made it possible for Departments to be more closely in touch with local conditions and more accessible to those affected by their work, while relieving pressure in London.

Purposes of Regional Offices
2. The main purposes which regional offices serve may be classified as follows:

(*a*) To maintain contact with local authorities or with industrial and commercial undertakings and to perform appropriate executive functions (e.g. Ministry of Housing and Local Government and the Board of Trade).

(*b*) To supervise a network of local offices providing services to the public (e.g. Ministry of Labour and Ministry of Pensions and National Insurance).

(*c*) To provide common services for other Departments (Ministry of Works and Central Office of Information).

3. Many Departments maintain regional offices for more than one of these purposes. For example, the Ministry of Works regional offices not only provide common services such as office accommodation, but also maintain contact with the building industry and perform execu-

tive functions in the control of building operations. All regional offices to some extent provide a two-way channel of information between headquarters and local units. In some Departments there are decentralised staff, other than those in regional offices, with direct responsibility to the headquarters of the Department.

Extent of decentralisation

4. One of the main problems which has faced Departments in the development of regional offices has been to decide the extent to which powers can be devolved to the regions. In the case of Departments concerned largely with policy issues, devolution is not so easy as in the cases of Departments with wide executive functions. As a regional organisation necessarily involves the employment of considerable numbers of staff, it has been important, in order to justify the expenditure involved, to reach a clear understanding about what each regional office can do without reference to headquarters: otherwise the regional office, apart from any information it may supply from its knowledge of local conditions, would tend to be merely an extra link in the chain.

5. Since one of the advantages of regional devolution is that Departments can consult together at the regional level on problems affecting a number of them, it has been important to secure a common measure of decentralisation among Departments which have frequently to consult together. One of the main purposes of decentralisation is lost if one out of a number of Departments insists on problems, which the others could settle at regional level, being referred to headquarters. So far as is known, the present regional organisation is working satisfactorily from this point of view.

Number of Regions

6. Before the war those Departments which had a regional organisation frequently differed in the number of regions they employed and in the boundaries of each region. As the risk of war came closer, successful efforts were made to secure common regions and common boundaries. During the war there were 12 standard regions (including Scotland and Wales). The Post Office had in the '30s built up an organisation based on 10 regions and it was not found to be necessary to propose that the Post Office should conform to the standard organisation.

7. In any future war, the 11 standard regions indicated in the map attached to this memorandum, plus a South Eastern Region based on Tunbridge Wells, would be used and the Home Office, for civil defence purposes, are organised on twelve regions. Other Departments have found it possible to dispense with a separate regional organisation

in respect to the South Eastern Region, and considerable latitude is given to Departments to amalgamate regions and to make adjustments in boundaries where this effects economies in staff and suits the convenience of the Department concerned.

8. The question has from time to time been considered whether all Departments should, for peace-time purposes, use a smaller number of regions than the eleven commonly employed at present. So far any development along these lines has not been found to be practicable; but the position is kept under review.

Scotland and Wales

9. Scotland and Wales present special features. In Scotland there are a number of headquarters Departments responsible to the Secretary of State for Scotland which operate alongside the offices of the Great Britain Departments. The position there is at present under review by the Royal Commission on Scottish Affairs.

Common offices

10. Departments keep under examination the question whether regional offices might with advantage be amalgamated. Thus, when the Ministry of Materials was set up, it was agreed that the Board of Trade regional offices should undertake the Ministry's regional work. The regional offices of the Board of Trade and the Ministry of Supply are now in process of being amalgamated. When this was first mooted last year, the question was also examined whether the regional offices of the Ministry of Fuel and Power and the Admiralty could be combined with those of the Board of Trade and the Ministry of Supply to form a single regional office for the Departments concerned with trade and industry: but the work of the Ministry of Fuel and Power and the Admiralty was sufficiently distinct from the work of the other two Departments to make this difficult and there is, of course, a limit to the span of work which a Regional Controller can effectively cover.

Pooling of Common Services

11. From time to time studies are made of the extent to which it would be more economical for services carried out individually for Departments to be pooled and managed by one Department as a common service. Thus a recent study was made whether routine clerical work, typing and duplicating, cleaning and messenger services, etc., could be performed on a common basis. The conclusions drawn were that there were no substantial economies to be gained in the regions by a large-scale centralisation of routine work and services, nor by any further pooling of those services which were already centralised to some degree. It is, of course, possible to effect useful but minor econo-

mies from time to time by sharing arrangements where a number of Departments work in adjacent offices in one building, and a great deal of such sharing is done.

Local Offices

12. A considerable number of Departments have networks of local offices for work involving contact with the public.

13. The numbers of staff involved in local offices are very much larger than in the case of regional offices and the possibility of amalgamating small offices or using one Department to act as an agent for another in its local work is kept under examination to see whether staff savings might be effected.

14. As opportunity affords, the Ministry of Works endeavours to bring small local offices together into one building, since this frequently serves the convenience of the public and may yield savings through lower accommodation costs and the pooling of some common services. The difficulties of finding suitable accommodation and those caused by restrictions on capital expenditure should not, however, be under-rated. Everyone has agreed that the objective is a desirable one but it is not always easy of realisation.

15. The local Post Offices have for many years done a considerable volume of agency work for other Departments.

16. As the work of the Ministry of Food has fallen off, arrangements have been made for the work to be carried out by the local offices of other Departments, notably the Ministry of Labour (paragraph 7 of the memorandum submitted by the Ministry of Food).

17. The amalgamation of the Ministries of Pensions and National Insurance and the consequent prospect of some amalgamation of local offices (para. 5 (5) of the memorandum submitted by the Ministry of Pensions and National Insurance) is another example of the same policy.

18. As mentioned in paragraph 2 (3) of the memorandum prepared by the Ministry of Pensions and National Insurance and paragraph 19 of the memorandum by the Ministry of Labour and National Service, experiments are in progress in 50 towns by which local services are being provided by one Ministry for the other. These are all towns in which the Ministry of Works had already been able to bring the offices under one roof. In addition the National Assistance Board have recently taken part in the experiment in fourteen of the towns. These experiments in joint working have not yet been running sufficiently long to allow their success to be judged.

H.M. Treasury,
2nd February, 1954.

Appendix 17
Memorandum from the Urban District Councils Association

REGIONAL ORGANISATIONS OF GOVERNMENT DEPARTMENTS

In response to the invitation from Sub-Committee D of the Select Committee on Estimates that the Association should submit their views upon the Regional Organisations set up by the Ministry of Fuel and Power, the Ministry of Works, the Ministry of Housing and Local Government, and enquiring as to whether the members of the Association have found that these Regional Organisations and others with which they may have had to deal still continue to perform a useful function or whether the members have found it in practice more expeditious to approach the headquarters of the Ministries direct, the Association express the following opinions:

(a) The regional offices of the Ministry of Housing and Local Government in relation to the erection of new houses perform a useful and valuable function especially, but by no means exclusively, with regard to those matters upon which regional level discussions and negotiation can take place and a settlement be arrived at. By the personal contact which arises a considerable saving in time is effected and more effective administration ensues.

Furthermore, upon a subject matter of this nature, the Regional Officers by spending their time in the region acquire a knowledge of and become acquainted with local customary requirements and preferences, become better able to understand local prejudices and are thereby more cognizant of the problems which from time to time confront the local authorities within the Region.

In addition, by reason of the proximity of the regional administrative offices to the areas of the local authorities with whom they have dealings, the Officers of such regional offices are able to make on-the-spot inspections and examinations which in themselves are a considerable saving of time and consequent expense and which give greater satisfaction to all concerned.

(b) Although not specifically mentioned in the invitation beforementioned, it is the considered view of the Association that Divisional Road Engineers of the Ministry of Transport and Civil Aviation perform a useful and valuable function in relation to the highway matters upon which they have dealings with urban district councils which it is difficult to perceive could be carried out from the headquarters of the Ministry. The Association would be opposed to any suggestion that the positions of Divisional Road Engineers should be discontinued. Particularly does this apply to unforeseen circumstances which from time to time arise when works are in progress. Here again, local knowledge acquired in the performance of duties is considered to be valuable.

(c) Following upon the concentration of Local Fuel Offices and the apparent limited power of the Regional Officers of the Ministry of Fuel and Power so far as matters affecting local authorities generally are concerned, their effective functional use to local authorities appears to be negligible.

(d) The Licensing functions exercised by local authorities as agents on behalf of the Ministry of Works having since 1st April, 1954, been limited to certain matters connected with operations of building works relating to housing repair and adaptation and the licensing in connection with houses exceeding 1,500 sq. ft., occasions seldom arise when it is necessary for local authorities to have dealings with the regional organisations of this Department.

(e) The Association therefore consider that the regional offices of all Government Departments with which urban district councils are concerned, with the exception of the Ministry of Housing and Local Government in relation to the erection of new houses and the Divisional Road Engineers of the Ministry of Transport and Civil Aviation, could, without causing any inconvenience to urban district councils, be dispensed with.

(f) The experience of members of the Association supports the view that the regional organisation of the Ministry of Housing and Local Government other than the part of it dealing with the erection of houses and the regional offices of the other Departments mentioned no longer perform a useful purpose such as to justify their continuance in that more often than not such regional offices are constrained to refer to headquarters on so many occasions that direct approach to headquarters would be more effective and expeditious.

Regional Economic Planning

From A. W. Peterson, 'The Machinery for Economic Planning: III.
Regional Economic Planning Councils and Boards', *Public Administration*,
Vol. 44, Spring 1966, pp. 35–41.

The author was Deputy Under-Secretary of State, Regional Policy,
in the Department of Economic Affairs, at the time he wrote this
article. It explains the regional economic planning organization set
up by the Labour Government in 1965 and the hopes then
entertained for this new machinery. Though these regional bodies
are still in existence, their light now burns dimly. The Royal
Commission on Local Government thought that the activities of the
planning councils were appropriate to the provincial councils which
it proposed; but developments in this area wait the outcome of the
proposals of the Commission on the Constitution.

Northern

Yorkshire and Humberside

North West

East Midlands

Wales and
Monmouthshire

West
Midlands

East Anglia

South East

South West

Economic Planning Regions as at December 1965

Fig. 1

REGIONAL ECONOMIC PLANNING COUNCILS

When, in December 1964, the First Secretary announced his plan for the appointment of the first Regional Economic Planning Councils, he said that they 'will be concerned with broad strategy on regional development and the best use of the region's resources. Their principal functions will be to assist in the formulation of regional plans and to advise on their implementation. They will have no executive powers'; and that 'the members will be appointed as individuals, and not as delegates or representatives of particular interests'.

The membership of the Councils has been chosen to represent a wide range of experience. Most of them have about twenty-five members, among whom are people with experience in local government (either as elected members or as officials) and in industry, together with members drawn from the universities in the region and those with experience in the field of social service. The members with local government experience have been selected from names put forward by the local authority associations and those with industrial experience from names put forward by the employers' associations and the Trades Union Council. In Scotland and Wales the Council members are appointed by the Secretary of State, and the Chairman of the Council is a Minister. In England, appointments are made by the First Secretary, and the Chairmen include men prominent in the fields of local government, industry, and the universities.

Except for the Councils for the South East Region and East Anglia, the members of which have only recently been appointed, the Councils started their work in the Spring of this year and have been meeting at monthly intervals. Most of the Councils have found it necessary to appoint sub-committees to consider particular aspects of regional planning such as communications, land use, industrial structure, and the problems of labour mobility.

The Chairmen of the Economic Planning Boards regularly attend the meetings of the Council, and regional officers of other departments are invited to attend for discussion of items of particular interest to their department. Officials also attend meetings of the Council's sub-committees, and the Planning Board Secretariat also service the Councils. This close collaboration between the Councils and the Boards is a most important feature of the new regional machinery.

REGIONAL ECONOMIC PLANNING BOARDS

The Economic Planning Boards consist of senior regional officers of the departments concerned with economic planning, such as the Board of Trade and the Ministries of Labour, Housing and Local Government, Transport, Technology, Agriculture, Public Building and

Works, Power, and Land and Natural Resources. On the Scottish and Welsh Boards, representatives of the Scottish and Welsh Offices take the place of representatives of those English departments that do not operate in those countries. Contact is maintained with the nationalized industries through the responsible departments. In England, the Chairman is an official of the Department of Economic Affairs. The Boards meet regularly at monthly intervals, and their meetings are attended, whenever possible, by the Chairmen of the Economic Planning Councils. Other meetings are arranged to consider particular questions in which several departments have an interest. Arrangements have been, or are being, made to house the staffs of all the departments with a major interest in regional economic planning in the same building. In Scotland, the Chairman of the Board is an officer of the Scottish Office, and in Wales, of the Welsh Office.

THE WORK OF THE COUNCILS AND BOARDS

The Councils and Boards, like the Department of Economic Affairs itself, are concerned with the long-term implications of economic planning. Their contribution will be made in two ways: first, by assessing the economic potential of each region, and the measures which are needed to realize it fully, including social measures, such as those designed to make the region more attractive; and secondly, by ensuring that full weight is given to the regional implications of national policies. These are complementary functions, but particular importance must be attached to the first, since it is by establishing a more detailed assessment of a region's potential that the Councils and Boards can make an increasingly useful contribution to the formation of national policy. Much of their work will therefore be concerned with the sort of economic analysis on which a start has been made in the regional studies published in recent years. This aspect of regional economic planning is difficult and time-consuming, and there is much scope for improving the techniques of analysis. It is best regarded not as something which can produce quick and definite results in terms of proposals for action, but as a dynamic process which will gradually enlarge and deepen understanding of the factors which may affect economic growth in each region, and of the policy measures which are needed to ensure that regional growth follows a pattern which is most likely to be of benefit to the national economy.

Meanwhile, decisions have to be taken by the Government, both on general economic policy and in the field of communications and physical planning which will have important long-term effects on the economy of the regions. Some of these decisions will be dictated by national considerations, but the Councils and Boards will be able to play an increasingly useful part in advising on the practical implications of national policy at the formative stage. Their advice has already been sought on the proposals of the National Ports Council for the development of major ports, and on the long-term road programme.

The regional organization has also an important part to play in the implementation of national policy. Thus, the Councils have been consulted about the regional implications of proposed railway closures and will be considering the effects of the re-organization of the coal industry which has recently been announced.

In addition to their main task of ensuring that national and regional economic planning marches in step, the Councils can do a great deal to encourage local authorities and unofficial organizations to adopt a regional approach to common problems. In many fields, such as technical education, the arts, tourism, and the rehabilitation of derelict land, the benefits are regional rather than local, and sufficient resources can be mobilized only by co-operative effort. With their wide membership, the Councils are particularly well fitted to take the initiative in stimulating action in these fields.

Finally, the Regional Boards can make an important contribution to the efficiency of government administration in the regions by strengthening the co-operation between departments and reducing delays which may be caused by the need for inter-departmental consultation at the Whitehall level.

FUTURE OF THE REGIONAL ORGANIZATION

Descriptions of bureaucratic machinery are like the instructions one gets with household appliances. The parts of the machine are listed more or less intelligibly, and the way in which they are intended to function is described in deceptively simple terms. It is only by experience that one learns how the machine behaves in practice and which parts of it are awkward to handle.

The new regional organization has not been in existence long enough to display all its capabilities and weaknesses, and it is a little early to judge how it may develop. It will be particularly interesting to see how the new machinery can usefully supplement the existing organization of central and local government whose powers, as has been emphasized, are not affected by its creation.

How far, for example, can the Economic Planning Councils, which have no executive powers and no elective responsibility, exert a real influence on the major decisions of policy which affect regional planning? They must ensure that the advice which they give commands general support in the region (although it will not always satisfy the aspirations of particular interests) and at the same time they must avoid putting forward claims for preferential treatment for the region which are manifestly inconsistent with a realistic national policy.

This is a delicate undertaking, and two things are essential to its success. First, the Councils will need to establish a reputation as bodies whose conclusions are supported by the best possible assessment of the region's economic potential. Secondly, they must enjoy the confidence not only of central but of local government, so that they are consulted about questions of policy which have regional implications, while these are under consideration either centrally or locally.

Given these two things, the Councils will be able to play an important part in ensuring that policy decisions take full account of economic considerations, as they affect the region as a whole, although the decisions themselves will continue to be the responsibility of the two executive bodies, central and local government.

Again, how far can the Planning Boards provide effective machinery for co-ordinating the execution of government policy at the regional level? There is a difference here between the position in England and that in Scotland and Wales, where the Scottish and Welsh Offices have direct responsibility for most of the physical services, and are represented on the Boards by headquarters officers, who are, moreover, all responsible to the same Minister. In England, all the members of the Boards are responsible to their own Ministers, and the Board is in effect an inter-departmental committee at the regional level. The effectiveness of the regional organization as a whole will therefore depend on the degree of delegated responsibility which central departments are prepared to give to their regional representatives, and the extent to which differences between departments can be resolved at the regional level. The limits of what is possible can only be discovered by experience, but it is reasonable to expect that the Boards will strengthen the machinery of government by giving a greater regional content to the consideration of policy issues and by providing a better instrument for working out the practical implications of policy as it develops. The quality of the material on which Ministers have to reach decisions should be improved, partly because the interdepartmental examination of planning problems at a regional level can be more exhaustive, and partly because the close links between the Boards and Councils will provide a more effective means of obtaining advice from people outside the government service, and of assessing local opinion. Co-ordination of executive action should also be more readily achieved at a regional level than it could be centrally, where the emphasis tends to be on broad financial control. As Sir Eric Roll has said of the Department of Economic Affairs as a whole, the function of the regional organization is to provide more selective economic tools to supplement the macro-economic approach to the problems of regional imbalance.

These questions about the effectiveness of the new regional organization assume the continuance of the existing pattern of central and local government. If that pattern is not regarded as immutable, other more fundamental questions arise. For example, would it be desirable or practicable to create in England a system of regional organization based on the Scottish pattern, in which the major functions affecting the regional development of physical services would become the responsibility of a single Minister? What would be the effect on regional planning of changes in the structure of local government, on which there has been much discussion in recent months? Is there a case for elected Regional Councils, or are there less radical changes in local government structure which would make regional planning more effective?

The fact that such questions are being asked suggests that it would be premature to regard the present form of regional organization as a final solution. They may to some extent have been stimulated by its creation, and the experience gained in its operation should certainly provide a useful indication of the need for structural changes of a more radical kind.

(c) Some Special Cases

When we look beyond the decentralization of the administration of the central government, we can find a number of regional bodies which have been specially created for particular purposes. Every instance of such regional machinery is a special case if we take the view that these *ad hoc* solutions have been necessary because there has been no system of multi-purpose regional authorities in existence which would have avoided recourse to specially created bodies. Most of these *ad hoc* creations have resulted from the same basic underlying cause, the incapacity of local authorities to continue to provide an efficient service. This has usually been related to size, either in the sense that most local authority areas did not provide a large enough demand in services experiencing rapid technological advances, such as electricity supply or because the large number of separate authorities resulted in too many differences in methods and standards of provision, as in the case of main roads, to give a satisfactory service to the nation as a whole.

There is a lengthy list of services which have been transferred from local government to other authorities since 1930. In some cases, particularly in electricity and gas supply, technical considerations are such that it is unlikely that the services would be transferred to any system of multi-purpose regional authorities which might be established. These services can be regarded as outside the immediate interests of this study. Yet there still remains a number of activities organized on a regional basis which could be absorbed into a multi-purpose regional system without much *organizational* difficulty, though there might be other objections as in the case of the health service. The regional hospital boards set up under the National Health Service Act, 1946, and the passenger transport authorities set up under the Transport Act, 1968, are two good examples of this type of regional authority.

Had the war-time Regional Commissioners ever functioned in their unique role as directors of regional governments in the event of invasion, we would have experienced a limited form of regional government as distinct from regional decentralization of central departments. The Commissioners were condemned for a variety of reasons, chiefly concerned with their interim war-time activities in relation to the supervision of the civil defence services of local authorities. Unfortunately, the real possibilities of this type of official, in providing a coherent direction and supervision of a number of administrative agencies at the regional level, were never explored. The cause of regional government would probably have been advanced if the regional controllers of the government departments in each standard region had been brought together under the effective supervision of a commissioner or a minister of some political standing, a status which the Regional Commissioners lacked.

The regional economic planning bodies set up by the Department of Economic Affairs in 1965 also tried, along with their other activities, to provide a co-ordinated governmental approach at the regional level, but this has probably been the least effective of their attainments. They have certainly not provided the sort of regional outlook and leadership that a commissioner-type of appointment could have developed.

There are, of course, some regional organizations whose origin does not stem from the inadequacies of local government areas. The regional railway boards are an example. Their ancestors were the four main line companies formed in 1921, though there have been some changes in areas as a consequence of the Transport Acts, 1947 and 1962. The British Broadcasting Corporation is another example. The Corporation's activities began with a series of local broadcasting stations which were later replaced by a national and regional network. Now, the nineteen-seventies look like seeing a return to a more localized pattern of broadcasting, a pattern which will inevitably raise the question of whether the monolithic national corporation should be abandoned and its responsibilities be transferred to regional councils.

In this chapter, we have reviewed the regional developments of the middle decades of the twentieth century according to their chief characteristics. We have also demonstrated that a good deal of regionalism has been developed as a result of practical necessity; and, as our last extract shows, there has been a great amount of common ground amongst the various regional institutions which have been established.

The National Health Service

From Ministry of Health and Department of Health for Scotland,
A National Health Service, Cmd. 6502, 1944, pp. 14–16 and 77–9.

This White Paper explained the reasons why the hospitals could not
be administered by the existing local authorities, but the regional
hospital boards which were eventually established did not follow the
pattern of 'joint authorities' suggested by the Government.

Local Organisation

Local organisation is inevitably more complex. The new service has to
include hospitals and institutional services for the sick in general, for
mental cases, for infectious diseases and tuberculosis, for maternity
and for every general and special hospital subject. It has to include the
many kinds of service usually provided in local clinics, a family
doctor service and many ancillary services – nursing, health visiting,
midwifery and others. It ranges from the one extreme of highly
specialised services, requiring relatively few centres for the country
as a whole, to the other extreme of services involving a large number
of local clinics and arrangements for care in the individual home.

Suggestions have been made for a completely new kind of local or
'regional' authority – sometimes proposed as a vocational or technical
body (like the special kind of central organisation already mentioned).
In so far as those suggestions would conflict with the principle of
public responsibility, they need not be considered here. Both the
principles applied to central organisation – that of democratic responsibility and that of full professional guidance – must be equally
applied to local organisation.

Service to be based on local government

The present local government system amply embodies the former of
these principles – that of democratic responsibility – and the existing
local authorities are already responsible for many kinds of personal
health service which will need to be incorporated in the new and wider
service in future. It is certainly no part of the Government's intention
to supersede and to waste these good existing resources, or needlessly
to interfere with the well-tested machinery of local government as it is
already known; nor would the record and experience of the existing
local authorities in the personal health services justify such a course.
On the contrary the Government propose to take as the basis of the
local administration of the new service the county and county borough

councils. But there are some requirements of the new service which the county and county borough councils cannot fulfil if they continue to act separately, each for its independent area; and changes will be necessary. In particular, for the future hospital service, it will be essential to obtain larger local areas than at present, both for planning and administration. The special needs of this service can be considered first.

Need for larger administrative areas for the hospital service

Broadly speaking the hospital services, so far as they are publicly provided now, are in the hands of the county and county borough councils, with the exception of isolation hospitals for infectious disease in the counties. The size of counties and county boroughs varies enormously – ranging (without counting London) from Rutland and Canterbury, with populations of some 18,000 and 26,000 respectively, to Middlesex and Birmingham with populations of over 2,000,000 and 1,000,000.

It would be theoretically possible to put upon the council of each county and county borough the duty to provide, or to arrange with other agencies for, the whole range of hospital services. This would impose responsibility for the services on authorities many of which lack the size and resources and administrative organisation to plan and conduct and pay for the service. What is more important, it would leave untouched the demarcation between town and country which is reflected in the system of administrative counties and county boroughs, but which has no meaning in relation to hospital services. The towns largely serve the country in the matter of hospitals. If for purposes of hospital administration they are kept apart by continuing the separate county and county borough basis, the result will be a complicated criss-cross pattern of 'customer' arrangements, since in most areas (particularly those of counties) it will be out of the question to secure the whole range of service – or even the bulk of it – inside the area boundary. These 'customer' arrangements will in turn involve complicated administrative arrangements and a mass of financial adjustments between different areas. Alternatively, if the provision of a complete service within each area were attempted, the resulting system would run counter to the whole conception of an ordered pattern of hospital accommodation and could only lead to wasteful competition in hospital building.

The need for larger areas has long been recognised by local authorities in many branches of hospital administration. The many combinations already in existence make this clear; indeed, the very existence of these combinations would in itself give rise to administrative difficulties if it were decided that the new hospital service as a whole was to be in the hands only of the individual county and county borough councils in future.

The essential needs of a reorganised hospital service, based on a new public duty to provide it in all its branches, are these:

(a) The organising area needs to cover a population and financial resources sufficient for an adequate service to be secured on an efficient and economical basis.

(b) The area needs to be normally of a kind where town and country requirements can be regarded as blended parts of a single problem, and catered for accordingly.

(c) The area needs to be so defined as to allow of most of the varied hospital and specialist services being organised within its boundaries (leaving for inter-area arrangement only a few specialised services).

In the majority of the areas of existing authorities none of the three conditions would be met.

It is therefore necessary to decide what the form of authority for these larger hospital areas should be. On this, various alternatives are examined in Appendix C to this Paper. The course most convenient – and indeed, in the Government's view, the only course possible at the present time – will be to create the larger area authorities by combining for this purpose the existing county and county borough councils, in joint boards operating over areas to be settled by the Minister after consultation with local interests at the outset of the scheme. There will be some exceptional cases (the county of London is the most obvious) where no combination is necessary at all; in such cases an existing authority will fulfil both its own functions and those of the new form of authority – but this will be unusual. Where the new form of joint authority is referred to in the rest of this Paper it should be taken as including any individual council which, in such exceptional circumstances may be acting in the two capacities.

While both planning and administration will usually need to be based on larger areas, this does not mean that a standard-sized area need be, or can be, prescribed for the hospital services. Local conditions – distribution of population, natural trends to various main centres of treatment, geography, transport and accessibility – must determine the size and shape of the optimum area. Sometimes simple combination of a county with the county boroughs within its boundary (i.e. the geographical county as a unit) will be sufficient; sometimes the linking of two or three small counties will be needed, sometimes other variations.

Special mention should be made of the isolation hospitals for infectious diseases, because in the counties these hospitals are with few exceptions owned and administered by the minor authorities and not by the county councils, and therefore a decision to transfer them to the new joint authority will not only remove them from their present owners (as with the hospitals of the counties and county boroughs) but will prevent their present owners from retaining even the part interest in them which membership of the new joint authority will afford in the case of the counties and county boroughs. (It is, of course, not practicable to give direct representation on the joint authority to these minor authorities, without at once duplicating the representation of all local government electors who happen to live in a county and not in a county borough.) The case for this absolute transfer of the isolation hospitals has nothing to do with the past record of the minor authorities, nor is it in any way a reflection upon the quality of the work which they have hitherto done. The whole trend of medical opinion has for some time been in favour of treating these hospitals, not primarily as places for the reception of patients to prevent the spread of infection, but as hospitals where severe and complicated cases of infectious disease can receive expert treatment and nursing. The small isolation hospital of the past century is not only uneconomic in days of rapid transport but cannot reasonably be expected to keep abreast of modern methods. One result of the new outlook will be the development, in addition to the larger isolation hospital serving the densely populated area, of accommodation for infectious diseases in blocks forming part of the general hospitals. These considerations all indicate that the infectious disease hospitals must in future form part of the general hospital system.

It may be, as time goes on, that for certain specialised hospital functions there is room for the development of a few particular centres which would serve national rather than local needs. In this field there may be a case for direct provision or arrangement by the Government centrally. But such provision or arrangement would be special and exceptional and need not be considered here as part of the normal organisation of the new service.

As will be seen, when the hospital services are fully considered in Chapter IV, the function of the new joint authorities will be to secure a complete hospital and consultant service of all kinds for each of the new and larger areas – partly by their own direct provision and partly by arrangement with voluntary hospitals, and all on the basis of an area hospital plan which they will formulate in consultation with the hospitals and others concerned, and which will require the Minister's final settlement and approval. The existing powers and duties of the present local authorities in regard to hospital services – including tuberculosis, infectious diseases and mental health – will pass to the joint authorities, together with the existing hospitals and other institutions concerned.

Appendix C
Possible methods of securing Local Administration over larger areas than those of present Local Government

On the assumption that for certain aspects of the health service, particularly the hospital service, there is need for larger areas of local administration than exist for these purposes now, and that the body responsible for the administration must be representative of and answerable to the electors of the area, there are, broadly speaking, three possible courses:

(1) to establish a directly elected body for the sole purpose of administering these parts of the health service;

(2) to establish a directly elected body for the purpose of administering a group of services including these parts of the health service;

(3) to secure joint action by the councils of the existing counties and county boroughs which make up the proposed area of administration.

The creation of a directly elected local authority for some particular purpose would run counter to modern developments in local government, which have been towards replacing the system of special authorities for the administration of particular services (such as Boards of Guardians and School Boards) by the system of authorities covering a wide range of functions. But, apart from that the process of electing a one-purpose authority operating over a fairly large area is not likely to arouse sufficient public interest to attract an adequate proportion of local voters to the poll. Moreover, the system – if generalised over all the social services locally administered – would create an impossible complexity of separate authorities for separate local administrative functions, each requiring separate local election, each operating over a different area, and each requiring separate arrangements for rating or precepting in order to obtain its local revenue.

An alternative suggestion, of establishing new local authorities over wider areas for a substantial group of local services, has been canvassed in recent years. For instance, a proposal for comprising in a single local administrative area the county of Northumberland, part of the county of Durham, and four county boroughs lying on either side of the Tyne, was made in the Majority Report of the Royal Commission on Local Government in the Tyneside Area (1937) and it was recommended that six of the major local government services – Public Health (Medical and Allied Services), Education, Public Assistance, Police, Fire Brigades, and Highways – should be administered by a body with jurisdiction over the whole of this area. Proposals of a similar kind have been made in various quarters since the outbreak of the present war.

An authority performing so many important functions would need to be directly elected. But its establishment would involve a major alteration of the structure of local government. It would deprive county councils of practically all their chief functions – if, indeed, the few minor functions left could be held to justify their continued existence at all, and it would so denude county borough councils of their powers as to leave them with functions in some respects less than those of the 'minor authorities' of to-day. Recent publications of the various local government associations and other bodies have shown that there is a wide divergence of view as to the future pattern of local government. It is clear that this must be the subject of a comprehensive inquiry, which could not be instituted under present conditions or completed in a short time. Settlement of the machinery of the new health service cannot await the conclusions of such an inquiry and the passing of any consequent legislation.

The only practical course – pending a general review of local government – is to use the present machinery and the existing facilities for securing such combinations of authorities as may be necessary. This means the application (and possibly some adaptation) of the well-established practice of securing larger administrative units by joint action.

The advantages and disadvantages of administering particular services by combinations of local authorities organised as joint boards have often been argued. The members of the Tyneside Commission, referred to above, differed on the point, the majority regarding the joint board system as 'undemocratic', the signatory of the minority report taking the opposite view and recommending the extension of the system as going a considerable way to meet the problems with which that area was faced. The general convenience of arrangements which make it possible to have an area of administration exactly appropriate to any particular service, and to set up an authority for that area, chosen by persons who are themselves direct representatives of the local electorate, cannot be denied. But it is true that the system, if completely generalised, would leave the constituent local authorities who choose the members of the boards with little to do beyond nominating those members, instead of administering services themselves.

Other objections are often advanced. It is said that joint boards tend to attract the more elderly and less effective members of the constituent councils, and that their efficiency is thereby diminished. This is a matter of impression. It may be that, even if it is true, it is due not to the nature of joint boards but to the subject matters with which they happen to deal. A joint board administering (say) an infectious diseases hospital or a sewage disposal system – although its activities may be not less essential to the public welfare – may well attract less interest than would be taken in housing or education, two subjects which excite the keenest interest among local administrators. In any case, this particular weakness of the joint board system, if it exists, is one for which the remedy lies in the hands of local authorities themselves.

Another common criticism is that the powerful weapon of precepting on constituent authorities for funds weakens a joint board's sense of financial responsibility; or – to put it another way – that the members of a joint board, being indirectly elected and therefore at two removes from the ratepayers, have not the same need to justify policy to their supporters as the members of a directly elected authority. There may be something in this, but it is a point which could be met; e.g. by requiring the joint authority to submit to its constituent councils (at intervals of, say, one or two or three years) estimates of their proposed expenditure, for the approval of all – or of a specific majority – of those councils. Some means of removing deadlocks (probably by way of arbitral powers vested in the appropriate Minister) would be needed, unless a majority decision were to be binding. This device, coupled with a more regular habit among the constituent councils of examining, and if necessary debating, the annual and other reports of the joint board, would go a long way to preserve a proper relation of the board to its constituent councils and the electors.

It is also said that the joint board system is bad in that it separates the services entrusted to it from the rest of the main machinery of local government. So far as the health service is concerned, the answer is the practical one – that the need to settle areas of proper size and resources for certain aspects of the service is urgent, and that (temporarily at least) the joint board seems to be the only practicable means of doing this. There need be no question of ruling out any wider development of local government which may later emerge, as the need for new services and extensions of existing services reveals itself. But that is a matter of long-term policy, for which the establishment of a comprehensive health service cannot be delayed.

The Regional Commissioners

From 'Regionaliter', 'The Regional Commissioners' in *Political Quarterly*, Vol. 12, No. 2, 1941, pp. 148–53.

This article was written, one suspects, by a senior public official and it appeared when there was still a strong possibility that an invasion might be attempted so that the prospect of one or more of the Regional Commissioners having to assume the direction of government in their areas was very real. The extract which is reproduced shows how keenly the author perceived both the dangers and the prospects of this development.

... Even as late as 1938, regionalism would have appeared to an en-quiring neophyte to be, not a dead political issue, but rather one which had never come alive.

Less than a year later, however, a full-blown system of regional administration came into existence as an essential part of the Govern-ment's war organisation.

This dramatic innovation is a striking illustration of the manner in which necessary social and political changes force their way in at the back entrance when they are shut out of the front door. It has happened again and again in the history of public administration that institu-tions which have resisted adaptation all too successfully have suddenly been confronted with an alternative solution which, while avoiding the source of conflict and thus evading opposition, in effect by-passes the old institutions and leaves them stranded. In such circumstances it is true to say that nothing fails like success. The apparently irrelevant solution may deal a mortal blow to the organs which have withstood all attempts at adaptation.

This is what has happened in the present instance. At one stroke there has been installed a fully-fledged system of regional government which, while leaving the local authorities apparently untouched, offers a formidable challenge to their future existence and status.

The Regional Commissions are twelve in number. The following list gives particulars of the areas into which Great Britain is divided for the purpose:

Region	Regional Commissioner
SCOTLAND	Rt Hon. Tom Johnston, M.P.
NORTHERN Northumberland, Durham and the North Riding of Yorkshire.	Sir Arthur Lambert, M.C.

Region	*Regional Commissioner*
NORTH-EASTERN The East Riding and West Riding.	Rt Hon. Lord Harlech
NORTH-WESTERN Cumberland, Westmorland, Lancashire, Cheshire, the boroughs of Glossop and Buxton and certain urban districts.	Sir Harry Haig, K.C.S.I., C.I.E.
NORTH MIDLAND Nottinghamshire, Lincolnshire, Leicestershire, Rutland, Northamptonshire, Derbyshire (excluding the boroughs and urban districts contained in the North-Western region).	Lord Trent
MIDLAND Shropshire, Staffordshire, Herefordshire, Worcestershire and Warwickshire.	The Earl of Dudley, M.C.
EASTERN Norfolk, Suffolk, Bedfordshire, Cambridgeshire, Huntingdonshire and the parts of Essex and Hertfordshire outside the Metropolitan Police District.	Sir Will Spens, C.B.E.
SOUTHERN Oxfordshire, Buckinghamshire, Berkshire, Hampshire, Isle of Wight, the part of Surrey outside the Metropolitan Police District, Poole and two urban districts.	Mr Harold Butler, C.B.
SOUTH-WESTERN Gloucestershire, Wiltshire, Somerset, Devonshire, Cornwall, Dorset (excluding Poole and the two urban districts contained in the Southern region).	General Sir Hugh Elles, K.C.B.
LONDON The Metropolitan Police District.	Sir Ernest Gowers, K.C.B. (Senior Commissioner) Admiral Sir E. R. Evans Alderman C. Key, M.P. (in charge of shelters) H. Willinck, K.C., M.P. (in charge of rehousing the homeless) Sir Warren Fisher (in charge of demolition and repairs)
WALES	R. Richards, M.P. Col. G. T. Bruce, C.B., C.M.G., D.S.O.
SOUTH-EASTERN Sussex and the part of Kent outside the Metropolitan Police District.	Rt Hon. Sir Auckland Geddes, K.C.B.

It will be seen that in most cases a region has been constituted out of entire (or almost entire) counties and county boroughs. The chief exception to this is the London region, which takes the quite inadequate Metropolitan Police District (created in 1839) as its area.

Much could be said concerning the merits and demerits of the particular areas which have been given to the Regional Commissions, but this article is concerned with the nature of the institution rather than with the details of territorial jurisdiction. Such a discussion would therefore tend to divert attention from the main question, and is therefore omitted.

IV

The fundamental purpose of the Regional Commission is threefold. First, to act as the eyes, ears and mouth of the central government in the region. Second, to be responsible for seeing that the Government's Civil Defence and A.R.P. measures are carried out in the region. Third, in case of a breakdown in communications, to take the place of the central government in the region.

It will be seen that the first of these functions involves intelligence and liaison; the second involves supervision and inspection; the third, administration and policy-making.

The Government departments concerned with domestic services have appointed Divisional Officers to represent them within each region. These include the Ministry of Food, Ministry of Information, the Post Office, Ministry of Health, Ministry of Labour and National Service, Ministry of Pensions, Mines Department, Petroleum Department, Ministry of Transport, Office of Works and Buildings, and the Unemployment Assistance Board. These officers continue to receive instructions from their respective departments in the normal way while maintaining close contact with the Regional Commissioner. In the event of a breakdown of communications a Regional Commissioner would assume supreme control of his area; the Divisional Officers would look to him instead of to their respective departments; and the Regional Commission would operate as a miniature Central Government within the region.

Pending the arrival – which may never come – of this final stage, in which supreme authority is assumed, the Regional Commissioner is in the meantime able to exert an enormous influence over the conduct of affairs. This is particularly the case in regard to A.R.P. and Civil Defence matters, because in this sphere the Regional Commissioner acts on behalf of the Minister of Home Security, who pays a very high grant to local authorities in aid of their expenditure on these services. The Regional Commissioners have attached to them as personal assistants a number of leading officials of the Ministry of Home Security in charge of various aspects of A.R.P. and Civil Defence work.

Outside this special field the Commissioners are able to exercise a powerful and often decisive influence over other branches of administration. The novelty of the institution, the critical military situation, the prestige of the office and the personal eminence of some of the Commissioners result in their authority often exceeding their powers. This is noticeably so in London, where the municipal structure is especially weak – a mere patchwork quilt – and the Regional Commission especially strong. Except in Wales, the Commissions elsewhere consist of a single member with a deputy. In the Metropolis two Commissioners were originally appointed, but the number was gradually increased to five.

The present Commission for London consists of Sir Ernest Gowers (Senior Commissioner) and Admiral Evans, who are charged with general duties; Alderman Charles Key, M.P., in charge of shelters; Mr H. Willinck, K.C., M.P., Special Commissioner for rehousing the homeless; and Sir Warren Fisher, Special Commissioner entrusted with demolition and repairs to houses, highways and public utilities. To the extent that these vital tasks have passed into the hands of the Regional Commissioners, the scope and significance of the work of the local authorities has been diminished, and their stature reduced.

V

The Regional Commissioners were established to fill an aching void in our system of government caused by the absence of a coherent and systematic form of regional organisation. In the war emergency we now confront they are without doubt a necessary and perhaps indispensable addition to the machinery of the State. This should not blind us to the fact that they represent a complete break in our constitutional tradition.

The Commissioners cannot be regarded as politically responsible in any genuine sense of the term. The Minister of Home Security answers for them in the House of Commons, and they can be dismissed by the Government. But the position occupied by men of this calibre filling positions of unique authority cannot be assimilated to that of Civil Servants, and no one can seriously imagine that the doctrine of Ministerial responsibility is applicable to them. Moreover, at the time of the fullest exercise of their powers they will be cut off from all contact with the Cabinet, the Minister of Home Security and Parliament. The fact that two or three of the Commissioners happen to be Members of Parliament is presumably an accident, and such an incidental connection with the legislature cannot be regarded as an adequate safeguard of their accountability.

An attempt is being made to arrange meetings between the Commissioners and the Members of Parliament representing constituencies within their respective Regions. This is better than nothing, but it cannot be regarded as an adequate safeguard of democracy, since the Commissioners are not answerable to the M.P.'s, and their statements cannot even be quoted in the House of Commons.

No less sharp is the contrast afforded between the Regional Commissioners and the system of democratically-elected local authorities. The Commissioners represent, indeed, a clear example of that dangerous trend in our political development which may be described as 'Government by Commission.' By this is meant some form of appointed board or officer exercising large administrative powers without direct responsibility to an elective body. They are the apotheosis of the movement which can be traced in the establishment of such bodies as the B.B.C., the London Passenger Transport Board, the Central Electricity Board and the Coal Commission.

Most important of all is the certainty that, whether they desire it or not, and regardless of their good intentions, the Commissioners must inevitably offer a serious menace to the future of local self-government. Our system of local authorities has many serious defects which are deserving of criticism and censure; but as instruments of democracy they possess merits of supreme value. The democratic process has been largely developed in and through the local council. The town hall and the council chamber is the first and indispensable link in the chain of our democratic institutions, the place in which the civic spirit is evoked and bodied forth in democratic shape. If these centres of local democracy are overshadowed and reduced to insignificance by the powerful new Regional Commissions created by the central government, the ultimate effect will be to weaken and undermine democratic government at the national and Imperial level.

It is difficult to propose an immediate remedy at this stage of events. The war makes it impossible to replace the Regional Commissioners by an elected council; and the local authorities themselves are in a state of suspended animation so far as a vital contact with the citizens is concerned. The method of indirect election is undesirable at the best time of times. To-day it would be hopelessly mistaken.

Hence, all we can do now is to watch the course of events carefully, to analyse the present situation in all its implications, and to make up our minds that as soon as the war is over we will abolish the Regional Commissioners and replace them with directly-elected Regional Councils. Only thus can we preserve and strengthen our system of local democracy on which so much depends.

Regional Economic Co-ordination

From A. W. Peterson, 'The Machinery for Economic Planning: III.
Regional Economic Planning Councils and Boards', *Public Administration*,
Vol. 44, Spring 1966, p. 38.

The evidence as to the extent of interdepartmental co-ordination at
the regional level, which should be one of the objectives of effective
regional government, has not been very substantial in the case of
the regional economic planning bodies. As the following extract
infers, more emphasis seems to have been placed on co-ordination
between headquarters and regional offices within the separate
Departments.

An essential requirement for the effective functioning of the regional
organization is a good system of communications with the central
departments concerned with regional economic planning. It has long
been the practice for departments with regional offices to have regular
meetings with their regional representatives, and since the Economic
Planning Boards were set up arrangements have been made for
monthly meetings with all Board Chairmen, under D.E.A. chairmanship, in which senior members of other divisions of the Department
of Economic Affairs besides the Regional Policy Division, and also of
other departments will take part. Formal arrangements also exist for
the discussion of questions affecting regional economic planning
between representatives of the central departments concerned.
Officials of the Department of Economic Affairs also attend meetings
of the Regional Boards.

The Chairmen of the Economic Planning Councils meet together
regularly, sometimes among themselves, and sometimes with D.E.A.
Ministers. The First Secretary and other Ministers will periodically
hold meetings with the Council Chairmen and representatives of both
sides of industry, local authority associations and other organizations
concerned with regional planning to discuss the work of the Councils
and Boards.

There is also close day-to-day contact between the Regional Policy
Division of the Department of Economic Affairs and the Chairmen of
the English Boards and their staff. The Regional Policy Division has
three functional branches, each of which deals with general policy on a
number of aspects of regional economic planning. Questions of
specific interest to a particular region are dealt with by the Board
Chairmen, who will if necessary consult the appropriate Headquarters
branch. It is often necessary to consult other departments, either

regionally or centrally. The system is designed to place responsibility for the implementation of regional economic planning on the Regional Boards, while ensuring that regional planning is integrated with national policy.

Broadcasting and Regionalism

From P. Beech, *New Dimensions in Regional Broadcasting*,
B.B.C. Lunch-time Lectures, Eighth Series, No. 5, March 1970, pp. 3–5.

Though we may dismiss Mr Beech's claim that the traditional
English Regions were created by the B.B.C. – C. B. Fawcett
expressed the ideas embodied in his *Provinces of England* at least a
decade before the Corporation was established – the regional
broadcasting organization has become a well-known pattern. It is
also of significance for our consideration of the development of
regional ideas, because the broadcast journalism of the regions *has*
had a part in the creation of a regional consciousness amongst the
people of the various parts of the country.

'I would like to begin by spending a few minutes reviewing the history
of the English Regions.

First of all, have they any validity? Is there logic in the way in
which they divide up the country? The answer is that the traditional
English Regions were artificially created by the B.B.C. Until fifty
years ago, the county was the largest unit below nationhood which
commanded any loyalty or acceptance, and I suspect that the concept
"region" – now so familiar to us in connection with British Rail,
Economic Planning Councils, the Gas Board, and so on – was practically unheard of before the B.B.C. introduced it in the 'thirties.

Radio's origins were far less complex. It started as local radio in a
number of independent city stations. In time it broadened out into a
two-tier broadcasting organisation – network and regional. But the
regional part of it was not created in response to cultural demand or
sociological pressure. It evolved as a result of the B.B.C.'s desire to
give listeners a choice of programmes. One network, the "National
Programme", covered most of the country on long wave. The second,
the "Regional Programme", had to be on medium wave, and in order
to cover Britain, five high-power transmitters on five frequencies were
required. The five transmitters made it possible to create five separate
regions, and it was their coverage which drew the regional boundaries.
If, in order to get the Regional programme, you tuned your set to
Moorside Edge, then, wherever you lived, you were in the North
Region; if 51T gave you the best signal, then the B.B.C. regarded you
as a Midlander. There's little evidence to suggest that these new
affiliations meant much to listeners; they were more united in an anti-
metropolitan attitude than bound by local patriotism.'

'By 1939 then, the reputation of the Regions was established and secure. Wherein lay its strength? In my opinion, English regional vitality didn't derive from any territorial consciousness or patriotism, but from a climate of healthy dissent. Regions have always held open house for the noncomformist and the buccaneer, and this policy brought them a lot of talent from among the millions living outside the metropolis. Independence was the soil which nourished their success.'

Coincidence of Regional Boundaries

From Association for Planning and Regional Reconstruction, *A Preliminary Analysis of 42 Maps of Regional Boundaries*, Report No. 42, March 1947.

The frequency with which public authorities have had to resort to regional units of organization leads to the speculation as to how far these regional units cover similar territories. This Report deals with this question in relation to those regional units which existed in the early post-war period. It is also of interest to note that it was the recognition of this frequent occurrence of similar territories for different administrative purposes which made an important contribution to the development of the 'city-region' concept.

The area of Britain has for centuries been divided into fragments of various shapes and sizes called Counties. These units have, more and more frequently of recent years, proved inconvenient for certain purposes and, for generations past, it has been found administratively convenient to form groups of counties into 'regions'. These regions have varied in size and composition according to the purpose for which they were formed and considerable emphasis is usually placed upon their points of difference.

This brief report discusses their points of likeness.

Maps have been made of 42 different regional boundaries: 24 of these have been boundaries devised and operated by Government Departments (from the Districts of the Major Generals in 1656 to the Regions of Food Distribution 1942): 7 have been boundaries employed by official organisations such as the National Association of Libraries, 1935, or the Congregational Churches, 1919: 2 have been boundaries with a definite physical basis, the Water Catchment Board, 1942, and the Meteorological Office, 1939: the remaining 9 have been proposals, made either by Government appointed committees or eminent individuals. All are listed in Table A.

Information supplied by the Board of Trade and entitled 'Normal Divisions of Government Departments' was chosen as the basis for the measurement of agreement. The boundaries on this map were divided into 40 segments, listed in Table B, and the degree of correlation of each of these with 39 other maps was noted. Map I 7, Post Office and Telephone Districts, 1938, and Map I 25, Proposed Electric Supply Area Boards, 1947, had to be omitted as their divisions seldom follow county boundaries, from subsequent analysis.

The results, which are tabulated in Table B, show that the division of England from Scotland is accepted by all and the division of England from Wales by almost all.

The most generally accepted lines of division within England are:

1. The demarcation of Yorkshire from the counties to the west and south (over 75% agreement on all sections).

2. The enclosure of the 5 counties of the West Midland Region (over 69% agreement on all sections).

3. The separation of the East Midlands from South East England by a line running south west from the Wash along the boundaries of Lincolnshire and Northamptonshire.

4. The separation of Southern England vertically along the eastern boundaries of Gloucestershire, Wiltshire and Hampshire.

These lines of division carve England up into the following 6 major divisions:

NORTH	Cumberland, Durham, Northumberland, Westmoreland, Yorkshire.
NORTH WEST	Cheshire, a part of Derby, Lancashire.
WEST MIDLANDS	Hereford, Shropshire, Stafford, Warwick, Worcester.
EAST MIDLANDS	Derby (but not the north west), Leicester, Lincoln, Northampton, Nottingham.
SOUTH WEST	Cornwall, Devon, Dorset, Gloucester, Somerset, Wiltshire.
SOUTH EAST	Bedford, Berkshire, Bucks., Cambridge, Essex, Hampshire, Herts, Huntingdon, Kent, London, Middlesex, Norfolk, Oxford, Rutland, Suffolk, Surrey, Sussex.

Within these 6 major divisions there is very little general agreement on the best lines of subdivision.

Most maps show some dividing line in the North, sometimes running north and south, sometimes east and west. The greatest variety occurs in the South East. Surrey and Sussex are sometimes separated from Hampshire, and Bucks from the counties to the east, but the varied ideas of the limits of Greater London cause great confusion.

In the South West, Dorset is sometimes divided from Wiltshire but the other counties are usually grouped together.

The West Midlands, the North West and the East Midlands are far less frequently subdivided.

TABLE A. LIST OF 42 MAPS OF REGIONAL BOUNDARIES

Group I: Regional Boundaries of Government Departments
I 1. Church of England
I 2. Districts of the Major Generals, 1656
I 3. Military Districts, 1803
I 4. War Transport and Civil Defence, 1942
      (Compare I 5, II 7, IV 7)
I 5. Ministry of Transport, 1933 (compare I 4, II 7, IV 7)
I 6. Normal Divisions of Government Departments, 1946
I 7. Post Office and Telephone, 1938
I 8. War Office for Purchase of Wool, 1914–18
I 9. Ministry of Works, 1939
I 10. Board of Trade, 1942
I 11. Census of Production, 1935 (compare I 14, I 21)
I 12. Ministry of Health, 1939 (compare I 13, II 5)
I 13. Proposed Hospital Boards, 1946 (compare I 12, II 5)
I 14. Registrar General, 1941
I 15. Ministry of Labour, 1918
I 16. Ministry of Labour, 1939
I 17. Ministry of Labour, 1942
I 18. Factory Inspectorate, 1938
I 19. Ministry of Education Inspectorate, 1941
I 20. Ministry of Agriculture Advisory, 1942 (compare I 21)
I 21. Ministry of Agriculture Statistics, 1942 (compare I 21, I 11, I 14)
I 22. Milk Marketing Board, 1939 (compare with I 24)
I 23. Ministry of Food Organisation, 1942 (compare I 18–20)
I 24. Ministry of Food Distribution, 1942 (compare I 23, IV 4)
I 25. Proposed Electric Supply Area Boards, 1947 (compare II 1)

Group II: Regional Boundaries of Official Organisations
II 1. Central Electricity Board, 1946 (compare I 25)
II 2. National Association of Libraries, 1935
II 3. Youth Hostels Association, 1937
II 4. Allied Societies of R.I.B.A. 1935
II 5. British Hospitals Association, 1937 (compare I 13)
II 6. The Congregational Churches, 1919
II 7. Automobile Association, 1939 (compare I 4, I 5)

Group III: Regional Boundaries with a Physical Basis
III 1. Water Catchment Boards, 1942
III 2. Meteorological Office, 1939
III 3. Alternative Programmes of B.B.C. 1939

Group IV: Proposals for Regional Boundaries
IV 1.   Ministry of Health, 1920
IV 2.   Royal Commission on Transport, 1929
IV 3.   John Dower, 1938
IV 4.   G. Cadbury, 1939 (compare I 24)
IV 5.   E. A. A. Rowse, 1941
IV 6.   E. G. R. Taylor, 1941
IV 7.   E. W. Gilbert, 1941
IV 8.   C. B. Fawcett, 1942

Chapter

3

Regional Structures

A unique academic contribution to the development of ideas about regionalism has come from the work of geographers, who have evolved regional structures by mapping the social and economic characteristics of the country. Two distinct features can be seen in these geographical works. First, there is the early recognition that the areas of the local government units which were established in the latter years of the nineteenth century bore little relation to the social and economic structure of the country. There is a general propensity on the part of most of the geographers towards regional or provincial forms of organization, and a common argument that these more accurately reflect the realities of the social and economic fabric than the nineteenth century institutions. Indeed, the rapid growth of regional elements in the organizational structure of all kinds of activity, public and private, civil, ecclesiastical and military, is recorded by the geographers as further evidence of the unsuitability of the local government areas for administrative purposes.

The second feature, and the more important one from an ideological point of view, is the development of an organic concept of the relationship between a town or a city, usually referred to as an urban centre, and the surrounding area. The system of local government which was created in stages between 1835 and 1899 embodied a cleavage between town and country, expressed in the dichotomy of administrative county and county borough and the differences in the powers of the urban and rural district councils. The organic ideas of the geographers have been based on the clear recognition of the interdependence of town and country, socially and economically. With the growth of communications and the development of a large number of service industries, this interdependence has become more entrenched with time. Yet, obvious though the development appears, the consequences have only slowly percolated through official thinking about the reorganization of local government.

The organic notion of interdependence is the basis of the concept of the city-region, the idea that a town is the hub of a complex of social and economic activities which extend beyond the administrative boundaries of its local government machine. This concept, in its simplest form, leads almost inexorably to a 'rational' solution: all one has to do is to draw on a map the factors which express the social and economic influence of the town, and these will duly indicate a 'real' area in which a local authority should operate.

But this proposition is too deceptively simple. The city-region concept cannot be applied to the delimitation of governmental areas without some qualifications. To begin with, as R. E. Dickinson has demonstrated, urban centres differ in the kind and the extent of the influences which they exert over the areas which surround them. As a result, there are smaller areas of influence within larger ones. Which of these is the more relevant for governmental purposes? Smailes conceived the idea of putting the towns in some kind of order, rating them according to the variety of service features which were centred on them. This was his 'urban hierarchy', which he used to indicate those places which possessed an adequate number of the features which he considered essential to merit the status of a regional centre.

Both Smailes and Dickinson proceeded by mapping a large number of activities which showed the area of influence of a particular place. From this succession of areas of influence it becomes possible to detect those areas which recur again and again in different services. For the large urban centres two or three different sized areas soon begin to emerge, according to the nature of the service facilities concerned. The significant fact is that these areas emerge from a host of different activities. It is on this facet that we discover one of the main weaknesses of Mr Senior's scheme for the reorganization of local government as embodied in his Memorandum of Dissent from the Report of the Royal Commission on Local Government in 1969. He chose to base his idea of a city-region on a very limited range of factors, those related to the use of motorized transport. He limited the area of his city-regions by the extent to which motorized transport determined the daily flow of people into and out of urban centres. But this is a very inadequate base for the concept of a city-region, because the extent of the physical movement of people in their daily lives, whether for work or for pleasure, does not sufficiently identify the social and economic relationships based on a given urban centre. There are many distributive, commercial and financial activities embraced by an urban centre's service facilities to which motorized transport is irrelevant

and which, therefore, escape Mr Senior's definition. A better approach
to the city-region concept had, indeed, been expressed by Mr Senior a
few years before he joined the Royal Commission, and it is these
earlier views which are reproduced in this chapter.

The main contributions of Smailes and Dickinson appeared nearly
thirty years ago, but another geographer, Fawcett, had expressed a
rather simpler approach thirty years before them. In the extracts
which follow, a more recent view of the development of the urban
hierarchy has also been included to provide the reader with a more
up-to-date picture.

Another reason why the city-region concept cannot easily be applied
to the reformation of local government structure is that the geographers have often been more concerned with the problem of finding
suitable areas for town and country planning purposes than with the
wider aspects of local government structure and services. Local
authorities are multi-purpose bodies and it is undesirable that their
structure should be dominated by the technical needs of one particular service. Moreover, environmental planning has developed in such
a way that it carries the danger that it will embrace the policy making
and administrative planning functions which are properly the duty of
the council of a local authority itself.

A further difficulty arises from the fact that local authorities, if they
are fulfilling their true role, should have some influence on the development of the communities they serve. This means that, in the long run
at any rate, the development of the social and economic relationships
which form the web of the city-region will be affected by the influence
of the governing authority. This, of course, is another way of emphasizing the organic nature of the city-region. It is not a static phenomenon, and in the long run it also means that there must be corresponding changes in the administrative areas.

As might be expected, since the different writers often use the same
range of indices of economic and social factors, there is a large measure
of agreement about the basic areas at the regional or provincial level,
though there remains scope for some argument about the precise
definition of boundaries. In this respect, some arbitrary decisions must
be taken simply in order to get boundaries drawn and the area of an
authority's operations adequately defined, but considerations of this
kind are hardly sufficient to vitiate the large measure of coincidence of
the general arguments.

In summing up the work of the geographers, there are three important features to remember. The first is that they have provided a vast
amount of evidence to show the irrelevance of the local government
system set up at the end of the nineteenth century to the social and

economic structure of the country. Within this general point, we may also note the sharp institutional division between town and country which has produced a whole series of strains and stresses within the system which have further aggravated the general deficiencies. The second point is the unanimity with which the geographers have resorted to regional or provincial units of organization as a remedy for the defects they have uncovered.

The third feature, however, is a negative one: the absence of any connection between the social and economic characteristics mapped by the geographers and any measure of the operational viability of the authorities which might be established for the areas so defined. It might be assumed that, since the general trend of the arguments is towards larger authorities than those now in existence, their operational viability can be inferred from the fact that the existing authorities are managing to carry on. Yet, this assumption is not entirely warrantable because many of the existing authorities are criticized for falling short of what is generally regarded as necessary for an efficient and effective organization.

Though this is the weak point of the geographical approach, it is also a deficiency shared with many other would-be reformers. Few of them give enough consideration to the question of whether the authorities that they would create would be operationally efficient. What needs to be considered is not just the demand factors which stem from various levels of population, which is the index generally used for indicating local authority viability, but whether the resulting authorities will have financial foundations, a credibility as employers of staff and an effective internal organization to permit of efficient and effective operation. These last-mentioned things are what measure the administrative health of an authority, not the size of population or area served. They cannot be ignored if a satisfactory system is to be established, but so far these are not the kind of things which the geographers have set out to measure.

Drawing Provincial Boundaries

From C. B. Fawcett, *Provinces of England*, Williams and Norgate, London, 1919, pp. 69–80.

The simple geographical principles which Fawcett laid down for the delimitation of provincial boundaries are much less complex in idea than the city-region principle, but not without some difficulty in their application to the map of England. Using these principles, Fawcett divided England into twelve provinces.

Our first principle: 'The provincial boundaries should be so chosen as to interfere as little as possible with the ordinary movements and activities of the people' – follows from the fact that a man's work-place and his residence should be in the same province. The division of interests which necessarily results when a man works in the area of one local authority and has his home in that of another is detrimental to the growth of any sane local patriotism. It ensures that his interest in local affairs and elections is divided, and often he takes practically no part in them. The apathy of the majority of the people, which is so great a handicap to London's local government, is probably due in great part to the confusion of local authorities in Greater London and the lack of any one authority for that vast urban area. Our boundaries should be so drawn that no suburban district is severed from its focal town; though in so small and crowded a country as England the complete logical application of this principle is impossible, for in some cases the outer or detached suburbs of different city areas overlap – London's detached suburbs extend to Bournemouth and Cromer, and those of Liverpool and Manchester along the coast from Llandudno to Blackpool and to the Lake District and the Pennines.

From this principle it follows that the boundaries should be so drawn that any area of continuous dense population should be kept as a whole in one province: and hence that the boundaries will in general be drawn along those more thinly peopled tracts of the country which do in fact form, relatively, areas of separation between the more populous districts.

Our second principle is: 'There should be in each province a definite capital, which should be the real focus of its regional life. This implies further that the area and communications of the province should be such that the capital is easily accessible from every part of it'.

This has led to the arrangement of two or three of the provinces round their capitals, and to some discussion of the capital for each. This particular principle bears so directly on the real unity of a province that it is, in our opinion, much more fundamental than any considerations as to the relative areas or importance of the provinces.

The third principle underlying our delimitation of the provinces is: 'The least of the provinces should contain a population sufficiently numerous to justify self-government'.

This principle is self-evident. Without a sufficient minimum of population it is impossible that the province could include such a variety of minds and opinions as to make democratic self-government a reality. The actual figure taken as the basis in this discussion is one million. This is a convenient round number which fits into English conditions; no special importance is claimed for it. In lands where population is spread more sparsely the minimum is necessarily lower, and the area over which it is spread greater, than in England. Here the million fits with the requirement that all parts of a province should be within a moderate distance of its capital, even in the more thinly peopled parts of the country.

The fourth principle set out is: 'No one province should be so populous as to be able to dominate the federation'.

This is one reason for advocating a division of England; since otherwise that country could, in a British Parliament, easily outvote the combined representatives of Scotland, Ireland and Wales. . . .

The domination of a single state in a federation is not likely to be favourable to the best interests of the other members or of the federal state as a whole. Hence it is not desirable that England should remain a unit in the proposed federation of the British Isles or of Great Britain. Also, there are in England several distinct regions, each of which is sufficiently populous and distinct from the others to form an individual member of the federation, such as, for instance, East Anglia, the North Country, Lancashire and Cheshire, and the Devonian Peninsula. These are at least as distinct from each other in many respects as any one of them is from Wales or Scotland; and we believe that the best interests of the people would be served by giving each such region full provincial self-government, on the same footing as Scotland or Wales. There is no reason whatever to assume that the representatives of such provinces of England would act together in a federal parliament in the way in which members sent there from one national parliament might tend to do.

The fifth principle is: 'The provincial boundaries should be drawn near watersheds rather than across valleys, and very rarely along streams'.

Among the most vital of the matters in regard to which we need to organize the resources of the country on a large scale and over wider areas than those of any existing Local Authority are:

(*a*) Water supply for our towns and villages.

(*b*) Drainage.

(*c*) The supply and distribution of electricity and gas for lighting and power.

(*d*) The provision and maintenance of roads and tramways.

The main lines of all these must normally and naturally be laid along the valleys; since there they meet with the easiest gradients and the minimum of natural obstacles. Hence also lines of travel and industrial and commercial establishments, factories, warehouses, offices, etc., are usually placed in the valleys. A valley is a natural unit area for most purposes of human organization, primarily because the higher ground which separates one valley from another is, to a greater or less extent, an obstacle to intercourse and less favourable to settlement and occupation. Our population is mainly in the valleys. From this it follows that the boundaries should be drawn near the watersheds. This is of much greater importance in areas of considerable relief, where the valleys are sharply cut off from each other by high ridges, than it is on low plains. Over most of England the valleys are distinct; but the dales of the Pennines are much more strongly separated from each other than are the valleys of the Costwold Hills or the Downs, and still more so than those of the Midlands; while in the Fenland we have a region so flat that the interstream ridges have practically disappeared, and the rivers, with their bordering strips of floodland, become the barriers. Thus the principle that boundaries should keep to the watersheds is of great importance in most parts of the country; but it ceases to be of much value in the lowlying plains about the head of the Humber and the Wash. . . .

Where the application of this principle would have led to delimitations contrary to those indicated by the principles stated above, it has been regarded as the less important one. The boundaries of our provinces cut across the valleys of the Trent and the Severn because to draw them on the watersheds would involve cutting up the densely peopled areas of South and North Staffordshire; and it is more desirable to keep such continuous areas of dense population each in one province than to keep to watershed boundaries.

The last of our six principles is: 'The grouping of areas must pay regard to local patriotism and to tradition'.

Any provinces of England must necessarily supersede and absorb the counties. Hence county patriotism becomes a factor of great weight in the delimitation of the provinces. Most suggestions hitherto made for the division of the country into major local government areas for any purpose have been limited to grouping the existing counties in various ways. These have sometimes been accompanied by suggestions for some transfers of districts from one county to another, for instance Ribblesdale from Yorkshire to Lancashire, in order to get rid of some of the worst of the existing boundaries. The writer made some scores of attempts at such arrangements of counties before coming to the conclusion that the only hope of an effective solution lies in abandoning all attempts to base the provincial boundaries on those of the counties, and starting afresh by applying the above principles to the existing state of distributions in England. The task of attaining a practical and satisfactory delimitation of provinces is a geographical one, and it can only be accomplished by a systematic application of geographical science to the existing conditions.

Concept of the City Region

From R. E. Dickinson, *City, Region and Regionalism*, Kegan Paul, London, 1947, pp. 165–7, 231–4, 253–4, and 273–5.

Dickinson provided one of the earliest and most comprehensive expositions of the city-region concept in this book. These extracts are taken to show first his exposition of the basic concept and its application to this country; and finally how it leads to the movement for regionalism as the modern basis of organization.

The city cannot be fully understood by reference only to its arbitrarily defined administrative area. It has to be interpreted as 'an organic part of a social group', and in approaching the analysis of the four main urban functions – dwelling, work, recreation and transport – 'it must be remembered that every city forms part of a geographic, economic, social, cultural and political unit, upon which its development depends'. The problem of the regional interpretation of the city, of defining and analysing the functions and limits of the city and the unifying relationships in the surrounding area, is one of disentangling the regional component and examining the multitude of tributary areas served by and serving the city. Each group of functions has its particular extent and characteristics. Many functional areas have no close relation with each other in their geographical extent – which is often difficult to define – or in their causes or characters. But they all have a common denominator in their dependence on the city and, in consequence, in the scientific sense, we may refer to this area that is functionally dependent on the city as the city-region.

The regional interpretation of the functions of the city involves a twofold approach: first, an assessment of the effects of the character of the region – its resources, and economic production – on the character of the activities of the city; and, secondly, an examination of the effects of the city, as a seat of human activity and organization, on the character of the region. There is also involved the question of the limits of the city, and its spheres of influence or tributary areas in its multitude of regional functions. Some attention has been paid in Part I to the question of defining the limits of the city as a regional centre, but this should be subordinated to the main aim of this approach which seeks to evaluate both the city and its region, however vaguely defined, in terms of their mutual relations and in the light of their historical development.

Settlement, route and area are the three facets of the geographical interpretation of urban economy. The commercial output of the area – farming of different types, forestry, industry, or combinations of these – calls into being centres differing widely both in their interests, their commerce and in the industries arising from the processing of the primary products marketed in them. The quantity of output that passes through commercial channels is the sum total of economic, political, and cultural intercourse. It is, in effect, a measure of the nodality of the urban centre. If all such intercourse is concentrated in one city, all the commerce for the area would pass through the city; and the sum total of this commerce would be the total of its exports and imports. This theoretical state of affairs is never reached because the degree of concentration of circulation in one city in any area depends on the suitability of the area for commerce relative to the location of the city and of its neighbouring cities, to the conditions of historical development, and to the physical build of the land, which may rigidly affect the orientation of routes. Nevertheless, the potency and extent of the sphere of influence of a city are to be measured in theory from the degree of concentration of the circulations of the area around it in the form of freight, passenger and general intercourse.

The city produces goods, and processes and stores imported goods not only for a nation-wide market, but also for the market in its surroundings – whatever it can sell in competition with its neighbours. The city, in addition to its own natural increase (by excess of births over deaths), draws the folk from its surrounding area to enjoy its special amenities – its shops, institutions, markets, art galleries, and theatres. With the great growth of cities in the early nineteenth century, the rural population has been drawn into the towns, with the resultant phenomenon of rural depopulation. The city is a melting-pot and fount of opinion. It disseminates its views on matters relevant to the life and affairs of its citizens and the people of the surrounding towns through the medium of the press. It is a home of learning, culture and political life. The city must be fed, with food for its people and materials for its industry. Before the development of cheap and rapid transport, every city was almost entirely dependent upon its surrounding area for both. Distant supplies of food or materials or immigrants were brought by the only cheap means of transport – water, and it is no accident that in the past, before the railway era, the chief cities in Europe and America were either ports or riverside cities at the heads of river navigation. In the modern era, however, although the movement of foodstuffs and raw materials is world-wide, there is, in fact, a still closer relation between town and country. For all perishable goods must be delivered quickly and daily to the city consumers. Moreover, the economic factor of accessibility to the best market dragoons farm areas to supply large urban markets, so that an even closer tie-up between the great city and its environs results. Again, with the ever-increasing complexity in the social and economic structure of society, in service and organization, the city has acquired a great increase of functions as a regional centre for the distribution of both consumer goods and producer goods, and as a centre of services – social, economic and administrative. The city makes its impact on the surrounding towns and countryside, especially since the advent of the automobile, by the expansion of urban built-up land – for residence, industry and recreation. It also affects the character and structure of their social and economic life.

. . . Let us now examine the regional functions of the chief English cities under pre-war conditions from the same point of view. Each of the seven conurbations, which rank among the greatest urban agglomerations in the world, has a dominant central city, which is the main focus of its activities; but they differ from each other in certain important respects. London, Glasgow and Newcastle have sites with marked nodality, i.e. sites on which there is a convergence of important natural routeways, so that each of them has been a principal centre of activities of a large surrounding tributary area for many centuries. As a bridge-town at the head of navigation of a river, where natural land routes converged, each city has been the nucleus of urban expansion to form the conurbation and a large tributary area around it. Merseyside has a similar unity, since it is grouped around the harbour on both its banks. Birmingham is similarly a dominant unchallenged focus: with respect to its administrative area it is the largest city in Britain. Manchester–Salford, though a great industrial centre, is also a metropolitan centre of the highest order, serving the many smaller industrial towns around it. The West Yorkshire conurbation is unique. It lies astride the moorlands between the Aire and Calder valleys, in which are the towns of Leeds and Bradford, Halifax, Huddersfield and Dewsbury. It has no natural dominant focus, and lacks a tradition of unity, but Bradford is the specialized commercial focus of the woollen and worsted industries, and Leeds is its general business and administrative centre.

The chief city in each of the conurbations, as well as the other larger cities in more rural areas, making a total of about fifteen, possess the following distinctive characteristics:

(i) Each is the principal focus of a densely populated and distinctive industrial region, and has a population much greater than that of surrounding towns. The latter tend to be grouped in a circle as on the rim of a wheel at the hub of which is the metropolitan centre.

(ii) Owing largely to the geographical factors of site and location, through the marketing organization of each is effected the world-wide distribution of what may be termed the primary specialized or basic industries of its surrounding area; and the collection and distribution of vital supplies. A metropolis, however, is not necessarily an independent centre of trade, for its pre-eminence in this capacity is dependent upon adequate transport facilities, and in the case of Leeds, Bradford, Sheffield and Birmingham the trade of the surrounding area is partly oriented towards competitive metropolitan cities, or finds its outlet in a port which is complementary to and serves the same hinterland as the inland city.

(iii) Each city possesses a great number and variety of miscellaneous industries which owe their origin to the demands of the regional market and their localization in the city to its reservoir of labour and its excellent transport facilities. These are the regional secondary industries, as their products are chiefly distributed throughout the surrounding area, though business transactions are by no means restricted to it, for the growth of an industry in production and reputation results in an ever-widening area of distribution. Examples are the printing and brewing industries and the manufacture of furniture and provisions.

(iv) They are all endowed with a varying degree of financial individuality, since they have served in the past as regional centres of banking and insurance. This independence, particularly with regard to banking, they have failed to maintain, with one conspicuous exception, owing to the overwhelming financial dominance of London and the advantage acquired through representation in London.

(v) In virtue of cheap and frequent travelling facilities, each is an outstanding shopping centre – an indirect form of areal commodity distribution for an extensive surrounding area. The maximum extent of the shopping area is roughly co-extensive with the area which is within two hours' journey of the centre (Fig. 2).

It is important to emphasize here a major contrast between the metropolitan regions of the United States and Great Britain which arises from the difference in their size. Britain is small and highly urbanized, comparable in both these respects with New England in the north-eastern corner of the United States. Its big cities are within 50 or 60 miles of each other. London, it is true, completely dominates southern England – metropolitan England as Mackinder appropriately called it – but even here the historical capitals have maintained their sway even though small in size over areas which are very distinct historical units – East Anglia with Norwich, Wessex with Salisbury, Winchester and the modern port of Southampton, the Oxford area, the West Country centred on Bristol, the South-West with its centres

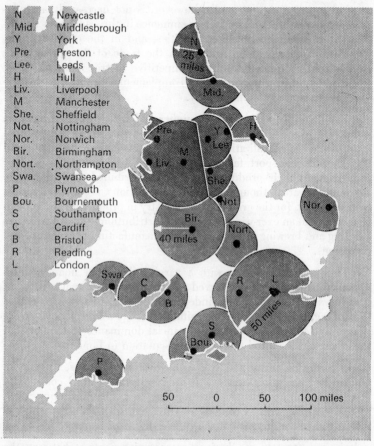

N	Newcastle
Mid.	Middlesbrough
Y	York
Pre.	Preston
Lee.	Leeds
H	Hull
Liv.	Liverpool
M	Manchester
She.	Sheffield
Not.	Nottingham
Nor.	Norwich
Bir.	Birmingham
Nort.	Northampton
Swa.	Swansea
P	Plymouth
Bou.	Bournemouth
S	Southampton
C	Cardiff
B	Bristol
R	Reading
L	London

FIG. 2. England and Wales. Distances from Great Cities (after E. G. R. Taylor).

Radii vary according to the size of the city – London 50 miles; cities over 1 million, 40 miles; cities over 100,000, 25 miles. Unshaded areas are remote from great cities.

in Plymouth and Exeter. In the north of England and central Scotland, however, the great urban agglomerations are close together and frequently are contiguous. Moreover, there is a deep-rooted feeling of civic independence as between one urban area and another and as between one smaller cluster and another. These facts have two results.

First, it is not possible to conceive of a clearly defined hinterland for a port or of a clearly defined marketing territory in which one city, because of its great geographical distance from competitors, holds undisputed sway. The threads of trade of any town or factory or port spread over a large part or all of the country. Secondly, the big urban agglomerations and their fringes often merge into each other, so that in theory, the midway line between two centres will be at once the limit of their 'region' and of their 'hinterland'. This will be the divide of suburban communities, and probably of urban associations on the one hand, and of trade associations and the movement of goods on the other hand. The Manchester region merges, in this respect, for example, into West Yorkshire (Leeds and Bradford) and Sheffield, and while on the west it merges with Merseyside. Again, the Potteries is an old and independent economic unit on the border of the influence of Manchester and Birmingham and has close relations with both.

The whole of Britain – like France, Germany and the United States – is divided into districts for a great variety of purposes – for the collection of statistical data, for administration by departments of State, for the organization of numerous trades and professions, and for military and civil defence. These districts, defined as a rule quite independently of each other, vary greatly according to their purpose. Many are based on the existing political divisions; others adopt quite new boundaries; some are simply determined by the amount of business which a single office staff can conveniently handle; others hinge on the distribution of one or more occupations, on questions of accessibility and distribution of population. Each country is divided into districts by numerous private concerns which have regional offices, depots or warehouses, to facilitate nation-wide organization and service. This procedure is adopted by State Departments, by trade and professional organizations, and by business concerns dealing in consumers' goods so as to ensure effective and regular contact with all retail dealers, and by nation-wide health services and water and electricity supply. Practically every aspect of business, commerce and administration is now 'regionalized' in this sense, with the services concentrated in the principal cities. It should also be noted that while these *ad hoc* regions differ widely, often necessarily so, from each other, many show a remarkable similarity in their geographical extent, especially around the great cities. They are built in large measure on existing administrative units which are often anachronisms. Regions are also under discussion for such special purposes as medical services, education, and industrial and social organizations, each demanding a set of units and authorities suited to its particular problems.

Regionalism has never been as popular a movement in Britain as in France. It has, in fact, been confined to a few scholars – geographers, economists and political philosophers – and it is only in the last few years that it has become a subject of wider interest and concern. This interest centres on the administrative aspect, that is, the question of reorganization of local government districts and the devolution of administrative authority from Whitehall. Indeed, Regionalism is usually considered in this country as synonymous with administrative devolution in a framework of new local government units.

The civil administration of England is carried out on a triple system – the County (with its urban counterpart in the County Borough), the Rural District (with its counterpart in the Urban District, which in country districts is usually a small town near the geographical centre of the Rural District) and the Civil Parish. The Rural and Urban Districts, formed in 1894 from the sanitary districts of 1872, were based upon the Poor Law Union districts which were created under the Poor Law Amendment Act of 1834. Before this date, the triple system consisted of the County, the Hundred, and the Parish, and it can be traced back to the Norman Conquest.

The County or Shire is the major statutory administrative unit in Britain. It was already in existence before the Norman Conquest. The counties south of the Thames and in eastern England were recognised as 'shires' in the time of King Alfred. Some of them correspond with the initial areas of settlement of the Anglo-Saxon tribes, so that each had a nucleus of open, settled land and a periphery of marsh and forest on the lower land. In the densely wooded and thinly peopled lands of central England, which was then the kingdom of Mercia, the shires came into being during the tenth century. Each was defined as a group of Hundreds conveniently accessible in one day to a fortified administrative centre, which became the county town. These midland counties, each with the suffix 'shire', are all approximately of the same size, and the shire bears the same name as its capital. The counties in the north and south-west of England are the largest; they were not organized as definite county administrative areas until the twelfth century, and were not effectively absorbed into England until after the time of the Tudors. In Wales the political divisions that existed before the English conquest were based on the ancient tribal groupings of pastoral communities who lived on the lower slopes of the hills below the moorlands and above the forested river valleys. The hierarchy of tribal space-groupings culminated in nine major areas each under the rule of an overlord. By the Statute of Rhuddlan in 1284, Edward created the Principality in west and north Wales with five new counties based on the tribal overlordships. The March remained under the disputed control of about 150 marcher lords until 1536, when by the Act of Union five more new counties were created, the boundaries of which were based on those of the lordships and not upon physical divides.

The main fact we would emphasize in connection with these counties is that they came into being before the Norman Conquest and already in the Middle Ages their boundaries had often become areas of close settlement. This has been greatly emphasized in the last hundred years, so that to-day there is often little relation between the county boundaries and the present distribution and movements of population.

Regionalism as a popular cultural movement (though not bearing this name) has been mainly associated with the linguistic revivals in Scotland, Wales, and Ireland, each of which has expressed itself, in more or less degree, in a Home Rule Movement. These movements are analogous to the claims to autonomy of groups inside the west European States, such as Provence, Brittany and Alsace-Lorraine in France, Flanders in Belgium, and Catalonia in Spain, although such movements on the Continent have been regarded as endangering the unity of the State and have been treated with suspicion. In England proper, there are no deep-seated cultural differences. There is, of course, a popular consciousness of regional association, as manifested by a regional literature – Hardy's Wessex novels, for example – and by differences of dialect, popularized in some measure by the wireless. There are also 'regional' or 'district' social, cultural and trade associations. But in its national and cultural life England is a unit, for reasons of history and of the small size of the country, and perhaps most of all in the last century, because of the overwhelming dominance of the urban way of life. Hitherto, the rural way of life – dialect, customs, temperament and the like – have been swamped by the influence of city ways.

There are big differences between France and Britain in socio-geographical structure. In France the old political divisions and the very names of the provinces were abolished in 1789 and the new and smaller Departments established. In Britain, the counties are historical provinces and have persisted, unchanged, with real administrative significance, to this day. Nevertheless, there have been periods when larger units were required. The chief of these were the military governorships established under Cromwell. Among the few popular names applicable to such larger areas are East Anglia, the Fens, Wessex, and the Weald. Britain, however, is lacking in geographical names that refer to permanent social groupings like the *pays*. Possible examples are the Craven, Hallamshire, Forest of Dean, and Holderness districts, but these are of little significance to-day. This whole question, it may be added in passing, deserves much more careful study than it has yet received. Lastly, with few exceptions, urbanism has not seriously affected the traditional social patterns in France. In Britain, especially in northern England, the Midlands, the Home Counties, and central Scotland, these have been profoundly changed. Yet the county has always been the chief social and political unit in Britain and still is a popular unit for trade, professional and cultural associations, army regiments, football and cricket clubs, and the like. It is most popular in rural reas, but in the vicinity of the great cities the old-time associations have been all but obliterated, and here the need for a reorganization is most urgent and most needed. Any scheme to introduce new divisions and abolish the old must contend with very real and valuable social forces of tradition and conservatism.

But if the movement for the creation of entirely new divisions to replace the counties has never been widespread in Britain, in practice, as we have already seen, regions exist for a great variety of purposes, and in recent years the need for new regions for many aspects of public life has become more obvious and urgent.

Regions for the Master Plan

From Eva G. R. Taylor, 'Land and Plan', *Architect and Building News*,
17 October, 1941, pp. 8–9, 23.

Professor Taylor was another geographer who was interested in ideas
similar to those involved in the city-region concept. She wrote a
great deal during and immediately following the 1939–45 war on
the case for carrying out town and country planning activities in
regional areas as distinct from the existing county and county
borough areas. This short article shows how much she shared the
same kind of approach as her fellow geographers.

There is no escaping the fact that the whole trend of population
movement during the present century has been towards the greater
cities and their environs. This is not to be explained simply in terms
of industrialization, for it is happening also in countries that have a
predominantly agricultural economy. In the State of Victoria, Australia, for example, where only about 10% of the population work in
factories, over 55% live in Greater Melbourne, the capital city, with
over a million inhabitants. In Canada, too, always looked upon as a
land of 'wide open spaces,' considerably more than half the population is classed as urban, while in Soviet Russia the streaming of the
peasantry into the cities, old and new, is becoming a torrent which
threatens to escape control. What can stop this world movement?
Certainly not the building of a few mis-called trading estates, or
country factories to house new industrial enterprises as they arise.
Certainly not the constant plugging in the press and on the air of the
theme that a country life is to be preferred to a town life, and that war
evacuees will never willingly return to the towns. Like the lady who
said: 'I accept the Universe,' we have to accept great cities, even
monstrous cities. Our problem becomes that of ensuring that the city
shall stop short at the 'city wall,' where unspoilt country should begin.

In England there is a school of thought that sees London as the only
city fatally overgrown and poisoning its surroundings. Their remedy
is regional devolution of government and administration, or, to put
it more crudely, the break-up of the hordes of civil servants clustered
about Whitehall. The method proposed is to extend the principle
introduced to meet the war emergency (and possible destruction of
London) whereby Regional Commissioners were appointed to control
the affairs of groups of counties termed Civil Defence Regions. The
various Ministries, of Education, Transport, Agriculture, Labour, and
so on, are to have representatives and staffs at the regional capitals,

the principal officers being given a large measure of independence and power to act without consulting Whitehall.

When we examine the names of the towns chosen as these petty government seats, we find, as we might expect, that they are the largest in their regions and are already growing rapidly. Only such towns have the necessary accessibility and facilities to fulfil their new function, only such towns enjoy the necessary prestige which alone can make them locally acceptable as capitals. The scheme involves, therefore, the direction of large new population groups into Manchester, Birmingham, Leeds, Newcastle, and other cities in which problems of congestion already exist. A rough estimate of the movement may be attempted, although the figures are uncertain pending direct research. Each hundred civil servants in good employment would probably bring with them an equal number of wives, children, and immediate dependants. These two hundred persons would require the services of doctors, nurses, teachers, architects, builders, transport workers, tradesmen, servants, and others, to the number of perhaps fourscore. The fourscore would have their equal number of wives, children and dependants, making a further hundred and sixty persons, who in their turn would demand all sorts of services, provided by perhaps sixty employed persons, making a new group of one hundred and twenty, including their families, and so on. Thus a thousand civil servants established at, say, Leeds might mean a growth of population by seven thousand. A proportion of these would be young people growing up to enter industry, a potential labour supply which might itself attract new industry. Thus the snowballing effect would continue, and apart from the initial two thousand the newcomers would be recruited, not from London, but from the neighbouring small towns and country districts.

Granted, however, that London needs a little 'blood-letting,' or alternatively that Regional Administration will allow of more rational planning and more economical local government than our present system, the question arises: Are the Defence Regions the ideal regional sub-divisions of England and Wales? Emphatically they are not. They have been arrived at by grouping three or four counties together, and they perpetuate the county boundaries which were established centuries ago in harmony with a long-vanished land tenure. These boundaries often run down or across streets in the great 'conurbations,' and again and again they place under different administrations areas which are indivisible from the practical standpoint of 'life and work.' But the scrapping of the old county boundaries, anomalous though they are, would arouse powerful local opposition. Vested interests, local tradition, existing governmental machinery, personal loyalties – these cannot simply be ignored or overridden. The eighth map, therefore, shows a set of eight Regions (with certain sub-regions) that represent a compromise between what is and what might be. The boundaries are shown as bold sweeping lines which, while respecting the county limits where possible, at the same time avoid splitting up districts that have a unified economic or social life.

On the positive side the Regions are sketched out so that each is as far as possible an epitome of national life. Each has its share of national resources and amenities, its industrial strength, its agricultural strength, its commercial strength. Each has its traditional centres of culture and religion, its recognized and developed recreational regions. The capitals are chosen so as to be easily accessible (in the sense of our seventh map) from all parts of the Region. They must also be of a size sufficient to negative any tendency to a 'small town' or provincial outlook on the part of the Regional Authority.

Some of the boundaries are easy to draw. The Pennine moorlands, for example, form a natural division between the North-eastern and Yorkshire Regions, on the one side, the North-western on the other. But it is less easy to decide where the West Midlands end and the East Midlands begin. Can Nottingham in actual fact compete with Birmingham as a functional capital? And does the more central position of Nottingham give it a final and decisive advantage over Leicester? South of a line drawn from the Bristol Channel to the Wash there are only two main 'natural' regions: the larger, South-east, dominated by the Metropolis, and therefore termed Metropolitan, and the smaller West and South-West, including Somerset, Devon and Cornwall, with parts of Gloucestershire and Wilts. For the latter region Bristol is hardly the ideal capital, if only because of its poor accessibility from many quarters, yet no other town there can touch it in respect of size, industry, and commercial activity. Sub-regions naturally suggest themselves to meet this case, and their boundaries have been drawn subject to the proviso that these are very tentative. Local research and enquiry alone can reveal what boundary lines and what capitals correspond to actualities of life and work. When Devonshire and Cornish folk want a first-class entertainment, or are doing important shopping or seeking the best professional advice, do they go to Plymouth or to Exeter or to neither?

Within the Metropolitan Region, too, it is clear that there must be an inner ring comprising the dormitory area, and an outer ring of sub-regions with a more locally centred life. But is Norwich or Cambridge the functional centre of East Anglia? It is the latter which is chosen as the *chef lieu* of the Civil Defence Region. Again, what is comprised in the Oxford Region? Will Dorset people resent the suggestion that the capital of Wessex is Southampton? Has the Southern Railway, by the device of electrification, made all Sussex part of Outer London? And what of Wales? Its separation by the political boundary line is anomalous, even injurious, nor has Cardiff any natural relation to the centre, West or North of the Principality. But here again personal feeling runs strong, and often runs counter to sound economic sense.

In fine, the formulation of a Master Plan for Britain demands first and foremost the development of Group Intelligence. It is by the creative functioning of the Group Mind that it will be brought into being. That is the lesson of these articles and maps: there is no simple or easy answer to our problems of reconstruction, no 'one man' solution.

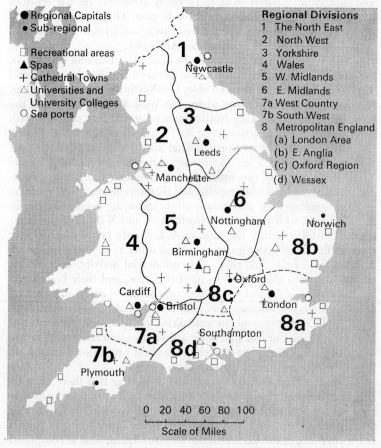

● Regional Capitals
● Sub-regional

☐ Recreational areas
▲ Spas
+ Cathedral Towns
△ Universities and
   University Colleges
○ Sea ports

Regional Divisions
1   The North East
2   North West
3   Yorkshire
4   Wales
5   W. Midlands
6   E. Midlands
7a West Country
7b South West
8   Metropolitan England
   (a) London Area
   (b) E. Anglia
   (c) Oxford Region
   (d) Wessex

0 20 40 60 80 100
Scale of Miles

FIG. 3. Regions of England and Wales.

City Regions for Administrative Purposes

From Derek Senior, 'The City Region as an Administrative Unit',
Political Quarterly, Vol. 36, 1965, pp. 82–91.

Mr Senior spent some years as a journalist with a special interest in
planning and local government, and might be described as a 'second
generation' city-regionalist. At least, his writings appear a good
twenty to twenty-five years after those of Smailes and Dickinson.
He revived interest in the city-region idea after a period in which it
had become almost forgotten, and he was fortunate that his interest
came at a time when the then Minister of Housing and Local
Government was cogitating about a more effective method of local
government reform than was allowed by the procedures of the Local
Government Act, 1958. This article was written just prior to Mr
Senior being appointed to the Royal Commission on Local
Government in 1966. The ideas which he expresses here should be
compared with the earlier views of Smailes and Dickinson, and
Senior's own proposals written into his Memorandum of Dissent
from the Royal Commission's Report (these are reproduced in the
next chapter).

'In conjunction with a progressive transport policy and a system of
comprehensive regional planning, these (housing and land acquisition)
measures will be directed to providing a fresh social environment in
keeping with the needs and aspirations of the time.'

    This is all the Queen's Speech had to say about regional planning;
the structure of local government was not mentioned. By the time this
article is printed the Government may have raised the curtain a little
further: it may, on the other hand, still be getting its intentions clear
in its own interdepartmental mind. At the time of writing these
intentions could be judged only from the statements, formal and
informal, made about them by the Ministers concerned before and
immediately after the election – among them Mr Crossman's repeated
statement that the sorting out of the relationship between his own
responsibility for 'providing a fresh social environment' and Mr
Brown's for 'regional planning' presented much greater difficulties
than the apportionment of functions between the Ministry of Housing
and the Ministry of Land and Natural Resources.

REGIONAL ECONOMIC DEVELOPMENT

What appeared to be intended was that Mr Brown's department should
plan the country's economic development, and in particular should

determine the priorities for national investment as between different fields and different parts of the country. Other departments would work out the policies for giving effect to this 'national plan' in their several fields – fiscal and monetary management, education and research, transport, land use and so on. This would involve not only the co-ordination of policies in Whitehall by a committee of the Ministers concerned under Mr Brown's chairmanship, but also the setting up of a corresponding 'Little Whitehall' in each 'region' to prepare a strategic development programme for the application of these policy decisions in the light of an analysis of regional trends and conditions. These 'Little Whitehalls' would be interdepartmental teams of civil servants – researchers, planners and administrators – led by senior officials of Mr Brown's department and advised by appointed 'regional councils' with members drawn from local government, industry, commerce, trade unions and universities in the regions.

It was evident that 'region' in this context meant 'standard region', or at any rate an area of standard-region scale: about one-tenth of England and Wales. It was not clear how the civil servant working in a 'Little Whitehall' would reconcile, in case of conflict, his loyalties to his regional leader and to his departmental superiors. Nor was it clear how the 'regional advisory councils' were to be constituted, or how they could usefully function without replacing the local authorities in the regional planning field. But it is not the purpose of this article to criticise the specific form of the arrangements proposed by central government for the exercise of its proper planning responsibilities and for the taking of whatever advice it thinks it may need. Still less is it my purpose to question the view that central government must be responsible for 'regional planning' of this sort and at this level. On the contrary, I am convinced that planning can make no headway unless central government does organise itself to think with one mind about all aspects of physical development and takes the initiative in formulating regional *strategies*, on whatever scale it finds convenient, for the timing and relative location of major residential, industrial, commercial and recreational developments and of the communications between them.

PLANNING AND LOCAL GOVERNMENT

I am equally convinced, however, that such strategies can serve no useful purpose unless competent agencies exist to discharge the quite distinct function of making land-allocating development *plans* within the framework so laid down; that while it is an inescapable obligation of central government to see to it that such agencies do exist, it is neither practicable nor proper for central government itself to assume their function; and that planning (as Dame Evelyn Sharp has said) 'must be a function of representative government', and in so far as it conditions the environment of our daily lives 'lies at the heart of local government'. I am also convinced that the only basis on which a plan-making authority can effectively operate in this motor age is the city region, and therefore that local government cannot long remain responsible for plan-making unless its major authorities are reorganised on this basis; that the loss of its plan-making function, on top of all the other functions which local authorities, as at present constituted, have been found incapable of discharging satisfactorily, would carry the decline of local democracy beyond the point of no return; and that this would be a national disaster.

THE CITY REGIONS

By a 'city region' I mean an area whose inhabitants look to a common centre for those specialised facilities and services (social, cultural, professional, commercial, educational and other) whose economic provision demands a user population of large but less than national proportions. Before the motor age the city itself and latterly the conurbation were the only areas that could make effective use of such opportunities; now their centres serve large hinterlands in the same way as they serve the surrounding built-up areas.

England and Wales can be conveniently divided into thirty-odd such units – mature, emergent, embryonic or potential. Apart from London there are five, based on the centres of Birmingham, Manchester, Liverpool, Leeds and Newcastle-upon-Tyne, which can be described as mature in the sense that the centre of each is readily accessible to a more than sufficient population (over two million) to sustain all humanly provided social facilities other than those which are so specialised that the whole nation must seek them in London or abroad. Another six, based on the centres of Nottingham, Sheffield, Preston, Southampton, Cardiff and Bristol, have ample dependent populations (over a million each), but their centres are as yet either not so readily accessible from some parts of their hinterlands or for various reasons less fully equipped. Preston, in particular, could hardly be included in this 'emergent' category but for the prospects opened up by the M6 and Lancaster University.

A dozen more, based on the centres of Swansea, Brighton, Hull, Leicester, Norwich, Stoke, Oxford, Exeter, Cambridge, Coventry, Middlesbrough and Gloucester, are developing along the same lines, with hinterland populations of between a third and four-fifths of a million. In the South East the proposed large-scale expansions in the vicinity of Ashford, Newbury, Northampton, Ipswich, Peterborough and Bournemouth could by the end of this century make their centres effective counter-magnets to London in respect of regional (as distinct from national) facilities, serving over half a million people each and thus reducing the London city region to an area extending only five to ten miles beyond the approved metropolitan green belt in all directions but the east. A Solway barrage and a Mid-Wales new town (if sensibly sited in relation to Dawley) would bring the Carlisle and Shrewsbury hinterlands within this 'potential' class, leaving only the fringe areas dependent on Plymouth, Lincoln, York and Bangor, with a combined population of little more than a million, unlikely in the foreseeable future to support services of regional standard – though nonetheless regionally 'structured' by their dependence on the centres named for such specialised facilities as their inhabitants can reach without making an expedition of it.

All these centres, save those of Newbury and Ashford, are already identifiable, by such indices as bus and rail services, newspaper circulations, store deliveries and rateable values, as dominant in their regions, which are virtually self-contained in respect of retail sales. Twenty-seven have universities in or near them, and the other nine are the strongest candidates for future academic foundations. Only in sparsely populated areas – West Cornwall, West Wales, Mid-Wales, the Welsh marches, the Lake District, the Cheviots and West Norfolk – are there people living more than an hour's drive from one or other of them, and the 1961 Census returns show a distinct tendency for these people to move to places within easier reach of them, as well as for people to move from the built-up areas round the bigger centres into the outer metropolitan zones.

COMMUNITIES IN THE MAKING

It cannot, of course, be pretended that even the mature city regions are yet communities in the corporate sense that towns and sometimes counties used to be in the pre-motor age. There is, indeed, a school of thought which colourably holds that no unit can inspire a sense of belonging until it has been defined, named and institutionalised. What *can* be claimed is that the city region, even in its embryonic form, is a social entity much more relevant to the concerns of local government than any other now that the motor-vehicle has come into general use. Its inhabitants may share no feeling of community with people living on the other side of its centre, but at least they all have a lively common interest in the quality and accessibility of the services that that centre can afford. Culturally speaking, townsfolk and countryfolk in the same region are ceasing to differ: both are demanding all the satisfactions, urban and rural, that modern technology and personal mobility are making available to all. Few of us can still be said, in any meaningful sense, to *live* in town or country, no matter where we may sleep: the range of our normal activities is region-wide.

Terms like 'city', 'town', and 'village' now mask the most important realities of social life and block the communication of ideas about them. The brief interregnum of the 'conurbation', too, is over and unmourned: 'from a planning point of view it cannot be looked at separately from the life of the region it dominates . . . the only valid concept is the city region, which effects a marriage between the built-up core and the area which comes under its direct social and economic influence, and which is shaped and held together by its system of communications'. So said the Ministry of Housing's chief planner at a summer school just three months before his department's Bill to set up a planning authority for the Greater London conurbation was given its second reading. Nothing, indeed, is now more irrelevant to the structure of contemporary society, or to the requirements of public administration, than continuous built-upness. Whether or not the city region will ever command such loyalty as is lavished on our Rutlands, it has emerged as the outstandingly significant unit of human settlement – or rather of human activity – in modern times. It is, indeed, the only unit in terms of which the problems of 'providing a fresh social environment in keeping with the needs and aspirations of the time' can fruitfully be formulated.

At the time of writing there was no overt sign that our new Government had yet looked beyond the standard-region strategy to the machinery by which it might be implemented. The Regional Advisory Councils could clearly be of no value for this purpose, except in so far as they might help to mobilise regional opinion in general support of the strategy proposed. Theoretically, no doubt, it would be possible for the planning section of the Ministry of Housing and Local Government to get the positive proposals of such a strategy tested and elaborated at city-region level, as it is doing in the case of the South East Study, by engaging teams of planning consultants (for the Southampton region) or putting its own staff on the job (for the Ipswich region). But in practice it could hardly build up a sufficient organisation to do more, over the whole country, than produce outline 'structure' plans covering the broad layout of each city region's main road system, the relative capacities of its main and minor service centres, the siting of major employment generators and large-scale overspill developments, and the disposition of regional open spaces.

These are, of course, the big problems; and they are problems which no existing administrative county or county borough is in a position to tackle. But every component of such a plan would inevitably be regarded by one or other of the city region's constituent counties and county boroughs as conflicting with its own sectional interests, and could be nullified by the mere inaction of the authority concerned, as the South East Study's proposals for the allocation of housing land in the outer metropolitan region are now being nullified. If a county planning authority simply omits to make such allocations the Ministry has no remedy but to allow appeals by developers against the county's refusals of planning consent, thereby transferring the initiative in the choice of site to the individual developer. This is the negation of planning.

So long as the local authorities remain land-allocating authorities it is therefore quite true, as Mr Crossman said at his first Ministerial press conference, that any form of regional planning has got to be acceptable to them. But it is equally true that the built-in antagonism between neighbouring administrative counties and county boroughs must normally make it impossible for the Ministry to win their acceptance for any 'structure' plan addressed to the needs of the city region as a whole. On six occasions in the last eighteen years a Minister has vainly 'decided' where a new town should be built to take the overspill from Manchester's slums. As a last resort the choice has now fallen (provisionally) on Risley, for no better reason than that it is expected to be less unacceptable to county opinion than any other, since nobody seems to want it for any purpose – least of all housing. This, too, is the negation of planning.

MR CROSSMAN FOLLOWS THE TORY LINE

At the same press conference Mr Crossman echoed his predecessor's rejection of the whole idea of elective regional authorities on the ground that it must involve the interposition of another tier of representative government between Parliament and the county and county borough councils. This, of course, is a complete misconception, such as could only occur in a mind conditioned to take it for granted that a regional authority must be of standard-region scale. In strict propriety this is the one scale of unit between the town and the country as a whole to which the word 'region' ought *not* to be applied, since it has no social, geographic, economic or other distinctive character of its own, but exists only as an administrative division defined for the decentralised exercise of national authority: its only proper appellation, therefore, is 'province', and 90 per cent. of the current confusion about regional planning would never have arisen if it had always been so called. And so it would be called if someone in Whitehall had not once hoped that the provincial proconsuls appointed to run the country in the event of invasion might escape the un-popularity of Cromwell's major-generals if they were dubbed 'regional commissioners' – and thereby caused the very word 'region' to stink in the nostrils of all good local democrats for twenty years.

'REGION' AND 'PROVINCE' DISTINGUISHED

But this is a lost cause. To the Whitehall mind 'region' will never mean anything but province. In order to insinuate the idea that elec-tive regional authorities should be based on city regions a quarter to a third the size of standard regions, and should supersede, not be superimposed upon, the top tier of local government, one has to call them something else. The only available alternative is 'counties'. What is proposed, then, is not the interposition of a *tertium quid* between central and county government, but the reorganisation of county government itself. What is proposed is the abolition of all existing county boroughs and administrative counties and their replacement by thirty-odd continuous counties, on average about the same size, geographically speaking, as the larger existing counties, but having the main urban concentrations included in their jurisdiction and located at their centres instead of astride their boundaries.

The drawback of this formulation is that 'county' also denotes the time-honoured *geographical* unit which inspires a loyalty so blind that county councillors can, by a simple confidence trick, induce its temporary transference to the *administrative* county wherever the boundaries happen to be roughly congruent. Looked at in historical perspective, Rutland's stint as an administrative unit is but an in-significant episode. Nowhere is county loyalty so strong as in York-shire, which has never been an administrative county, or Lancashire, three-fifths of whose inhabitants are citizens of seventeen gaps in the administrative county. This admirable sentiment would remain entirely unaffected by any change in administrative machinery once the change was made; meanwhile we shall just have to put up with the difficulties created by its misappropriation.

THE 'STANDARD REGION' OBSESSION

Even when it is made plain that what the regionalist wants is not the interposition of another governmental tier, but the modernisation of an obsolete one, the official reaction is one that still shows how impenetrable is the Whitehall mind's obsession with the standard-region scale. As voiced by Sir Keith Joseph (and echoed by his opposite number at the time) it runs: 'Can we really accept areas *as big as regions*' (my italics) 'for the services now undertaken by coun-ties?' It is, of course, essential that an elective authority should be concerned not merely with a single function, however important, but with the general welfare of its electors over a sufficient range of functions to command their interest and to attract the services of councillors and staffs of high calibre; but that is the strongest of all arguments for the reorganisation here proposed. It is precisely because the scale and scope of the functions appropriate to top-tier local government, developing in step with the scale and scope of our social organisation, have far outstripped its capacity to discharge them that it has been found necessary to withdraw or withhold an increasing number of such functions from local government and entrust them to *ad hoc* bodies, or leave them undischarged. And it is precisely for this reason that central government has recently been driven to institute official inquiries into the quality of the councillors and staffs that our present local authorities attract.

Eight years ago, when the current review of local government areas and boundaries was put in train, the Government rejected any idea of radical reform on the ground that the existing system had not shown itself incapable of discharging the functions entrusted to it. This would, of course, be true of any system, however obsolete, so long as care were taken to entrust to it only those functions which it was capable of discharging. But in fact there is not a single major function now undertaken by counties and county boroughs that can be discharged in all its aspects as effectively as we have a right to demand by any authority smaller in scale or less comprehensive in scope than the city region. Nor is there now any occasion to sacrifice effectiveness in the interests of convenience, since the motor-vehicle has made the largest city region's centre as accessible to its remotest inhabitant as that of Rutland was when county councils were constituted. Much more than that, continuous counties based on city regions would be ideally equipped in catchment area, case-load and financial resources to be responsible for the management of a unified, positive health service (including health centres and hospitals), of traffic, commuter transport and regional motorways, of seaports and airports, land drainage and water supply; for all higher education short of university standard; for organising the demand for house-building components on the scale required to make possible a user-centred system of industrialised building; for the comprehensive renewal of city centres; for the abatement of air and river pollution and the reclamation of derelict land; for crime squads and multi-purpose sports centres; for the promotion of regional development – and for the making of development plans. These are all important functions which either have been, are being, or are likely soon to be transferred from counties and county boroughs to *ad hoc* bodies covering wider and more suitable areas, or which have been neglected for lack of competent agencies to take responsibility for them, or which have nominally been entrusted to local authorities but suspended, abandoned or never even undertaken by them.

LOCAL GOVERNMENT IN DECLINE

Local government, in short, has ceased to be the agency of choice for the conduct of public affairs. Whitehall has accepted the overwhelming evidence that most existing local authorities would rather join the guilds and livery companies in the limbo of picturesque relics than let local government be dragged into the motor age; and Whitehall regards the existing local authorities' conception of their corporate self-interest as the only valid expression of the public interest in local democracy. That, in effect, was the pretext on which a structural reform, though recognised to be overdue, was deferred twenty years ago – that and the Government's view of the tasks confronting it in the social field as being far too urgent to be put off until we had got ourselves organised to deal with them. When we did have leisure for reform the pressure had evaporated, so the local authority associations were allowed to set limits to the current reorganisation which prevent the establishment of continuous counties except for the built-up conurbations. In consequence even this almost uselessly restrictive application of the continuous county principle is now totally opposed by county councils (such as Lancashire's) which fifteen years ago would have welcomed the benefits of its general application. And in consequence we now find ourselves in the same position as before: because local government could not be reformed in time to take charge of a comprehensive health service it has not been reformed in time to take charge of regional planning; and for that reason it is not going to be reformed in time for the next urgent development within its proper field. And so it will go on.

There are, indeed, signs (such as Burnley's recent initiative in the Association of Municipal Corporations) of a death-bed repentance among local authorities. But only a complete reversal of their collective policies, a positive pressure from them for radical reform, could make it practical politics in the next ten years. Two faint hopes remain, however. One is that the Minister of Housing, confronted with the manifest absurdity of any other possible course, will spare the time for a single-clause amendment of the Local Government Act that would permit the Local Government Commission to recommend the constitution of continuous counties for Merseyside and the Manchester city region, embracing their quite compact commuter hinterlands as well as their built-up cores, and will then instruct the Commission to reconsider its proposals for the other conurbations in the light of the possibilities thus made available. The other is that, in setting up the plan-making and development agencies that will in any case be required if the strategies worked out by the Regional Planning Boards are to be put into effect, he will define their areas of operation and fields of responsibility on the only appropriate basis – the city region. The result of the first step would surely be a resurgence of local democracy in the new continuous counties, relieving his own staff of the local decision-making that now keeps it from its proper work. As a result of the second step, the transfer of plan-making and other major functions to new elective city-region authorities might proceed smoothly as each emergent, embryonic, and potential city region attained a respectable degree of maturity. Provided these things were done, it might not greatly matter if in the meanwhile the rest of the country continued to exemplify the pitiful irrelevance of top-tier local government as we have it today to the 'needs and aspirations of the time'.

The New Urban Hierarchy, 1968

From R. D. P. Smith, 'The Changing Urban Hierarchy', *Regional Studies*, Vol. 2, No. 1, September 1968, pp. 2–17.

A generation ago, Smailes pioneered the idea of plotting factors to indicate a ranking order of town to show the characteristics of a 'regional capital'. The availability of new data from surveys and censuses has made it possible to revise the 'urban hierarchy' first formulated by Smailes. The following extracts from the most recent work on this theme enable us to take account of the developments in social and economic structure which have occurred in the quarter century since Smailes produced the original ideas.

There have been many important influences at work since 1938 which could be expected to have had their effect on the overall pattern of central places. War damage and reconstruction, overspill estates, new and expanded towns, a growing population, increasing motorization, the decline of the railways, the drift to the south, lower densities of development, changing social habits and innumerable economic changes, not least the advent of overall planning control – all these have been at work to change the pattern.

This enquiry aimed to borrow enough of the techniques and classifications of the earlier studies to ensure comparability, but the range of data studied had to be limited to those which could be handled by one person in a limited time. This inevitably limits the value of the results, and the conclusions must therefore be regarded with caution. No attempt has been made here to study either the areas served by the centres, or to assess the reasons for apparent changes in their particular status.

In addition to studying directories and guides to the distribution of most of the facilities studied by Smailes, other readily available data were used where they seemed relevant. In doubtful cases two or more sources were consulted, and personal visits made where possible. As some 2500 places were identified, however, this approach had its strict limits. Broadly speaking, the data relate to 1965, although some are earlier and others come right up to date.

There have naturally been some important changes in the relative status and distribution of particular indicators. For example, cinemas have lost much of their significance as central activities; where Smailes (1944) found more than one in most small towns it is now usual for there to be only one, and this can no longer rely on the

Table 1. Characteristics of orders and sub-orders of central places (1965)

	2A	2B	2C	3A	3B	3C	4A	4B	4C	5A
Banks open daily (excluding S.B.'s)	115	100	40	20	14	9	7	5	4	3
Accountants (firms)	150	75	30	20	10	7	5	2	2	1*
Cinemas	13	18	9	5	4	2	2	1	1*	
Postal:										
Head P.O.: P	P									
Post town: p	Po	Po	Po	Po	Po	Po	Po	po	po	p*
Principal P.O.: o	(10)	(4)								
General market (days/week)	6	6	6	6	3	2	1	1	1	1*
Woolworth store	2	2	2	1	1	1	1	1	1*	
Boots chemists	4	5	3	2	1	1	1	1	1*	
Rail passenger station:										
Large R; small r	R	R	R	R	R	R	R	r	r*	
A.A. hotels and garages:										
a at least 1 each	A	A	A	A	A	A	A	a	a*	
A at least 5 in all										
Grammar/Comprehensive schools	G	G	G	G	G	G	G	G	G*	
Ministry of Labour office	L	L	L	L	L	L	L	L	L*	
Local weekly newspapers:										
N two or more	N	N	N	N	N	N	N	n	ne*	
n one only										
ne edition only										
Acute hospital:	H	H	H	H	H	h	h	h		
H over 300 beds										
h under 300 beds										
Best hotel (star class)	4	4	4	3	3	3/2	2	2		
Further education	F	F	F	F	F	F	F*			
Telephone group centre	T	T	T	T	T	T*				
Shopping order (Carruthers, 1967)	2B	2C	3A	3A	3B	3B/C				
Marks & Spencer store	M	M	M	M	M	M				
Employment (thousands)	500	250	150	65	50	25	(under 25)			
Rail sundries depot:										
D main; d secondary	D2	D	D/d	d	d					
Special shopping (thousands of persons engaged, see text for definition)	15	8	5	2·5	1·5	0·75	(under 0·5)			
Theatres	5	2	2	1	1	1*				
Chamber of Commerce	C	C	C	C	C	C*				
British Home Stores	B	B	B	B	B					
Association Football League Division	1	1	2	3	4*					
Evening newspaper	E	E	E	E	E*					
General hospital, over 500 beds	H	H	H	H						
Telephone Area H.Q.	T	T	T	T						
University/Higher education	U	U	U	U*						
Television studio	TV	TV	TV*							
Morning newspaper	M	M								
Stock Exchange	S	S								
Teaching hospital	T	T								
Bank of England branch	B	B								
Principal orchestra	O									

* Indicates about half the centres have this facility.

necessary economic support to remain open indefinitely. Conversely, branch banks have grown in number with the increasing financial sophistication of the present age and with continuing competition up to 1967 between the leading national and regional banks. Secondary schools are classified differently since the 1944 Education Act, and only grammar and comprehensive schools were considered to be comparable with the schools noted by Smailes. General markets have held their place in trading to a much greater degree than seemed likely in 1944, and have been included in this study though apparently excluded by Smailes at a late stage in his enquiries.

The present study excludes all the administrative aspects of local government, while including education. It was felt that the comparison between commercial and social indicators on the one hand, and local authority organization on the other, should be made possible and that this might be of value in the reorganization of local government. This comparison has not been made here, however.

It would have been possible, given more time, to study the distribution of almost every central function. This being out of the question the selection was made of those data which were readily available and demanded a minimum of processing, while covering a wide range of activities. Classifications based on these alone cannot be regarded as wholly definitive, but broadly indicative of the general function and grading of central places.

Table 1 shows the range of facilities or aspects studied. Certain others were examined in less detail. *Special shopping* as here defined includes the following kinds of business for each whole town in the Census of Distribution and other Services 1961, Area Tables: General stores, Clothing and footwear shops, Furniture and furnishing shops, Booksellers, stationers, Jewellery, leather and sports goods shops, and other non-food shops.

For a study of this kind one must clearly start from some firm idea of what constitutes a central place. The conventional definition by name recognizes centres as the public sees them, and the common usage of a name for a place which has a collection of varied central activities (whereas particularly in suburbs there may be several different interpretations of the same name), helps to point to significant groupings. In rural areas there is normally no such difficulty, although one or two instances exist of a place of some central status which is often found listed under a city some miles away, due to the postal address structure. Thornbury, Gloucestershire, is one such.

Facilities which do not generally locate in central places, though related to their functions, have to be omitted from a study of this kind. Airports, motels, training colleges in former country houses, crematoriums on the outer fringes of towns all defy inclusion. Theatres and universities are normally central or fairly central but the Glyndebourne Opera and Keele University are typical of the exceptions which prove the rule. With increasing mobility and the advocacy of 'out of town' shopping centres, it may be that the old order will change drastically, but so far there has been little definite movement in this direction in Britain. In fact, an out of town shopping centre is a new central place. More in evidence has been the dispersal of various facilities, particularly secondary schools which are required to have large sites, from the congested centres of cities and towns. This means that one must be prepared for each central place to have a considerable and often growing physical extent, and the more important the centre the wider its components may be flung.

Some centres have identity problems. Stoke on Trent Head Post Office is at Hanley, principal shopping centre of the Potteries. Similarly, Ascot is at Sunninghill and Harwich at Dovercourt. Earlestown and Newton le Willows can be confused. Shaw is Crompton.

Suburban centres which are separated from their parent city centres by largely residential or industrial areas have been given separate listings where they can be recognized, but this is not possible in every case without personal knowledge of the city. Even residents are mystified by the whereabouts of the 'Radial' shopping centre in Bristol. On the other hand, it is relatively easy to identify the components of some twin or complex systems of centres, for example Liverpool–Bootle–Birkenhead, Middlesbrough–Stockton, Camborne–Redruth, Wolverton–Stony Stratford, and to grade each separately. This was not always done in the earlier studies, which makes comparison impossible in these cases.

Smailes distinguished only five orders of central place besides London, i.e.

Major Cities
Cities
Minor Cities or Major Towns
Towns
Sub-towns (four types).

It is possible to go further, as Bracey (1952) did in his study of Wiltshire and distinguish orders of importance in service village centres; this would be possible for the country as a whole, but only with great labour. However, an examination of his results shows the general validity of the distinction between a Town and a Village as a central place, and it is at the margin between the two that the present study ends. In this it is in complete accord with Smailes, but it is worth mentioning that in suburban locations there are many shopping centres of greater status than those of small rural towns, which are more completely provided with a range of facilities other than shopping.

Later workers, notably Green (1950), have developed the concept of orders and sub-orders, and this is adopted here. The basic range is from the first or Metropolitan Order through Provincial, Regional and Local Orders to Fifth Order or Village centres. Each order is assumed to possess characteristic functions, as well as more or less the complete range of functions associated with each lower order. Within each order of centre there are three sub-orders, i.e. those which are stronger than average, average and weak. Stronger members are relatively rare, and may possess more of the particular services characteristic of their order, or they may have no more than the usual number of these but in addition have certain services more appropriate to higher orders. Weaker members are numerous and characterized in many cases by gaps in the services expected of their order, or by possessing branch activities such as localized editions of newspapers published elsewhere, rather than the full facility. Finally it is possible to recognize, as Bracey did in Wiltshire, a sixth undifferentiated order of grouped settlement without significant services. These are no concern of this study.

In England, London is the sole and undisputed First Order centre. It may be regarded internationally as a strong metropolis, and described therefore as 1A. Below this level, however, there is a blurring between the orders as there is between colours in a rainbow. This is due to such underlying factors as differences in topography, demography, and in the evolution of each centre. Secular changes occur as the cumulative effect of innumerable decisions taken daily on the problems of whether to provide, or continue to provide, services of particular types in particular places on the basis of need, cost, profit, convenience, benefit and other considerations.

Having abstracted and tabulated the data, and made some preliminary comparisons of results, the following classification was eventually chosen for its close relationship to Smailes' and Carruthers' work. The classes do not precisely correspond, due to differences in the basic data and secular changes in the nature of central facilities themselves; but a close general comparison is readily made:

Smith	*Smailes*
2A	
2B	} Major Cities
2C	

Smith	*Smailes*
3A	Cities
3B	}Minor Cities or Major Towns
3C	
4A	}Towns
4B	
4C	Sub-towns
5A	Urban Villages

The last category was identified, but not mapped. It was clear that the data studied enabled those places which perform higher order functions, albeit inadequately, to be recognized more readily than those with a strong provision of Fifth Order services, and this would only mislead if portrayed on a map. Similarly it is felt that there is no great need to repeat the detailed sub-division of the weak local centres or Sub-towns according to the nature of their weaknesses, but rather to attempt a firmer and more detailed grading of the more important centres, on the lines of Carruthers. Hence four categories of Smailes are treated here as eight sub-orders. This makes comparison with Smailes no more difficult, and may make future comparisons easier.

Table 2 shows the more important centres – Orders 2 and 3 – and indicates the apparent changes of status which have occurred.

Table 5 summarizes and compares the numbers of centres of each grading as at 1938 and 1965, in England except Greater London. 770 centres in all are or were of at least Fourth Order status.

PROVINCIAL CENTRES – THE SECOND ORDER

To Smailes these were all Major Cities, though his article does rank them in some detail. . . . In England it is in fact possible to recognize three sub-orders of Provincial centres: the three strongest centres lead in very many respects, there are five others which usually hold a similar rank in relation to each other and to the three leaders, and finally there are a few rather weaker centres which have an incomplete range of the characteristic services.

Smailes recognized fourteen Major Cities in England outside London, and thirteen of these are certainly in the Second Order now. One – Bradford – has declined appreciably, to be replaced by another, so there are still probably fourteen. Great stability is certainly characteristic of the large city, which will come through fire and water to re-emerge with unimpaired status. Warsaw is the classic example, but war damage on the more piecemeal scale in England has left little mark on the relative status of our leading cities. Coventry seems to be emerging as the new Second Order city: yet its centre was damaged at least as severely relative to its size as any other town in England.

Manchester, closely followed by Liverpool and Birmingham, is the leading Second Order centre. This is just as Smailes found it. These three may be classed as 2A. There is also a fairly clear ranking within the 2B centres, in the order Leeds, Newcastle upon Tyne, Sheffield, Bristol and Nottingham. As with all classifications these are generalized, and must obscure significant facts such as Liverpool's weakness in Regional television, and Leeds' outstanding shopping facilities. Nottingham and Bristol are relatively weak as shopping centres, and Carruthers (1957) found Sheffield to be only a 3A bus centre.

The weaker Provincial Cities are less easy to rank but still include Leicester and Hull, each of which is clearly of 2C rating, and with fair assurance Southampton, Plymouth, and Coventry. This last is probably a really significant change from pre-war conditions. The phenomenal growth of its industries, and the redevelopment of its centre on revolutionary lines, followed by the establishment of major new cultural and educational facilities, have together brought this about; but, in various respects it is still relatively weak. Norwich is apparently holding its own as the smallest of the Second Order centres, being highly specialized in services.

By contrast Bradford seems to have suffered a decline. Smailes regarded it as a rather exceptional case, an auxiliary metropolis; but these days its dominance as the centre of the wool trade means less than it did. Even the future of the Wool Exchange is in some doubt, and importance as the Northern centre of the new Pakistani community in Britain is perhaps not yet so meaningful. There was a sharp decline in the numbers employed full-time in Special shopping between 1950 and 1961 in Bradford, and its morning newspaper has disappeared. Bradford's Association football teams languish in the Fourth Division – perhaps not a very important indicator, but one very much in the public eye. There is no doubt, however, that quantitatively Bradford is still stronger than any other centre in the Third Order, in terms of the number of its central facilities, which have been extensively redeveloped.

In attempting to draw a line between orders and sub-orders, the range of facilities available seems more relevant than the intensity of provision of those present. Quality, again, cannot readily be measured, and a new facility of any type may mean more in material terms than an old one, while actually playing a less integrated role in the community. The rise and fall of the Ten-pin Bowling centres is a good current example of this. A mass circulation newspaper or a very large hospital may mean no more to a city than smaller but more specialized examples elsewhere do to their own cities. The presence of even small individual representatives of facilities characteristic of an order, but not of those below, may be more significant than the absence of some features normally expected even in lower orders: a small university may raise the status of a town but the lack of a general market from an important seaside town may not mean a lowered status. Generally speaking, however, the presence of one facility characteristic of a much higher order, such as the Bournemouth Symphony Orchestra, will not make much difference to the general ranking of a place. Several such facilities, if present, may well do so even if there are deficiencies in more mundane services. This general approach has been followed throughout, and a normal range of facilities for each order and sub-order has been established against which deviations may be checked (Table 1). It should be emphasized that very few towns adhere precisely to any such 'normal' pattern.

REGICAL CENTRES – THE THIRD ORDER
REGIONAL CENTRES – THE THIRD ORDER

The strongest centres in this order are quite distinctive when compared with the normal run of large towns, and it is very significant that Smailes chose to label them with a special use of the word 'City'. Not necessarily very large in themselves, they possess a range of specialized facilities, many of a cultural type such as theatres and universities, but also a more varied range of banks and a concentration of offices, professional services, department stores and good hotels, such as are found scattered rather than concentrated in the remaining Third Order centres. The 3A grading is used here for such places, which are apparently increasing in number, and is fully compatible with Smailes' 'Cities'.

Apart from Coventry, which has risen out of this sub-order, all Smailes' Cities are still to be found as 3A centres in the 1960s. After Bradford the strongest are possibly Brighton, and Hanley–Stoke on Trent. These last two distinct central places, only 1½ miles apart, have to be taken together as their facilities are complementary rather than in competition; taken separately Hanley would be 3B and Stoke 3C. To the outsider the whole is one city. Newcastle under Lyme, only 2 miles from Stoke, is just below the threshold of the Third Order.

Middlesbrough, a strong 3A centre, and Stockton on Tees which is a weak 3B centre with a subordinate relationship to its partner, are less complementary, both having a near-complete range of facilities; but taken together with their smaller neighbours their combined facilities are the equivalent of the 2C sub-order, which represents an advance on the position as recorded by Smailes.

Wolverhampton and Bournemouth are now exceptionally strong

3A centres, and they are joined by the latter's Northern rival Blackpool, which was regarded by Smailes as a member of the Major Town category, i.e. 3B. Promotion is evident here.

Most of Smailes' 'Cities' now rank near the middle of the 3A group, but Gloucester and Carlisle are significantly weaker than the others, and Blackburn comes nearest to losing its 3A status. The outcome of the major central redevelopment now in progress there, and the relative effects on Preston of planned large-scale expansion, will be interesting to watch. Promotion to 3A is evident in Chester, Bolton, Huddersfield, Doncaster, and with less assurance may be added Lincoln, Bath and Southend.

Except for the two last-named, these are all Northern rather than Southern centres, and it may be asked how this apparent rise in status can be equated with the generally-accepted weakness of the North against the economic strength of the South. Apart from the somewhat different range of indicators studied as compared with Smailes, other factors may have a bearing on this anomaly: the relative congestion and obsolescence of certain of the larger Northern cities and the decline of small towns in that area.

Table 2. Central places of Second and Third Orders in England 1965 (excluding Greater London)

Second Order Centres—listed in descending importance:

2A Centres	2B Centres	2C Centres
Manchester	Leeds	Leicester
⎰ Birmingham	Newcastle on Tyne	Hull
⎱ Liverpool	Sheffield	Southampton
	Bristol	Plymouth
	Nottingham	Coventry
		Norwich

Note: All the above centres were in Smailes' (1938) classification regarded as Major Cities, except Coventry (City).

Third Order Centres—listed alphabetically within groups of descending importance. Smailes, (1938) grading shown thus:

(B) Major City, (C) City, (M) Major Town, (T) Town.

3A Centres		
Bradford (B)	Wolverhampton (C)	Bolton (M)
Bournemouth (C)	Blackpool (M)	Cambridge (C)
Brighton (C)	Derby (C)	Chester (M)
Middlesbrough (C*)	Oxford (C)	Doncaster (M)
Portsmouth (C)	Preston (C)	Exeter (C)
Potteries † (C)	Reading (C)	Huddersfield (M)
	Sunderland (C)	Ipswich (C)

---

* Stockton included in 1938.   † i.e. Stoke on Trent and Hanley centres.

Table 2.—continued

Northampton (C)	Chesterfield (M)	Truro (M)
Southend (M)	Rochdale (M)	West Bromwich (‡)
York (C)	Salisbury (M)	Winchester (M)
Bath (M)	Wakefield (M)	Yeovil (T)
Blackburn (C)	West Hartlepool (M)	Barnstaple (T)
Carlisle (C)	Crewe (M)	Boston (M)
Gloucester (C)	Dudley (M)	Bridlington (M)
Guildford (M)	Great Yarmouth (M)	Bury St Edmunds (M)
Lincoln (M)	Harrogate (M)	Dewsbury (M)
3B Centres	Hastings (M)	Morecambe (M)
Grimsby (M)	St Helens (M)	Newton Abbot (T)
Luton (M)	Scunthorpe (M)	Rugby (M)
Oldham (M)	South Shields (M)	
Swindon (M)	Stockton on Tees (‡)	Aldershot (T)
Watford (M)	Worthing (M)	Basingstoke (T)
Birkenhead (‡)	Lancaster (M)	Dartford (T)
Cheltenham (M)		Durham (M)
Darlington (M)	*3B Centre forming part*	Keighley (M)
Halifax (M)	*of composite centre of*	Kendal (M)
Medway Towns (M)	*a higher order:*	Macclesfield (M)
Slough (T)	Hanley (Potteries)	Newark (T)
Stockport (M)		Newbury (T)
Walsall (M)	*3C Centres*	Weymouth (M)
Wigan (M)	Canterbury (M)	Workington (M)
Eastbourne (M)	Mansfield (M)	Ashford, Kent (T)
Southport (M)	Burton upon Trent (M)	Bishop Auckland (T)
Worcester (M)	Bury, Lancs. (M)	Bognor Regis (T)
Burnley (M)	Folkestone (M)	Crawley (Sub-town)
Chelmsford (M)	High Wycombe (T)	Dover (M)
Colchester (M)	King's Lynn (M)	Loughborough (T)
Hereford (M)	Nuneaton (M)	Oswestry (T)
Leamington (M)	St Albans (M)	Stafford (M)
Maidstone (M)	Weston super Mare (M)	Whitehaven (M)
Peterborough (M)	Ashton under Lyne (M)	Windsor (T)
Rotherham (M)	Aylesbury (M)	
Scarborough (M)	Banbury (T)	*3C Centres forming*
Shrewsbury (M)	Barrow in Furness (M)	*parts of composite*
Taunton (M)	Chichester (M)	*centres of a higher*
Torquay (M)	Gateshead (‡)	*order:*
Tunbridge Wells (M)	Gravesend (T)	Chatham (Medway
Warrington (M)	Kettering (M)	Towns)
Barnsley (M)	Kidderminster (T)	Stoke on Trent
Bedford (M)	Lowestoft (M)	(Potteries)
	Margate (T)	Salford (Manchester)

‡ Not separately distinguished.

Table 4. Central places classified by Smailes (1938) but no longer having Fourth Order status

Alcester, Warwicks.	Neston, Cheshire
Arundel, Sussex	New Mills, Derbys. (Smailes
Bedlington, Northumb.	*Town*)
Budleigh Salterton, Devon	Padstow, Cornwall
Burford, Oxon.	Penistone, Yorks.
Craven Arms, Salop.	Petworth, Sussex
Egremont, Cumb.	Rothbury, Northumb.
Ellesmere, Salop. (Smailes *Town*)	Royston, Yorks.
Emsworth, Hants.	Shifnal, Salop.
Hayle, Cornwall	Soham, Cambs.
Heathfield, Sussex	Tetbury, Glos.
Kirkby Moorside, Yorks. (less than 5A by	Thornbury, Glos.
1965)	Thrapston, Northants.
Kirkby Stephen, Westmorland	Watton, Norfolk
Littleborough, Lancs.	Wells next the Sea, Norfolk
Lymm, Cheshire	Wem, Salop
Lyndhurst, Hants.	Wirksworth, Derbys.
Lynton, Devon	Wotton under Edge, Glos.
Mablethorpe, Lincs.	

Table 5. Comparison of Gradings, 1938 and 1965

Smith (1965)	Smailes' Gradings – No. of Centres as at 1938							
	Major City	City	Major Town	Town	Sub-town	Un-graded	Not shown*	Total
2A	3							3
2B	5							5
2C	5		1					6
3A	1	19	9					29
3B			46	1			3	50
3C			32	19	1		5	57
4A			5	77	3	1	4	90
4B				150	30	10	23	213
4C				37	127	63	55	282
5A				2	32	Omitted for		34
Ungraded					1	clarity		1
TOTAL	14	20	92	286	194	74	90	770

* Centres in congested areas obscured by symbols for larger centres; including those 15 miles or less from central London but not within the Greater London Council area.
  The totals above include a small number of composite centres made up of centres of a lower order which are also included.
  There are also numerous 5A centres which Smailes' study did not record.

The Reorganization of
Local Government

The local government system which was created for England and Wales by the Local Government Acts of 1888 and 1894 was very much a second best. The county areas were unsatisfactory because they were divisions which were then some centuries old, and they were not adjusted to take account of the social changes of the industrial revolution. The concept of the county borough which was introduced by the 1888 Act, that of a town separately administered from its adjoining county, was defective because it involved splitting off an urban centre from its economic hinterland, whilst the criterion for its definition, a population of 50,000, meant that many of the county borough units which were created were too small in terms of demand and internal organization for the effective performance of services. The division created by the administrative county/county borough dichotomy produced stresses and strains which the system could ill afford, because the administrative weaknesses of operating units which were too small in an age of rapid technological change were aggravated by the institutional rivalry of the two types of authorities.

The urban and rural district councils were for the most part the outcome of mid-nineteenth century events which were irrelevant to the purpose of the 1894 Act, which was to rescue something from the wreck of the original proposals on which the 1888 bill was founded. Though the Local Government Act of 1888 marked the successful victory, after half a century of struggle, to establish popular representative government in the counties, it was a signal defeat in the administrative sense. This is to be seen in two factors. The first was the gradual erosion of the population requirement for county borough status, from the Government's original intention of 150,000, through the figure of 100,000 which appeared in the bill, to that of 50,000 which was eventually enacted. The other was the failure to transfer to the county councils, as provided for in the Act, the powers of supervision over the *ad hoc* sanitary and other authorities which were exercised by various Ministers in the central government.

The consequences of this defeat were threefold. First, as we have already noted, there was the division between town and country, and relatively small towns at that, which still persists in the structure of local government. The Government's original intention of making the county the basic local government unit, with few exceptions in favour of the very large towns, was completely thwarted both by the large number of towns which were admitted to this exceptional status by the 1888 Act and the ease with which their number and the size of the existing ones could be increased – a process which could only take place at the expense of the administrative counties. The inability of the Government to carry through, in 1889, the transfer of supervisory powers over the vast array of *ad hoc* authorities to the county councils further weakened the councils' role in the new system.

The Local Government Act of 1894 which created the urban and rural district councils to replace the *ad hoc* authorities produced the second consequence of the breakdown of the reform movement, because it allowed the two-tier arrangement within the counties to develop so that the lower tier authorities, the county district councils, could assume an autonomy vis-à-vis the county councils in relation to their powers. So far from the county councils having powers of supervision over their lower-tier authorities, as the provisions of the 1888 Act contemplated, the new district authorities were able to claim that their powers and functions were directly bestowed on them by Parliament, and as a result neither tier owed anything to the other in the way of allegiance, co-ordination or co-operation.

The third outcome of the events of 1888 to 1894 was that existing areas were used as the areas of the new units. A large number of the urban sanitary authorities, which became urban district councils by virtue of the 1894 Act, were very small places which had acquired that status, not because of their 'urban' character, but because of a loophole in the Highway Act of 1862. Thus at all levels, county borough, county, and county district, many authorities were too small even at their creation. The gathering pace of technological development in the closing years of the nineteenth century and the early years of the twentieth soon emphasized the social and economic artificiality of these small units.

The early Fabians, who were so keen to develop socialism through the medium of municipal enterprise, were realistic enough to understand that their claims rested on their being able to demonstrate that municipal trading could be efficient. They saw that small operating areas, such as would be provided by many local authorities, militated against efficient operation of the utility services, and they provide our first example of the plea for regional administration as the means of overcoming the structural defects of local government.

A further difficulty existed in that the procedures for effecting changes in local government areas which were laid down in the two statutes were inevitably weak. They generally demanded the agreement of all the local authorities which might be involved in a change, and there was little likelihood of that happening as each local authority was naturally intent on self-preservation. In effect, the only changes which could be achieved within the existing legislative framework were the creation of additional county boroughs and the expansion of existing ones. This, of course, had the effect of further weakening the county system no matter how justified an individual borough's claims might be.

The congenital deformities of the local government structure were soon aggravated by the new tasks thrust upon it. The development of additional public services, particularly in the fields of education and public health, in the years between 1902 and 1919 forced attention on the structural deficiencies. The creation of the Ministry of Health in 1919 emphasized the concern of the central government with the efficiency of the local government system, and it was followed by the first large-scale inquiry into the system as a whole for nearly a century. The Royal Commission on Local Government, whose investigations took six years from 1923 to 1929, looked at the problems arising from the vast array of local authorities bequeathed by the nineteenth century, but it did not go beyond making recommendations for rationalising the structure into fewer but larger authorities of the *existing types*, and for ameliorating the county/county borough tension by making it more difficult for new county boroughs to be created and for existing ones to expand. The first official proposals for a recognizably regional solution to the problem of Lilliputian authorities within an extensive urban complex were put forward by the Royal Commission on Local Government in the Tyneside Area in 1937. These were never acted upon and, in any case, they dealt with the problems of a small part of the country and not with the general problems of the system.

A recognition of the need for a regional solution to be applied generally throughout the country came in 1940 from the Royal Commission on the Distribution of the Industrial Population. The Royal Commission brought a wider view to the problem because it was not solely concerned with local government issues. Indeed, it marks the introduction of a new dimension to the debate about local government. From this point onwards, the arguments go beyond the relatively narrow field of seeking more suitable areas for the administration of the existing functions of local authorities to a review of the wider role of local government in the state. Though the 1939–45 war caused the cessation of the regular reviews of county district authorities, which had been introduced by the Local Government Act, 1929, it gave a filip to proposals for post-war reconstruction in local government, as in a wide variety of other fields. Some reformers looked to regional solutions, not only as a means of creating a more efficient system of subordinate units of government but also as a means of providing the wider areas of administration which the newer functions of the state, in such fields as economic planning and the social services, often demanded. The manner in which the particular requirements of a variety of services led to the creation of *ad hoc* authorities on a regional basis outside the sphere of local government has already been examined in Chapter 2. Here we refer to three different views about the development of regional authorities for general purposes.

The Government's attitude, as expressed in the 1945 White Paper, hardened against regionalism, and perhaps the mild regionalist tendencies of the Local Government Boundary Commission which were detected in its 1947 proposals for single tier counties were a small contributory factor to its eventual demise without it having achieved a single change in the structure of local government. But there is no doubt that there was a growing volume of opinion amongst competent observers in favour of some form of regional government. The ideas of the geographers have been examined in Chapter 3, but the powerful academic voice of Professor W. A. Robson, undoubtedly our leading scholar in the field of public administration, came out in support of regional institutions in the second edition of his *Development of Local Government* in 1948.

After the demise of the Local Government Boundary Commission in 1949, the local authority associations once more displayed their full range of differences on the subject of how to reorganize local government. Far from any of them countenancing the development of regional authorities, the scheme outlined by the boundary commission in its report for 1947 was much too radical for most of them. The Government took advantage of this disarray and it did not again show any public interest in the problem of reform until it published a White Paper in 1956 on *Areas and Status of Local Authorities* (Cmd. 9831). From our point of view this document was singularly lacking in interest since it did no more than propose a new method for achieving a reorganization of local government structure without venturing into the realms of regionalism. Subsequently, the Local Government Act,

1958, established two review bodies, a Local Government Commission for England and one for Wales. The Commission for England was excluded from a widely drawn metropolitan area which became the subject of investigation by a third body, the Royal Commission on Local Government in Greater London. The incompatibility of town government by a single chartered municipal authority with the problems of a gradually extending urban sprawl had been recognized in the case of London by the middle of the nineteenth century. The uniqueness of the metropolis, its character and its problems, had long been one of the bases which differentiated London government from the rest of the country, and this differentiation was preserved in the local government reforms of the late nineteenth century.

This is not the place to examine the respective peculiarities and the governmental implications of the terms 'metropolitan' and 'conurbation', both of which have been used to describe the London situation. Clearly, however, there are regional characteristics in both terms, and the extended metropolitan area consigned to the care of the Royal Commission implied a territory which was more regional than local in character. As a result of the Commission's recommendations the larger metropolitan area was given a new system of subordinate government: a two-tier structure in which the upper tier, the Greater London Council, was marked by important differences from the administrative county councils which had formed the upper tier in the previous system. The differences have been further emphasized by the transfer from the central government to the Greater London Council, of responsibility for London Transport and for a number of traffic and highway duties previously undertaken by the Ministry of Transport.

In the remainder of England, the Local Government Commission had two tasks. One was to review the structure of local government in five special review areas, corresponding to the major conurbations outside Greater London, and for these areas it was able to suggest whatever institutional arrangement it thought most suited to each area, even though its proposals might not follow the general pattern of local government in the remainder of the country, that is, a pattern of administrative counties and county boroughs. The idea of the special review areas also implied regional characteristics, and it was widely felt that the solution proposed by the Royal Commission for Greater London would set a precedent for the provincial conurbations. However, in the event the recommendations for the Black Country (which turned out to be the only ones to be implemented), west Yorkshire and Merseyside were all based on the continued use of the general pattern of local government and showed how strong was the attraction, for existing authorities and the central government alike,

of the more parochial institutions. Only in the case of Tyneside and
the south-east Lancashire/north-east Cheshire areas were suggestions
made for two-tier solutions which involved regional authorities on the
London pattern. In the event the processes of review under the 1958
Act were brought to an end before any action was completed in these
two areas.

Outside the five provincial conurbations the Local Government
Commission for England (and so also the Commission for Wales) was
restricted to reshaping the areas of the counties and the county
boroughs. Some proposals were put into effect, but the smallest
English county, Rutland, managed to survive in spite of the Commission's proposals to merge it with neighbouring Leicestershire. The
failure to get rid of Rutland from the administrative map, in itself a
major defeat for the objectives of local government reform, was
symptomatic of the deficiencies of the review procedures established
by the 1958 Act, which allowed many opportunities for obstruction
and delay. In order to get out of the procedural impasse which had
inexorably built up, the Labour Government which came into office
in 1964 decided to bring the work of the Commissions to an end, with
many sets of proposals unimplemented, and to institute a more
radical process of review.

This was done by the setting up of the Royal Commission on Local
Government in 1966. The chairman was Lord Redcliffe-Maud, who
had just previously chaired the Committee on the Management of
Local Government. The manner in which this committee had made
proposals for a startling shake-up of the internal organization of local
authorities raised hopes that, with the same chairman, the new Commission would be equally radical in its proposals for structural reform.
Unfortunately, the Royal Commission's terms of reference confined it
to a review of local government with its existing functions. This
effectively prevented the Commission from giving any serious consideration to regional machinery, since any proposals of this nature
would almost inevitably have involved consideration of such bodies
taking over activities at present performed by various *ad hoc* regional
bodies, and perhaps some devolution from the central government,
and this would have taken the Commission beyond its terms of
reference.

Before the Royal Commission could complete its task, the Government established the Commission on the Constitution, with a notice-
able regional ring about its terms of reference. These referred to the
governmental needs of the various parts of the United Kingdom, the
offshore islands (the Isle of Man and the Channel Islands) and the different regions of England. The setting up of the Commission on the

Constitution did not represent a recognition on the part of the Government of the restrictive nature of the terms of reference of the Royal Commission on Local Government, neither did it represent a sudden conversion of the Government to the virtues of regionalism. The real impetus toward the creation of the Constitutional Commission was a combination of the electoral successes of the Scottish Nationalist Party and Plaid Cymru at bye-elections, with the restiveness of the Channel Islands and the Isle of Man at the prospect of their being dragged along by the external policies of the United Kingdom just when they were beginning to gain a large measure of control over their own affairs. The attempt by the Isle of Man Government to establish a commercial broadcasting system against the wishes of the United Kingdom Government had made both sides realise that this new exercise in freedom was not without problems. Both the rising tide of nationalism and the fractiousness of the islands gave cause to the Government to consider how best to maintain its own superior position. In setting up the Commission on the Constitution, the central government provided time to allow the steam to get out of the situation, and gave itself the opportunity to take a more deliberate look at the problem without being hastened into panic measures which it might later regret.

The inclusion in the terms of reference of the Commission of the problem of regionalism in England was probably a matter of form, though events were to show that in the long run there was more to this aspect of the problem than the Government was at first prepared to admit. The Liberal Party had argued strongly about 'power to the provinces'. The regional economic planning boards and councils, set up by the same Government, had demonstrated both the significance of the regional approach, and their own inability to meet the political and administrative requirements that such an approach necessitated. Also both the main report from the Royal Commission on Local Government and the dissenting memorandum from Mr Senior (in spite of their advocacy of the unitary principle and the city-region concept respectively), showed that resort to some form of regional organization could not be avoided.

In retrospect, it seems as though the creation of the Commission on the Constitution was both the saviour and the executioner of the local government Commission. On the one hand the Commission, both in majority and in dissension, had to admit that any reasonably satisfactory attempt to reform the structure of local government, even with the limit of its existing functions, had to look beyond what the local authorities did to facets of regional strategy, especially in physical and service planning. Recognizing this, it becomes impossible to produce a local government reform which does not involve a regional level of administration and of decision-taking. On the other hand, the fact that the Constitutional Commission was created before the local government body had completed its work clearly cut the ground from under the latter's feet. It was obvious that the creation of regional machinery would have to take precedence in any rational scheme of things to a re-ordering of local institutions. And as the local government Royal Commission clearly recognized, if as a result of the Constitutional Commission's work there was to be some form of devolution from the central government, then their terms of reference for the reform of local government were no longer relevant.

Fabian Provinces

From W. Sanders, *Municipalization by Provinces*, Fabian Society, London, 1905. Fabian Tract 125, pp. 2–5.

This was the first of a series of tracts published by the Fabian Society under the title of *The New Heptarchy Series* and it is the earliest recognition of the unsuitability of the areas of local government for modern administrative needs. The Fabians were, of course, concerned with the efficiency of the public utility undertakings but it is easy to see that the argument for larger areas could be extended to other local government services.

(The first Report of the Committee of the Society appointed to consider the Reform of Local Government, presented to the Society on 26th May, 1905, by Wm. Sanders, L.C.C., the Chairman of the Committee, and subsequently adopted.)

INDUSTRIES AND LOCAL GOVERNMENT AREAS

With the growth of municipal enterprise it has become obvious that the development of the collective control of the economic life of society is largely dependent upon the capacity of the community to adapt its local government machinery to changing social and economic conditions. Much of the existing machinery in England was created for the purpose of dealing with conditions widely different from those of to-day, and for exercising powers far narrower in scope than those which are now imposed upon it by legislation, or which the community demands that it should acquire. Local authorities are given duties to perform, or are allowed to assume duties, without due consideration of their fitness for the responsibility. Thus experiments in municipal activities are entered upon under unfavourable circumstances which preclude the possibility of complete success, whereby opportunities are given to the anti-Collectivist to vaunt the superior advantages of private enterprise.

One of the first points, if not *the* first point, to be considered in connection with any further extension of the powers of municipalities, or of the collective organization of industry in any form, is that of the area over which a municipal or other local governing authority should govern. Under the old conception, or want of conception, of the duties of local government authorities this appeared to be a matter of small importance, although in connection with main roads and sewers it was sometimes borne in mind by the legislators. When a local authority was appointed to deal solely with paving, it was a matter of minor importance whether it should have authority to pave fifty yards of the Strand only, or the whole of the streets and roads of London. But when the community proceeds to provide through its own administrative machinery water, gas, electric light and power, means of communication, educational facilities, and many other services, and, moreover, must compete with private undertakings, the promoters of which are anxious and willing for a consideration to relieve the community of the burden, the question of area becomes of paramount importance.

Tramways and Light Railways

This can be seen at once in the case of tramways and light railways. There is no existing government area which is generally suitable for the effective and profitable management of a publicly owned tramway system. Unless a town council can persuade the neighbouring local authorities to agree to some arrangement under which joint action can be taken for ownership and control, a dwarfed and crippled public service is created, comparing unfavourably in reality, as well as in the public mind, with a privately owned system which, by Act of Parliament, can, within wide boundaries, run where it listeth. The town council unit as a tramway area is obviously inadequate in the crowded centres of the North; the county council area, although less open to objection, would not be wholly satisfactory. For instance, an efficient tramway service for London and the surrounding district ought to extend over country governed by the five county councils of London, Middlesex, Surrey, Essex and Kent, and many county boroughs within their boundaries. This area is served at present by disconnected, incomplete systems, partly under public and partly under private ownership. In the existing dismembered condition of the metropolitan and extra-metropolitan tramway service, it is impossible for the community to secure the full advantages of this form of transit in either convenience or economy. The big centres of population in the Midlands and the North suffer in the same way, and provide equally convincing evidence of the imperative need for the establishment for transit purposes of new authorities having control over areas, the boundaries of which might in no case be coterminous with those of existing local government areas.

Municipal Electricity and Industrial Progress

Another service which, in order to be economically administered under public ownership, requires new authorities and areas is the provision of electric light and power. The municipal electric light and power works now in being were, in many cases, prematurely born, and, unless they can be given room to expand beyond the limits which now confine them, they are likely to become, not only horrible examples of the failure of public enterprise, but also serious obstacles to industrial advance. The metropolis offers a striking example of the failure to appreciate the importance of area in relation to the generation and supply of electricity. The metropolitan borough councils were made the authorities for this purpose, and several of them have erected generating stations and laid down their own self-contained systems. The limitations of the usefulness of their parochial installations are now obvious. For instance, the Battersea Borough Council approaches a railway company with an offer to light a huge goods station with municipal electricity. The goods station lies on the confines of the Battersea Borough Council's area, and unfortunately a small part of the station to be lighted is within the borders of a neighbouring borough council which has sold to a private company its powers to supply electricity. This company refuses to come to terms with its Battersea rival, and the railway company naturally declines to have two installations on its premises, with the result that the Battersea Borough Council loses an excellent customer and the railway company has to set up its own more expensive installation. Many other instances of this kind could be given, showing the administrative difficulties which arise through the piecemeal system of managing municipal electric light and power in the metropolis.

Area and Cost of Production

But administrative difficulties are small matters compared with unnecessary costliness of production arising from the adoption of the view that the ancient boundaries of the authority of an ecclesiastical institution enclose an area which is convenient as a unit for the production and distribution of electric energy. A Committee of the House of Lords has now (1905) discovered the foolishness of Parliament in not recognizing that London should have had one authority for this purpose. The private syndicates that are asking power to supply the whole of the metropolis, or large portions thereof, can bring overwhelming proof from the North of England, where such syndicates produce electricity in bulk, that they could bring about a considerable saving in the cost. The London County Council ought to have been the authority for electric light and power purposes. Not only would the administrative difficulties have been far less, and the economy secured which the companies promise, but London could have been lighted in a far more efficient manner. The poorer districts, which are now often neglected in this respect, could have been better served, without extra local expense, by means of an equalized lighting rate over the whole of the metropolis, and by the equalized distribution of the surpluses accruing from the districts with a large number of private profit-giving consumers. Moreoever, with the London County Council as the authority, further economy would arise from use of the generating stations to make electricity both for tramway and other purposes and for supplying light.

But even the London County Council area does not offer the most advantageous sphere. The movements and aggregations of population pay no heed to municipal landmarks, not even to those fixed for the L.C.C. London, as a unit for a well-organized, publicly owned transit service, already stretches from Uxbridge on the west to Upminster on the east, and from Potter's Bar on the north to Purley on the south; and the area of the public authority dealing with electricity should, in the main, coincide with that dealing with transit facilities. An authority controlling a province of this magnitude would have been able not only to supply the power for tramways, lighting, factories and work-shops, but should have had the monopoly right to supply the tubes and the railways that are now electrifying their local lines. It is hardly necessary to point out the important step that this would have been in further co-ordinating the control of transit services.

The great centres of population throughout England present the same problems in respect of area as London. The case of the Birming-ham tramway fight, in which the city was hampered and to some extent crippled as an efficient provider of means of transit by the action of surrounding minor local authorities, shows the need that the problem of local government area be dealt with on other than parochial or narrow municipal lines. The great towns of Liverpool, Manchester, Birmingham, Newcastle, Nottingham, Leeds, etc., must be considered as centres, and not as self-contained units for all local government purposes.

With regard to the supply of water new areas and authorities are urgently needed. The large towns through their greater wealth are able to annex the best water-bearing districts to the potential if not to the yet actual detriment of the smaller towns and villages.

Direct Employment and Wider Areas
Then there is the complex question of the direct employment of labour by the local authorities in those forms of industry in which under private enterprise steady, continuous demand, with corresponding regular employment is seldom found. Here again population and area play a considerable part in determining whether municipal under-takings of this nature can be carried on so as to ensure greater per-manence of employment, together with efficient and economical working. It is of course easy for a local authority, with a small popula-

tion and area, to estimate with comparative certainty the number of men it will permanently require to make up its roads and keep them clean; to clear away dust and house refuse and the like; and therefore to employ the men and carry out the work more efficiently than a contractor, with the added advantages of affording continuous employment with a fair wage to the men engaged. But in connection with the more intricate and fluctuating work of building, which requires a well-organized works department with expensive plant and an experienced staff, a large and well-populated area is indispensable for lasting success. The metropolitan borough council area is too small for a works department which would be really effective in adding to the number of men engaged continuously in profitable employment. Nor, under present conditions, could sufficient work be found to keep the plant in use long enough to repay its first cost. A borough council may build a bath and wash-house, a library, a coroner's court, lavatories, electric power station, stables for its horses, a town hall, houses and shops for the working classes, and a disinfecting station; but when these have been erected it has no more building to be done. It cannot do work for another public body nor for private customers. When it approached the end of its career as a useful institution there might arise a tendency to make work for the works department because it was there and because men were unemployed, regardless of consideration whether the proposed buildings were really required.

Regionalism on Tyneside

From Report of the Royal Commission on Local Government in the
Tyneside Area. Cmd. 5402, 1937, pp. 38–41 and 54–7.

This Commission was established as a consequence of the harsh
economic conditions experienced in the north-east during the early
nineteen-thirties and was really concerned with considering how far
a more unified system of local government could contribute to an
improvement of the conditions of the area. This Commission
produced the first official proposal for a regional authority outside
the metropolitan area, but no action was taken to give effect to the
recommendations.

127. Having dealt with the general system of local government and
the changes which have taken place therein, we now turn to the
particular system in force in the area which falls within the ambit of
our Terms of Reference.

128. The position on Tyneside at the present time is somewhat unique.
In an area not much larger than the City of Birmingham there are no
less than sixteen local authorities responsible for the administration of
all or some of the local government services. As a result of this it is
found that there are six different authorities responsible for services
such as public assistance, police, higher education, care of persons
suffering from mental diseases, tuberculosis and venereal diseases,
and the maintenance, repair and improvement of classified roads;
ten different authorities are responsible for elementary education;
nine of the sixteen authorities maintain fire brigades; and there are
eleven separate hospitals throughout the area for the treatment of
persons suffering from infectious diseases, while eight hospitals exist
to deal with smallpox cases.

129. This extraordinary multiplicity of authorities is not due to any
desire of some body or person to create a complicated system of local
government in this part of the country. While the areas of local
government have remained substantially unaltered, confusion has
arisen owing to the development of the several districts, which in
many cases are now contiguous, combined with the subsequent
devolution by Parliament to local authorities of powers in connection
with additional or reallocated services.

130. On the north bank of the River Tyne there are two County
Boroughs, namely, the City and County of Newcastle and the Tyne-

mouth County Borough. There are, also, the Municipal Borough of Wallsend and the Urban Districts of Gosforth, Newburn and Whitley and Monkseaton. In addition, the Northumberland County Council is responsible for the administration of certain services in the Borough of Wallsend and in the three Urban Districts. The Councils of the City and County of Newcastle and the County Borough of Tynemouth, being County Borough Councils, are autonomous for all local government purposes within their respective areas, although certain agreements exist between the County Borough Councils and other local authorities in regard to certain services to which reference has already been made.

131. On the south bank of the River Tyne, and forming part of the Tyneside area, are the County Boroughs of Gateshead and South Shields, also the Municipal Borough of Jarrow and the Urban Districts of Hebburn, Felling, Whickham, Blaydon and Ryton. The County Council of Durham administers certain services within the Borough of Jarrow and also in the five riparian Urban Districts, and the reference in the preceding paragraph to the duties of the Councils of the County Boroughs applies equally to the County Borough Councils of Gateshead and South Shields.

132. After a close study of the written evidence submitted by the various local authorities, and having heard the oral evidence of witnesses from all such authorities, we formed the opinion that the system of local government now in force in the Tyneside area does not allow of the numerous local government services being administered in the most efficient and economical manner, and that, therefore, the full benefits capable of being derived from such services are not available over the whole area.

133. With the various considerations in mind to which we have already referred, and as a result of our deliberations, we decided that the best way to approach our task was carefully to examine the requirements of each individual service and to determine the best manner in which such service should be administered in accordance with modern standards, so as to obtain the best possible advantages for the greatest numbers.

134. The great advances which have been made in certain local government services, and the legislation which has been passed with a view to improving the health and welfare of the people, coupled with the fact that many of the services cannot now be described as local in character, brought us to the conclusion that local government services should be divided into two categories, namely, those services which

are preponderantly national in character and which should be administered more economically and efficiently over large areas (and which for convenience may be termed 'regional' services), and those services which are local in character conferring upon ratepayers direct benefit more or less commensurate with the equivalent rate burden.

135. It was by no means easy to determine how services which may be termed 'regional' were to be distinguished from those which might be left to local administration. While we have decided that the services should most certainly be divided into two categories, we are agreed that the distinction cannot be drawn with logical precision, for the reason that there are some services which, though national in character, can more conveniently be administered by a minor local authority. On the other hand there are services which are hardly national in character and yet are more than local in their broad effects.

136. We have dealt in detail with such of the services as may be regarded as 'regional' in a separate part of this Report, from a study of which it will be seen that, in each case, we have arrived at the conclusion that it is desirable for such services to be administered over an area larger than any local government area at present existing on Tyneside.

137. We further decided that the area of administration should include both urban and rural districts, as by this means the benefits and advantages to be derived from the services referred to would be within the reach of all the inhabitants, regardless of their environment.

138. One possibility that presented itself to us at an early date was that it might be desirable to have different areas for different services in order to obtain the greatest benefit. Ample legislative provision exists whereby two or more local authorities may combine for the administration of particular services, e.g. under the Education Act local authorities can form a federation for the purpose of the administration of education over the united areas, and there are numerous other statutory provisions enabling joint boards and joint committees to be formed for particular purposes. It cannot be said, however, that any of these provisions have proved popular among local authorities. From our observation we think it would be a truism to say that local authorities zealously guard the rights which have been conferred upon them to administer particular services; and consequently the advantages which might possibly accrue to the public by the unified control of the administration of a service over a greatly extended area are liable to be lost sight of in the laudable desire to maintain the status and dignity of the local authority. Apart from this we hold the view,

which was shared by many of the witnesses who appeared before us, that difficulties would be created by the constitution of a number of *ad hoc* authorities, whereby the democratic character of English local government might be seriously affected. Taking all points into consideration, it appeared to us that the disadvantages would outweigh all possible advantages, and our conclusion, therefore, was that the better solution would be the creation of a single central authority with power to administer the 'regional' services over a considerable area.

139. Our next problem was to decide as to the area best suited for the purpose of a regional authority, and we have accordingly given attention to the needs of the particular services specified in paragraph 144, and to each of which we refer in the succeeding chapter. Our view is that the area should be of sufficient size to allow of equitable distribution of benefits over the entire district, to ensure efficient administration and to secure that the local authority should have ample financial resources. We feel that the grouping of important services under one central authority would tend to attract to that authority the type of men and women who are qualified and capable of undertaking the responsibilities attaching to the office of membership of such a body.

140. As regards the remainder of the local government services, which speaking generally give local benefit, we are of opinion that these services should be administered by local government units having jurisdiction over a more restricted area contained within, and forming part of, the wider or regional area. Such minor authorities should be possessed of sufficient financial resources and cover an area large enough to ensure efficient and economical administration.

141. It will be appreciated that the creation of a regional authority having jurisdiction over a wide area will, of necessity, deprive the County Boroughs within the Tyneside area, of their status. We have given careful consideration to the question of county boroughs and to their rights to self-government, and while we are of opinion that, in the case of the larger county boroughs, local government is well administered within their respective areas, there are to-day objections to such a system.

142. The area covered by a county borough is usually well-developed, containing valuable industrial and residential property with a proportionately high rateable value, and corresponding benefits to the inhabitants. Although the boundaries of a county borough are defined, experience shows that, as the districts contiguous to it develop and thus increase in rateable value, boundaries are extended to absorb the newly-developed area. This extension may be of advantage to the

districts so acquired, but at the same time it reacts on the county council by reducing the area under its control, with a corresponding loss in rateable value.

143. We are convinced that the establishment of a regional authority would not only allow of further development, increased facilities and better administration over the whole area, but also it would not be in any way detrimental to the areas at present covered by the county boroughs.

144. In dealing with local government in the area under our purview we have classified certain services as 'regional', as we regard them as services which should, on Tyneside, be administered with advantage over the wider area already adumbrated. The services which we consider should be so classified are: Public Health (Medical and Allied Services) including Mental Hospitals and Mental Deficiency, Education, Public Assistance, Police, Fire Brigade and Highways (except unclassified roads in urban areas).

187. We have already stated our reasons for the adoption of a wide area for the administration of certain regional services. We now proceed to deal with the extent of that area, and also with its component parts.

188. We have come to the conclusion that the regional area should consist of the following existing administrative areas:

Areas North of the River Tyne
The Administrative County of Northumberland.
The City and County of Newcastle-upon-Tyne.
The County Borough of Tynemouth.
The Borough of Wallsend.
The Urban District of Gosforth.
The Urban District of Newburn.
The Urban District of Whitley and Monkseaton.

Areas South of the River Tyne
The County Borough of Gateshead.
The County Borough of South Shields.
The Borough of Jarrow.
The Urban District of Hebburn.
The Urban District of Felling.

and in addition certain portions of the Urban Districts of Whickham, Blaydon and Ryton in the County of Durham. These portions have been selected because of their urban character, their proximity to

C.R.R.—6*

Newcastle and the community of interests which exists with other Tyneside areas.

189. It will be observed that this regional area includes the whole of the geographical County of Northumberland and, in addition, certain areas on the south bank of the River Tyne.

190. Our proposals will necessarily deprive the County Boroughs of Newcastle, Tynemouth, Gateshead and South Shields of their status as such, and we have already set out in detail in other paragraphs of this Report our reasons for recommending this procedure.

191. The precise delimitation of the regional area is a matter to which we have given much consideration. In the early stages of our inquiry it became apparent that a decision would have to be taken as to whether the River Tyne is a natural boundary between administrative as well as geographical units or, whether, as has been suggested to us, it is a 'spinal cord' from which the social and industrial life of a large area radiates.

192. Centuries ago, and in particular at about the time when the present geographical counties of England came to be delimited, it is quite understandable that a river such as the Tyne formed a natural and proper boundary between the Counties of Northumberland and Durham in the area under our review. In due course, however, improvements were carried out to the river, the sides were embanked, thus narrowing the water-covered area, the bed deepened by dredging, natural obstacles were removed, ferries provided and bridges built. The result of these works and improvements was that populous centres began to develop on the banks of the river, particularly at the points where the first bridges were built. This growth along the river has proceeded steadily, and to-day shows no signs of diminishing.

193. Development on the River Tyne, throughout its history, discloses no variation from the normal procedure, and, as will be seen by reference to the map which is included as Appendix IV, a very large centre of population in which, in our opinion, there is a decided community of interest, has grown up on both banks of the river. In spite of this, however, the River Tyne, in its lower reaches, remains the dividing line between two counties and several local government units, no changes having been made in an arrangement which, although doubtless satisfactory in the past, does not necessarily meet the altered conditions which exist to-day.

194. We have given most careful consideration to the question of whether the River Tyne should remain the boundary between local

government units. We have heard much conflicting evidence upon this point, but we have unhesitatingly come to the conclusion that the River Tyne is not now a suitable frontier between administrative areas, and that our proposed regional area must embrace the territory on both banks of the river.

195. This question being settled, a more difficult problem arose, namely, to decide how far to the southward of the river the boundary of the proposed regional area should extend. No convenient natural boundary presented itself, and we were, therefore, faced with the fact that any boundary which might be drawn reasonably near to the River Tyne must be, almost entirely, an artificial one. Having given much thought to the matter, we have decided that the southern boundary of the regional area should be the existing southern limits of the County Boroughs, Municipal Borough and Urban Districts at present abutting upon, and to the southward of, the River Tyne, with certain exceptions as indicated in paragraph 188.

196. We have reached a conclusion that the southern boundary which we have selected, while by no means ideal, is the only feasible one for the present. We should, however, like to express the opinion that it may well be desirable, at some future date, that the new regional area should be further extended in a southerly direction. We are not prepared to make any definite suggestions as to how far this extension should go, but in certain events it might be desirable to place the final limits of the new regional area considerably further to the southward. This we regard, merely, as a plan for the future which could be put into operation when further improvements in transport facilities and rapidity of communications allow of such an extension.

197. It was suggested by some witnesses that the ideal solution of the problem would be to establish one large county borough on Tyneside, leaving the remainder of the geographical County of Northumberland, and also the remainder of the County of Durham, as separate units. This scheme has patent attractions if it is regarded purely from the point of view of the populous districts of Tyneside, and we have no doubt that, if it were to be adopted, the several existing towns on both sides of the river would benefit thereby.

198. It is necessary to bear in mind the effect which such a scheme would have upon the Administrative Counties of Northumberland and Durham. In the case of Durham the population is large, and the districts which would be removed from it form a minor portion only of the Administrative County. It was, nevertheless, pointed out to us that although only one-twentieth part of the area of the County is

involved, that area contains, approximately, one-sixth of the population and of the rateable value of the Administrative County. We were informed that, on the latest figures then available, the direct financial loss occasioned by such a transfer would not be serious.

199. In the case of the Administrative County of Northumberland the position is substantially different, since the total population is much smaller than that of the County of Durham, and the areas to be included in the suggested Tyneside County Borough, and thus taken away from the County, would constitute a substantial loss, with the resultant serious effect upon the rateable value, financial stability and the prosperity of the remaining part of the County. It is not too much to say that Northumberland would be largely crippled by the formation of such a County Borough on Tyneside.

200. Added to this there are the inherent disadvantages and drawbacks of the system of county boroughs, which we have dealt with elsewhere in our Report, and which would apply with equal force to a Tyneside County Borough. For these, and other reasons which we have enunciated when dealing with the individual services, we decided, after some reflection but without any doubt, that the whole of the geographical County of Northumberland must be included in the proposed regional administrative unit.

201. We have considered the most appropriate name for the Regional Authority, and have come to the conclusion that it should be designated The Northumberland Regional Council. The creation of this new authority will, of necessity, involve the reconstruction of the present Northumberland County Council. We think that the existing administrative machinery of the Northumberland County Council should form the nucleus of the Northumberland Regional Council.

202. We have now reached the stage at which the thickly populated areas on the south bank of the River Tyne have been included, together with the geographical County of Northumberland, in the new regional area which is to contain no county boroughs.

203. As stated elsewhere in our Report, it is our view that all local government services, other than the large regional services already enumerated, should be administered by other administrative units having jurisdiction over areas contained within the regional area. We have given consideration to the administration of these minor services in the area under our purview. On the question as to whether the various authorities should remain as at present, or whether there should be any amalgamation or other changes, we have heard a considerable body of evidence. Having carefully weighed this evidence

we are unhesitatingly of the opinion that the whole of the districts which may fairly be designated as forming the Tyneside area should be amalgamated so as to form one large unit for the purposes of the administration of the remaining local government services not included in those allocated to the Regional Authority. The areas which should be so amalgamated are:

Areas North of the River Tyne

The City and County of Newcastle-upon-Tyne.
The County Borough of Tynemouth.
The Borough of Wallsend.
The Urban District of Gosforth.
The Urban District of Newburn.
The Urban District of Whitley and Monkseaton.

Areas South of the River Tyne

The County Borough of Gateshead.
The County Borough of South Shields.
The Borough of Jarrow.
The Urban District of Hebburn.
The Urban District of Felling.

together with certain parts of the Urban Districts of Blaydon, Whickham and Ryton.

Regionalism and Distribution of Industry

From Report of the Royal Commission on the Distribution of the
Industrial Population. Cmd. 6153, 1940, pp. 178-84.

The Royal Commission came to suggest regional authorities not
because of the defects of the local government system in relation to
its existing functions but because regional authorities would enable
more activities to be undertaken in relation to the development of
the industrial and economic infra-structure of the country. The
opening up of new fields of activity was not pursued any further
until the regional economic planning bodies were established in
1965.

Regionalism and the Distribution of Industry

INTRODUCTION

371. Regionalism as usually understood involves primarily issues
relating to the reform of local government in Great Britain which lie
beyond the scope of this Commission. But if such reform of local
government should take place, especially in the reasonably near
future, material assistance would be given towards the solution of
several difficulties inherent in the issues before the Commission. These
two aspects of regionalism, (*a*) the reform of local government, (*b*) the
relation of such reform to problems before the Commission, must be
kept distinct: it is not, however, possible to appreciate the latter
without some explanation of the former.

372. Regionalism may also be viewed from a somewhat different angle
and its basis analysed, and the regional areas defined, in relation to
industrial rather than to local government considerations. On this
basis, for instance, a metal trade area or region might be defined in
the Midlands pivoting on Birmingham, or a textile region in South
Lancashire with Manchester as its centre. This basis for the regional
idea is further considered in paragraphs 384 and 385.

REGIONALISM AND LOCAL GOVERNMENT

373. The principal units of local government in Great Britain are:

(*a*) in England and Wales the county, the county borough, the non-
county borough and the urban and rural districts, and

(*b*) in Scotland the county and the large and small burghs. In recent
years doubts have arisen in some quarters whether those units are not
proving for many purposes too limited; and the possible adoption of

larger units, generally referred to as 'regions,' for administrative and other purposes has been a matter for discussion.

374. Experience in the last decade or so shows that, whether the machinery of local government be viewed (a) from above, i.e. vis-a-vis the central government authorities, or (b) from below, in relation to the public served, a larger and more comprehensive unit tends to thrust itself into the picture.

(a) From the point of view of the central authorities, Government Departments which are concerned with local administration – the Ministries of Health, Labour and Transport, the Post Office, etc. – have all found themselves forced to adopt for administrative purposes large regional divisions and to place responsible senior officials at the regional centres; the areas chosen for England and Wales have varied according to the needs of each Department from, e.g., seven used by the Ministry of Labour up to 13 or 14 by other Departments. For purposes of civil defence the country has been divided into regions each with its own regional capital.

As regards Scotland there has lately been introduced a considerable measure of devolution of Scottish Office (London) business to Edinburgh.

(b) From the point of view of the public and the services rendered, the advantages of wider areas of administration than are afforded by the ordinary units of local government have been recognised in respect of particular services, e.g., establishment of Joint Boards for water supply, hospitals, etc., joint electricity authorities, regional planning committees, regional smoke abatement committees, etc.

In Scotland, a regional system of medical services embracing the city of Aberdeen and the two counties of Aberdeenshire and Kincardineshire has been established and is in successful operation.

375. The case for a larger or regional unit of administration found definite expression in the Report of the Royal Commission on Tyneside, 1937: the area under review included the county of Northumberland and part of the county of Durham, four county boroughs, namely, Newcastle-on-Tyne, Gateshead, Tynemouth and South Shields, with various boroughs, urban districts, etc. The Majority Report declared that the existing system of local government in the area considered did not allow of the numerous local government services being administered in the most efficient and economical manner, and a re-classification of services into 'regional' and 'local' was therefore recommended; the regional services were to be administered by a new regional authority for the whole area (paragraph 139). The grouping of important services under one central authority would tend, it was

argued, to attract the type of men and women qualified and willing to undertake the work. The regional services were to include public health, medical and allied services, education, public assistance, police, etc.; the remaining – or local – services were to remain in the hands of the existing local authorities. The retention of existing local authorities for non-regional services would be an essential feature of any such proposals, though some adjustment of powers might be necessary.

376. In Scotland the Scottish Economic Committee have, under the Chairmanship of Sir Steven Bilsland, recently reported in favour of a Planning Authority with a scope extending to Scotland as a whole, assisted by regional bodies representing wider areas than those comprised in existing local government boundaries.

377. It is claimed that development of local government along regional lines would have various advantages:

(a) The definite establishment of regional areas would do much to preserve valuable local traditions and local culture, and their capital towns would become important centres of urban life for the region, where administrative, business, financial, educational and artistic ability could all find scope without drifting in so many cases, as at present, to London.

(b) Moreover, responsible representatives of the great Departments of State – the Board of Trade, the Ministries of Health, Labour, Transport, and the Post Office, etc. – could be located in these capital towns; and with the co-operation of the big Banks and of the 'City' authorities, these towns would become, even more than at present, important wheels in the financial and industrial machinery of the country.

(c) It is important to have high cultivation near large centres of population and if agriculture were considered regionally, the regional authority might be expected to ensure that the best possible use was made of the agricultural land in the region. A proper local balance would be secured between rural produce and urban needs, and the authorities in the regional centre would see to it that building schemes or location of new industries did not encroach on rich agricultural land necessary for fruit and vegetables to supply regional consumption so long as other less rich land otherwise suitable was available. The regional amenities would also be safeguarded.

378. Difficult questions in regard to:

(a) the constitution of the Regional Council – whether by direct election or by delegation;

(*b*) the powers and duties of that body and the financial readjustments involved;

(*c*) the basis of the delimitation of areas;

would eventually arise, but do not require consideration here.

REGIONALISM IN RELATION TO THE PROBLEMS BEFORE THE COMMISSION

379. A regional system if adopted would be of assistance in the consideration of several of the problems that face the present Commission. For instance:

(i) The Special Areas. Depressed localities within a region would be able to call upon the co-operation and sympathy of the regional capital and of the whole region. It would be to the direct interest of all in the region to promote recovery, and some provision for regional adjustment of rates would be desirable.

(ii) The problem of planning would be greatly simplified; the Regional Council would become the principal planning authority for the region, certainly for major regional requirements, leaving probably to joint Committees where existing, or to existing local authorities, the detailed administration of schemes. Planning would receive a great stimulus and on more comprehensive and better organised lines than is at present possible with the multiplicity of small planning authorities; and housing could be better related to industry. Larger financial resources would be available and decentralisation in proper cases could be encouraged, e.g., to satellite towns.

(iii) Regionalism has an important bearing on future policy with regard to balanced distribution and diversification of industry. Any scheme for regulating the location of industry would be materially assisted if regional areas were established. Thus, if certain industries were prohibited in a particular town they might suitably be located in another part of the same region and in that way the objection on the part of the town to the prohibition might be modified.

380. A good deal of evidence before the Commission has given support to the regional idea:

(*a*) Evidence has been offered indicating that much interest is being taken in proposals for regionalism in certain areas, e.g., in Manchester: it has been suggested that Merseyside should be under one regional authority, and also that Greater London needs a common local authority.

(*b*) The regionalising of certain services on the lines proposed by the Majority Report of the Royal Commission on Tyneside, would tend to remove or reduce the urge which draws people to the town, for reasons other than those connected with employment. A regional scheme of public health administration which is in successful operation over the whole area of the city of Aberdeen and the two counties of Aberdeen and Kincardineshire has already been referred to.

(c) Each region should have diversity of industry with a proper proportion of primary and secondary industries and with due proportion also of urban and rural population.

381. Some evidence was given that the calibre of those who administer the larger units of local government to-day is tending to decline. Councils and committees to be manned are numerous, alike in county and borough; the work is arduous, and volunteers of good administrative ability are not always easy to find. The establishment of councils, few in number and with considerable powers over wide regional areas would, it was anticipated, tend to attract those possessing a high standard of administrative ability, both in town and country life; this was in fact what occurred at the end of the last century when the London County Council took the place of the former Metropolitan Board of Works.

382. The international crisis of September, 1938, directed attention to the strategical danger involved in connection with the densely peopled urban areas in the South and East, and particularly Greater London; industrialists, banks, insurance companies, etc., found themselves forced to consider the problem of dispersal. This may tend in future to weaken, especially for the newer light industries, the magnetic pull of London and the South-East area, but the attraction for industry of the *big city* will remain: if the draw of London weakens, facilities in regard to labour, market, transport, supplied by the big urban areas other than London will still prove attractive to employers: Bristol, Cardiff, Birmingham, Manchester, Liverpool, Glasgow, especially if they become Regional capitals (and if these Regional capitals become important governmental, administrative and financial centres) may gather what London scatters.

383. The earlier town planners proposed a limit of 50,000 to 100,000 for the optimum size of a town: some modern experts go further and accept, say, a million as a limit for certain purposes. But for towns of large size the necessary conditions of any growth on the lines indicated are the abolition of slums where still existing, and adequate planning, provision of recreation space, and so on.

REGIONS BASED ON INDUSTRIAL CONSIDERATIONS

384. From the industrial point of view, and when dealing with problems of location of industry, there might be advantages in taking an

industrial rather than a local government groundwork as the basis for regional definition. Industries and industrial areas spread and develop irrespective of county or other local government boundaries. But, equally, if regions are to be set up, it by no means follows that their boundaries would coincide with any existing county or county borough boundaries; the regional scheme proposed by the Majority Report of the Royal Commission on Tyneside, which was framed after carefully weighing both industrial and local government points of view, deliberately disregarded local government boundaries and indeed cut across the county of Durham. Moreover, if regions are to be defined purely in relation to industry and industrial development, it would be difficult to fit certain purely non-industrialised areas such as North Wales or portions of the Highlands into a national scheme of regionalism.

385. These difficulties are probably, however, largely unreal: any scheme of regionalism, if it is to be sound in construction and effective in operation, would have to reckon with the forces alike of local government and of industry, as well as other factors such as geography, transport, and so on. In many cases most regions would probably assume much the same shape, whether constructed mainly on an industrial or a local government basis; South-east Lancashire with Manchester as its capital, a Midland region with Birmingham as its capital, or a Clyde Valley region with Glasgow as its capital indicate obvious regions whatever basis is assumed.

CONCLUSION
386. It seems clear that by the adoption of a regional system the solution of several of the problems before the Commission would be materially facilitated.

The Labour Party and Regionalism

From The Labour Party, *The Future of Local Government*, The Labour Party, London, 1943, pp. 7–9 and 15–16.

The Labour Party was one of many organizations which published views about the reform of local government, and in common with most 'outside' observers it suggested some form of regional authorities. On the other hand, no such ideas came from the associations of local authorities.

Proposals for Reorganisation

REGIONALISM

There is now a widespread recognition of the need for a change in Local Government, but there is by no means agreement as to the form of change desirable. Discussion of the subject tends to become confused with the war-time expedient of dividing the country into twelve Civil Defence Regions, and the appointment of Regional Commissioners. This development, however, cannot be regarded as a regionalisation of Local Government. It is rather a devolution of the responsibilities of the central Government, so that the functions of government can be carried on in a war emergency. This form of regionalism is more than a war-time measure, however; it is a tendency that has grown throughout the present century. Before the war there were regional organisations for electricity, the Ministry of Labour, the Ministry of Health, the Advisory Services of the Ministry of Agriculture, Milk Marketing Boards, Assistance Boards, etc., while during the war a number of Ministries have adopted the Civil Defence Regions for special administrative purposes. This is not the place to discuss the future administrative set-up of the central Government. It must be emphatically stated that this type of organisation cannot be permitted to supplant a system of democratically elected Local Authorities. Nor must these Regions condition the area of the new, bigger Local Government Authority, since they are much too large and unwieldy and therefore too remote to maintain a common interest.

THE SINGLE ALL-PURPOSES AUTHORITY

Among the proposals for reform is one which suggests the reorganisation of Local Government on the basis of a single all-purposes Authority, similar to the existing County Borough Council. This view is unacceptable because:

(1) In rural areas the resources available would be so limited that the area required would be too large for all purposes, with a danger of the structure becoming remote, particularly in relation to purely local services, and would necessitate the delegation of some of the responsibilities upon co-opted Committees. Purely local services, with other responsibilities delegated from the major Authority, should be administered by a democratically elected Local Authority.

(2) In the large conurbations, there is a two-tier system in being which will continue to be necessary in all centres of large population if local interest is to be preserved.

It is imperative that any change in Local Government should seek to fuse the interests of town and country, and to have within each major unit a well-balanced grouping, actual or potential, of diversified industry, agriculture, commerce, and residence. This cannot be done by merely adding tracts of rural land to an existing town, because this would merely accelerate urban sprawl, often over good agricultural land. In this connection, it is significant that the Land Utilisation Survey revealed that of the 30,000,000 acres of farm land, not more than 2,500,000 acres were of the highest quality capable of intensive cultivation. Some of this land had been built on during the housing boom, while a considerable proportion of the remainder was on the fringe of great cities, and was in the market as building land. If the exercise of planning powers is to ensure the best use of land, the planning Authority must operate in an administrative area wider than would be possible by the proposed extension of town government.

PLANNING THE NEW STRUCTURE
Any change in Local Government structure must vest full authority in the elected representatives of the people. The democratic tradition in Local Government is very powerful, and nowhere more so than in the ranks of the Labour Movement. It is not enough merely to affirm this principle. Efforts must be made to translate Labour's ideas and ideals into a constructive system of government that will conform to the necessities of historical development. Due regard must therefore be paid to the organisations which now exist, all of which have played a vital part in developing the social services and in training large numbers of people in the art of public administration. Nevertheless, the immensity of the task of post-war reconstruction must be recognised. It will require a smaller number of Authorities than now exist, since no change adequate for modern needs could avoid their supersession. Suitable machinery should be established by the Central Government to survey the country as a whole to determine the areas suitable for a Regional or Major Authority, adequate for the efficient performance of

large-scale services, particularly those which need for their efficient and economical development considerable area, population, and sufficient financial resources. It should be emphasised that the use of the word 'Region' in this connection is in no way related to the organisation or area of the Regional Commissioners, but is used merely to indicate a suitable geographical area. The new Regions must not be so large that the sense of a common interest in their government would be lost, or cause various areas on their outskirts to feel that they had too little in common, but must be large enough to permit an adequate area for development. Their resources must be such that they can with little difficulty command administrative and technical staffs of the highest efficiency. They may well be adaptations of the existing administrative County areas, provided that present boundaries, many of which were determined by historical conditions which bear no relation to modern needs, are not regarded as sacrosanct or unalterable. Where necessary, amalgamations and absorptions of existing Authorities should take place to achieve a satisfactory unit.

AREA AUTHORITIES

Within each Region there should be a suitable number of Area Authorities to administer the purely local services, and others delegated to it by the Major Authority. The size and number of the areas could be determined by population, rateable value (actual and potential), administrative convenience, and the balance of town and country. They should be as few as will make efficient democratic Local Government reasonably possible. This would require amalgamations of many Urban and Rural Authorities, and where possible these would be based upon existing County Boroughs.

DIVISION OF FUNCTIONS — STANDARD OF SERVICE

In addition to revising the structure of Local Government, steps should be taken to extend its powers to enable it to play a full part in the democratic government of the people. Thus, in addition to ensuring a minimum standard of performance by the exercise in suitable cases of the powers of default by the Region in the case of default by the Area Authority, and by the Minister in the case of the Regional Authority, a general Enabling Bill should extend the opportunities of development by Local Authorities. In the allocation of powers to the respective Authorities two principal considerations will have to be borne in mine. These are:

(1) The control and administration of such services as are best provided and administered by, and the cost borne equitably over the Region, must go to the Regional Authorities.

(2) The powers and duties of the Area Authorities must be such as will give them a status and their powers such an importance as will attract the right type of person as members.

PUBLIC UTILITIES
A number of services which are now being administered by Local Authorities such as gas, transport, and electricity, ought to be part of a national scheme under public ownership, if effective national planning is to be ensured. Provision must be made within such a scheme for a proper locus to be given to Local Authorities on prices and services.

LOCAL GOVERNMENT FINANCE
It is an axiom of democracy that autonomy should be accompanied by financial responsibility; therefore the region and its component areas must, subject to Government grants, provide the money they respectively spend. This is essential if Local Government is to retain an adequate measure of independence and liberty of action.

Where a service is completely dependent upon Government finance, there is an increasing measure of central control and a diminishing opportunity for local initiative. Improvements in the system of local rating, particularly in the machinery of valuation, are essential. The establishment of the type of major organisation advocated will make for a greater degree of uniformity in valuation and will contribute to the removal of some of the difficulties now being experienced.

It is of prime importance that the boundaries of each Region and of its component areas should be delimited in such a way as to secure as far as possible that each would be able to provide much the same standard of services, at much the same cost, and that its rateable resources would be of sufficient size and financial 'specific gravity' to be reasonably capable of meeting the cost of its services without entailing excessively high rates or unjustifiable disparities of rate burden between either the Regions themselves or the areas within the Regions. As regards the Regions, any such disparity could be minimised by an equitable scheme of Government grants, in view of the fact that most of the grant-aided services would be regional; as regards the component areas it might well be that any exceptional disparity would need to be met by a financial contribution from the Region under appropriate conditions; that is to say, by an 'easement of rate' arrangement within the Region.

Appendix
Division of Powers and Functions between Regional Authorities and Area Authorities

(As listed in the Provisional Proposals issued in July, 1942)

Service	Powers to Regional Authorities	Powers to Area Authorities
Town Planning and Building	Making of Regional Planning Schemes.	Supervision of operation of Planning Schemes, consents to erection and user in accordance with Schemes.
	Making of Building By-Laws.	Administration of Building Acts and By-Laws, grant of consent to buildings. Dangerous structures, temporary structures, sky signs, etc.
	Power of approval of street naming.	Street naming. Street numbering.
Housing	Major Housing Schemes, slum clearance, Development Schemes, etc. Default Powers. Small Dwellings Acquisition.	Local Schemes, including reconditioning. Small Dwellings Acquisition.
Main Drainage, etc.	Main Drainage. Supply of water and management of rivers to be dealt with together.	Sewerage. Minor Water Courses.
Highways, etc.	Trunk Roads. Major Improvements. Major Bridges. Ferries. Tunnels.	Minor Bridges. Minor Ferries. Subways. Local roads and streets, scavenging, and paving of streets. Lighting to standard settled by Region. Street Markets.
Fire Protection	Fire Brigade. Fire prevention inspections, means of escape, etc.	

Service	Powers to Regional Authorities	Powers to Area Authorities
Open Spaces	'Green Belts' and large spaces.	Small spaces.
Hospital Services	Hospitals and Health Centres. Ambulances. Mental Treatment. District Medical Service. School Medical Service. V.D. Scheme for Region. Nursing Homes registration and inspection.	Midwives. Maternity and Child Welfare. Infectious diseases notification. Vaccination. Births notification.
Public Health	Diseases of Animals. Lodging houses.	Nuisances. Bakehouses. Canal boats. Child life protection. Dairies. Disinfection. Offensive trades. Slaughter houses. Food and drugs. Factories inspection. Mortuaries. Public Baths. Cemeteries.
	Refuse disposal and regulation of local collection as to frequency and types of vehicles. Smoke prevention. Port Health (power to devolve administration to Health Authorities).	Refuse collection and provision of dustbins.
Education	Schools and Institutions.	
Museums and Libraries	Concurrent powers.	Concurrent powers.
Small Holdings		Small Holdings. Allotments.
Public Assistance	P.A. Institutions. Out-relief. Training of Blind Persons. Domiciliary assistance.	

Service	Powers to Regional Authorities	Powers to Area Authorities
Shops, etc.		Inspection, hours of opening. Sanitary conditions. Petrol storage. Explosives. Weights and Measures.
Entertainments	Licensing of theatres, cinemas, etc.	
By-Laws generally	By-laws on matters under Regional control.	By-laws on matters under local control.
Electricity and Gas	Meter testing. Locus on prices, supply, etc.	
Finance	Valuation, Precepts, Loan Sanctions, etc.	Rate-making. Rate-collecting.

NALGO and Provincial Councils

From Nalgo Reconstruction Committee, *Reform of Local Government*, National Association of Local Government Officers, London, 1943, pp. 26–8.

This Report, which caused some controversy in the Association, did not go as far as the Labour Party's proposals in regard to regional authorities, but was nevertheless more revolutionary than anything that the local authority associations proposed. In the Nalgo scheme the main work of local government would be carried out by a series of all-purpose authorities throughout the country with provincial councils carrying out only limited functions as described in this extract. This pattern was almost exactly that suggested twenty-five years later by the Royal Commission on Local Government in 1969.

59. The division of the whole country among a number of all-purpose local authorities of the type suggested would solve many of the problems indicated above. Without further provision, however, it would fail adequately to meet the needs of those specialised or large-scale services which call for planning and co-ordination over a wider area than any single all-purpose authority of the size suggested could cover.

60. To ensure this co-ordination, we therefore further recommend that there should be established by law a number of Provincial Councils.

61. These Provincial Councils should be composed of representatives appointed by the all-purpose authorities within the province, in proportion to the population of each. Their function should be solely to secure efficient planning and co-ordination of the services remitted to their consideration. They would thus possess no executive or administrative powers – but their recommendations, subject to the approval of the government departments concerned, should be mandatory upon all the local authorities within the province.

62. The services over which the Provincial Councils would exercise their planning and co-ordinating function would include:

Town and Country Planning

General Hospitals, Specialist Hospitals, Mental Hospitals, and certain Public Assistance Institutions

Major Highways Developments

Provision for Specialist and Technical Education

Main Drainage and Sewage Disposal

Provincial Library Provision

The Development and Co-ordination of Public Utility Services; and

Any other services whose adequate provision requires a larger population than the local authorities in the area can provide individually, or which would benefit from broad planning and co-ordination over wide areas.

63. The area covered by each Provincial Council should be that within which co-ordination of the services remitted to it is desirable. It is probable that this would, in respect of most services, coincide with the Provincial Planning area. There may, however, be some services which would require different areas and for which it would be necessary to have different Provincial Councils. In general, however, it should be the aim to concentrate as many services as possible under one Provincial Council.

64. As has already been explained, the Provincial Council would possess no executive powers. Its function, as we visualize it, would be to consider the needs of its area in regard to each of the services enumerated above, to determine the nature of the provision to be made, and to select the appropriate all-purpose authority or authorities which should make that provision. The cost both of provision and maintenance would be apportioned among the areas served on an agreed basis. Institutions which already serve, or would serve, an area more extensive than that of a single all-purpose authority would be administered by the authority in whose area they are situated, the costs being similarly apportioned on an agreed basis among the authorities making use of the institutions. In some instances, one all-purpose authority might provide the institution and make charges for user by others, on lines already familiar in some services.

65. With regard to Town and Country Planning, once a provincial scheme had been agreed for the Provincial area, it would be the duty of the all-purpose authorities within the area to incorporate it in their statutory schemes. It should be made clear that, while the Provincial Council will be concerned with the key plan for the wider area, the all-purpose authorities will be associated with the preparation and application of the local elements and details of the scheme in their own areas.

66. In making these recommendations, we wish to emphasise that we do not consider that either the functions or the areas of the suggested Provincial Councils would be, in size or in any other way, comparable with those of the existing Civil Defence Regions. We do not envisage

any organ of local government at the regional level, considering such an organ altogether unsuited to local government.

67. Nor do we consider that the establishment of Provincial Councils on the lines here suggested would in any way deprive local authorities of the right to direct access to government departments. We attach much importance to the close relationship between the local authority and the central government department, and we consider it desirable to emphasise that regional contacts are an inadequate and irritating substitute for direct communication with, and easy access to, the central government department.

White Paper Vetoing Regionalism

From Ministry of Health, *Local Government in England and Wales during the period of Reconstruction.* Cmd. 6579, 1945, pp. 4–6.

The final war-time view about the reorganization of local government was expressed by the Government in this White Paper. The Government took advantage of the division of opinion amongst the local authority associations about the nature of reorganization to propose only the mildest of schemes for boundary changes, whilst the associations' singular unanimity about their dislike of regional ideas gave the Government an opportunity to dismiss them without any serious consideration whatever.

The reasons which have led the Government to the view that the time is not opportune for a general recasting of the local government structure have been stated in Parliament and were elaborated in a letter addressed in September, 1943, by Sir William Jowitt, then Minister without Portfolio, to the Association of Municipal Corporations and the County Councils Association. Broadly, they may be stated in two propositions – first, that there is no general desire in local government circles for a disruption of the present system, or any consensus of opinion as to what should replace it; and secondly, that the making of a change of this magnitude, which would by common consent have to be preceded by a full-dress inquiry, would be a process occupying some years and would seriously delay the establishment of the new or extended housing, educational, health and other services which form part of the Government's programme.

As against this it may be – and, indeed, has been – said that the present local government structure was not designed to bear the weight of these new and extended services and will prove inadequate; and that to establish the services in advance of a reconstruction of the system is to pour new wine into old bottles. This argument is usually based on two main contentions, both of which call for examination:

(1) that certain of the services, such as town and country planning and hospital services, need to be planned, and in some cases administered, over a wider area than a county or county borough; and

(2) that the reconstruction programme will place an impossible burden on local government finance.

Wider Administrative Areas

Interest and apprehension on this subject have been aroused by one important war-time institution, the creation of civil defence regions and the appointment of Regional Commissioners. This change did not alter the system of local government itself. Its purpose – and effect – was not to alter, or transfer to the State, any of the functions of local authorities but to decentralise the machinery of Government Departments in relation to civil defence and other war-time services. The system was established because it was thought that conditions might arise in which it would not be possible to maintain communications between the seat of central government and the rest of the country. Although, happily, these conditions have not arisen, there is no doubt that the decentralised Government machinery provided by the regional system has proved an effective instrument to meet the urgent needs of war and that the Commissioners have formed a valuable link between the Government and local authorities. But there is no question of maintaining the system in peace. Some Government Departments – whether responsible for services directly administered or concerned with services administered by local authorities – will no doubt find it advantageous, or indeed necessary, to maintain and perhaps to develop their own localised staffs and offices; but it can be stated definitely that it is no part of the Government's policy in dealing with post-war reconstruction to perpetuate the system of Regional Commissioners.

But, apart altogether from the needs and expedients of war, it has been asked, 'If the new or enlarged services which form part of the reconstruction programme call for planning or administration over wider areas, how is that compatible with the present local government structure?'

There are various alternative ways in which it would be possible to plan or administer over wider areas services which cannot be planned or administered efficiently within a single county or county borough. The alternatives include nationalisation, regionalisation and the creation of joint authorities for planning or for executive purposes.

TRANSFER OF FUNCTIONS

As regards nationalisation, fears have been widely expressed that there is a growing tendency to divest local government of its responsibilities by transfer of functions to the State.

In actual fact the only permanent transfers of functions from local authorities to the State during the last decade are those made by the Unemployment Act, 1934, and the Old Age and Widows' Pensions

Act, 1940, by which, with general approval in local government circles, the maintenance of the able-bodied unemployed and the supplementation of old age and widows' pensions were vested in the Assistance Board, and by three Agricultural Acts. The last mentioned Acts provided for the establishment of a National Veterinary Service and a National Agricultural Advisory Service and for the transfer to the Minister of Agriculture and Fisheries of certain functions relating to conditions in which milk is produced on the farm. In addition, by the Trunk Roads Act, 1936, a small mileage of county roads was converted into trunk roads and placed under the direct responsibility of the Minister of Transport.

The Government are not prepared to rule out altogether the possibility of transferring certain other functions, if on merits a good case can be shown for this course. Some extension of the system of trunk roads, for example, has already been foreshadowed; and the White Paper on Social Insurance proposes to transfer to the State certain of the residual functions of public assistance. Moroever, the Government have at present under consideration the future organisation of the fire service and certain of the public utility services. These latter are in a rather different category from the other local government services and their control is at present fortuitously divided between municipal and private enterprise.

The Government are however opposed to any general policy of centralising services hitherto regarded as essentially local.

Nor do they believe that a solution is to be found in the creation of regional authorities. This system would involve the establishment of directly elected bodies to administer certain services over areas larger than those of counties and county boroughs, and would introduce a two-tiered system in county boroughs and possibly a three-tiered system in counties. This is a matter on which the Local Government Associations have shown a unanimity which is in marked contrast to the diversity of their views on other possible lines of development.

JOINT AUTHORITIES

The Government consider, therefore, that where co-ordination of services between two or more areas, whether counties or county boroughs, is necessary, it should be sought by the established procedure of Joint Boards or Joint Committees. To this procedure there are, admittedly, objections – objections which are well known and need not be described in any detail in this Paper. Briefly, Joint Boards are open to the criticism that they are not directly elected and that they must rely for their finance upon precepting, a system which has been said to weaken financial responsibility. Joint Committees constituted solely for the planning of services are open to the criticism that it is unsatisfactory to divorce such planning from executive authority. Moreover, it can be argued with force that, as the need for wider planning and better co-ordination is more fully realised, the field in which joint action is required increases, and there is consequently a danger of creating a multiplicity of *ad hoc* authorities covering a variety of areas and services. The Government have no desire to underrate these objections; but they do not believe that the difficulties are so great as to warrant delay in the working out of the reconstruction programme. The number of services in which joint planning or joint action is essential is, after all, limited, and where in the development of the programme combined action is required, it should be possible to find acceptable means of ensuring it. To proceed in this way does not rule out ultimate integration of the joint bodies in any area into a single compendious unit, if experience should show this to be desirable.

It is for these reasons, and after considering the various suggestions of the Local Government Associations, that the Government believe it to be inexpedient to contemplate drastic innovations, such as the constitution of regional bodies, in re-shaping the local government system to fit post-war needs. They prefer to rely on the existing structure based on the county and county borough, with appropriate machinery, where necessary, for combined action.

Robson Advocates Regionalism

From W. A. Robson, *The Development of Local Government*, 2nd edn.,
Allen and Unwin, London, 1948, pp. 50–7.

After more than twenty years of campaigning for improvements to
the structure and organization of local government, Professor
Robson came to accept the fact that an adequate reform would have
to go beyond the limitations imposed by the primary structure of
administrative counties and county boroughs. This account gives
his reasons for this development of his views.

The Regional Problem

While recognising the advantages of the Boundary Commission, I
have suggested that its powers are insufficient to enable it to deal
effectively with the most pressing aspects of the regional problem.
This statement requires explanation.

When I wrote this book in 1930 I was under the impression that the
grave defects in local government structure described in Part I could
be sufficiently overcome to yield reasonably good working results if
joint action by local authorities were undertaken on a far more
ambitious scale than had been previously attempted. I therefore concluded that the primary elements in the structure should be the county
councils and county borough councils, linked together for particular
services by a ubiquitous network of joint boards and committees.

I no longer believe this solution to be adequate. The need for
regional planning and regional administration of large-scale services
has become far more insistent in recent years. The areas of circulation
for economic and social purposes have become more pronounced
owing to further development in transport and communications and
the 'areas of consciousness' more definite. The progress of thought in
the physical planning movement has moved towards the closer integration of town and country life. In consequence, the administrative
dichotomy embodied in the Local Government Act, 1888, which
introduced the distinction between county council and county
borough, is an outworn conception. The regional surveys and plans
which have been made for London, Birmingham, Manchester, and
other conurbations, have shown that proper areas cannot be obtained
by any simple combination of county boroughs and county councils.
Above all, the full-length study which I made of the metropolitan
region has convinced me that it is hopeless to expect any high degree
of co-operation between county boroughs and county councils.

Within the present framework the large towns, especially those which suffered heavy war damage, can put up a strong case to incorporate within their boundaries outlying areas for rehousing at lower densities and deconcentrating congested industrial districts. But the needs of the large town can be met only by ignoring the county problem. The county councils have an unanswerable argument. They have been asked to accept new responsibilities in the spheres of education, police, planning, fire brigades and health services. How can they perform these tasks if they are continually losing the wealthiest and most populous parts of their territories? The Scott Committee rightly urged the need to raise the standard of local government services in the rural areas so as to give the countryman and his children an equal opportunity with the town dweller. How can the counties improve services if they are left with only straggling, sparsely-populated areas of low rateable value? They could, of course, become almost wholly dependent on central grants, but that would be the virtual end of local government in those areas.

Take again the question of decentralizing large numbers of persons – a million in the case of London – together with industrial establishments from the overcrowded and congested central cores of the great cities to the new towns which are to be built on virgin soil or developed from villages and towns designated for planned expansion. How can these vast movements of population take place smoothly and successfully unless they are dealt with on a regional scale by regional organs which will transcend the conflicting interests and limited powers of county boroughs and county councils? These unprecedented aspirations demand new ideas and new measures in the sphere of public administration.

The position which has been reached in all these matters is one which calls for a much higher degree of *physical* separation between town and country than has prevailed during the past 20 or 30 years; indeed, all planners are agreed upon the need to re-establish the age-long distinction between urban and rural communities which has become blurred and even obliterated as a result of the sporadic building and uncontrolled development during the period between the two World Wars. At the same time there is need for a much greater integration of town and country for administrative and financial purposes of common interest.

For these reasons I am convinced that a far more radical solution is now required, particularly in the areas surrounding the great urban complexes. No wise or just solution is possible in terms of the present set-up, shuffle the boundaries as you will. The only remedy is to raise local government to a higher plane by creating regional organs which will comprise areas large enough to harmonise the conflicting interests of county boroughs and county councils. Those interests are at bottom essentially complementary. By this means we can obtain areas and authorities adequate to administer the regional services such as planning, technical education, water supply, refuse disposal and the rest. Such conurbations as Birmingham, Manchester, Merseyside, Tyneside, Glasgow, Leeds, Bradford, Bristol, and, above all, London, cry out for treatment on these lines.

Broadly speaking, I favour the creation in these and other conurbations of directly-elected regional councils covering both the industrial, commercial and residential core and also a wide stretch of rural and semi-rural hinterland, extending far beyond the suburbs and comprising dormitory settlements, outlying villages and farms, a green belt or a brown agricultural belt, garden cities or smaller towns and so forth. These regional councils would be responsible for regional planning and the administration of a few services requiring large-scale administration, such as the larger housing projects, main drainage and sewage disposal, main highways and bridges, water supply, hospitals, gas supply, electricity distribution, the provision of large parks and open spaces, the disposal of refuse, civil airfields, river conservancy and flood prevention, technical education, passenger road services.

In order to establish general regional councils of this kind it will be necessary to compromise between the needs of the various services in the determination of appropriate areas. This will involve the sacrifice of perfection in some spheres of activity, but my study of the Metropolitan region has persuaded me that, while all boundaries present some anomalies, it is possible to delimit areas which will broadly satisfy the main regional needs, the alternatives to a solution of this kind are so calamitous to local government that we must not allow action to be impeded by the technical difficulty of ascertaining suitable regions. In re-reading Part I of this book I feel that I accepted somewhat too readily the conflicting demands of the specialists in the various services for areas of particular sizes and shapes without paying sufficient regard to the over-riding needs of the local government system as a whole. Or possibly I failed to examine sufficiently the possibility of compromise.

Below the regional council there will need to be a second tier of municipal authorities administering the local services in town or country areas respectively within the region. The regions will be too large to be administered by a single authority and a double-deck system will therefore be required. The principle of major and minor authorities which is embodied in county government would thus be preserved and projected on a larger scale. It would be applied to the conurbations which, apart from London, are largely administered by county borough councils. The conception of a two-tier system for the great conurbation is right in principle, though in the case of London it has been badly applied for political reasons. I have described elsewhere in some detail the distribution of functions between major and minor authorities which I propose for the metropolis and the relations between them. This type of organization could equally well be applied to the other conurbations.

There are two points which may be emphasised. One is that we should not contemplate more than two tiers of authorities. A three-deck system would be wasteful and cumbrous. The other is that I do not propose the whole country shall necessarily be dealt with on the lines suggested above. The practicable method of approach is to deal first with the conurbations, which are in dire need of regional government for the reasons I have explained, and then to consider what is the best organization for the residue which will comprise the smaller and less industrialized towns and the more rural counties. It is by no means necessary that we should have only a single uniform pattern of regional and local government in areas possessing widely differing characteristics.

On the other hand, it is possible that some areas which cannot be described as conurbations may be susceptible of treatment on similar lines. Wales, for example, is generally recognized to need regional government, though there are differences of opinion whether Wales should form a single region or be divided into two regions for the North and South respectively.

To attempt to go beyond this rather general outline of the reforms which are urgently needed would take me beyond the limits of this prologue: I should, indeed, have to write a new book. The material for such a book unfortunately does not at present exist, for there has been no official investigation and insufficient unofficial research into the problems of areas and authorities since the Royal Commission on Local Government of 1925–29. More information is badly needed.

A scheme on the lines of the proposals set out above is at present under discussion in the Manchester region. At a conference of 64 local authorities held in July 1946, the suggestion was made that a Manchester County Council should be constituted in an area centred on Manchester and extending far into the surrounding territory, both urban and rural. A resolution was passed in favour of the matter being further examined. This resolution did not commit the local authorities concerned, but 33 of them afterwards signified their desire to have the matter pursued further. A meeting was subsequently arranged between representatives of the Manchester City Council and members of the Boundary Commission to discuss a memorandum submitted by the City Council on the local government problems confronting the region.

This memorandum emphasized the inter-relationship between Manchester and those parts of South-east Lancashire and North Cheshire of which it is the centre, and the impossibility of divorcing the interests of the city from those of the surrounding area. The local government problem facing Manchester to-day has two aspects. One is that of securing the proper provision and administration of the major local government services over a wider area while creating at the same time a more closely-knit municipal system which would stimulate local interest in civic affairs. The other aspect is to ensure adequate arrangements for the local government of the outlying areas which under the Manchester City Council's housing programme will be developed to receive the overspill population that cannot be properly housed within its boundaries. The needs of the city are estimated at 76,000 houses, of which 43,000 will have to be built outside its present boundaries.

The Manchester memorandum recognizes that 'the fuller development of the major local government services such as, for example, health, education, water, highways, the treatment and disposal of sewage, and town planning, necessitate a wider area of service and change than has hitherto been the case,' and it draws attention to the way in which Manchester City Council has come to provide numerous services to neighbouring areas. The local government problem would not be solved merely by extending the boundaries of Manchester, since to do so would not be likely to foster local interest in civic affairs. Local interest requires a unit of administration of a reasonably small size. In consequence, the solution of the problem should be sought in an arrangement which would both extend the area of administration for major services and also stimulate local interest.

For these reasons the Manchester City Council regard the creation of a county council for Manchester and district as the most satisfactory solution. This would make the county council responsible for the provision and administration of the major services while leaving local services to the county district councils. 'In effect it would mean that the county boroughs would give up certain powers in favour of the county council; and the county boroughs, boroughs, and urban and rural districts would perform the functions not assigned to the county council.'

If regional councils were established there would be a practicable alternative to the transfer of functions from local authorities to central departments or special bodies. After all, the hospitals have been nationalized in order to be regionalized. Unless a bold step of this kind is taken, we may well repeat the mistake which was made in the 19th century of creating a series of separate bodies for individual services; boards of guardians, health boards, school boards, improvement commissioners, highway boards and several others. This is certain to lead to confusion, extravagance and inefficiency. We have already repeated the error in London, with its separate authorities for water, police, transport, the port, electricity and other services. The metropolis has in consequence developed in a chaotic manner.

In the last quarter of the 19th century nearly all the statutory authorities for special purposes were swept away and their functions transferred to the general local authorities which were set up to replace them. Only the Boards of Guardians lingered on until 1929, when they, too, were abolished. We must not, however, assume that a similar process will happen in the 20th century. Such a complacent view leaves out of account the vested professional, technical and vocational interests which are brought into being by the creation of *ad hoc* regional or national machinery to deal with hospitals and the health service or public utilities. These vested interests may well prove extremely tenacious of their separate and independent modes of administration, irrespective of the fact that they all constitute forms of public ownership and operation. They may thus present an insuperable obstacle to any subsequent attempt to integrate these single-purpose bodies into a general system of regional government. Those who console themselves for what is now happening or threatening by the thought that the 20th century, like the 19th, will have its happy ending, may well be disappointed.

Fortunately there are signs of a growing realization of the extreme danger which is threatening the whole system of local government from the process of erosion and denudation. The conference on local government held by the Association of Municipal Corporations in September, 1946, at Eastbourne revealed a state of acute apprehension and alarm on the part of almost every speaker and contributor to the discussions except the Minister of Health.

Three main causes of disquiet were stressed by the Mayor of Lincoln (Alderman Hill). First, the trend away from the elected body to the selected body, or in some cases to the *ad hoc* body, which may be elected but is not a part of the ordinary local government structure. Second, the trend towards centralization. Third, the trend towards transforming local authorities from independent operating bodies to mere agents of the central government.

Local Government in Crisis

From W. A. Robson, *Local Government in Crisis*, Allen and Unwin, London, 1966, pp. 69–73, 75, 93 and 146–8.

Nearly twenty years on from our last extract, Professor Robson writes a short collection of sharp essays in which he expresses amazement that the obvious has been ignored for so long and little has been done to bring the local government system into the twentieth century. These various extracts which follow display both anger and frustration on the part of the author, but they also help to explain to the reader of the present volume how much inaction and double-talk characterized the post-war period. Ninety-five years before Robson wrote these words Goschen, in introducing his attempt to reform the local government system in 1871 (which also yielded little in practical results) described the system as 'a chaos of areas, a chaos of authorities and a chaos of rates' – a description which still holds good in large measure despite the reforms of 1888 and 1894.

A Diagnosis

The reasons for these drastic symptoms of decline are clear. For more than forty years the organization of local government has been growing obsolete and is now hopelessly out of date.

The local authorities in England and Wales on April 1, 1965 comprised:

58 county councils
82 county borough councils
276 non-county borough councils ⎫
548 urban district councils　　 ⎬　a total of 1298
474 rural district councils　　 ⎭　District Councils
About 7,500 parish councils
About 3,400 parish meetings

The list does not include Greater London, which has the Greater London Council, 32 London Borough Councils and the City Corporation.

If we classify the local authorities according to population, we get the figures on page 191.

The differences in population among areas of the same constitutional class are almost grotesque. The counties range from Lancashire, with more than two and a quarter million, to Rutland with less than thirty thousand. The West Riding of Yorkshire has 1,696,220 in-

TABLE II: POPULATION OF LOCAL AUTHORITIES IN ENGLAND AND WALES (mid-1964)

Population	Number	
Above 1,000,000	4	County councils
	1	County borough council
500,000 to 1,000,000	14	County councils
	3	County borough councils
250,000 to 500,000	15	London Borough councils
	17	County councils
	10	County borough councils
100,000 to 250,000	17	London borough councils
	14	County councils
	33	County borough councils
	1	Non-county borough council
	2	Urban district councils
	2	Rural district councils
50,000 to 100,000	5	County councils
	34	County borough councils
	45	Non-county borough councils
	17	Urban district councils
	27	Rural district councils
20,000 to 50,000	3	County councils
	1	County borough council
	94	Non-county borough councils
	130	Urban district councils
	164	Rural district councils
10,000 to 20,000	1	County council
	53	Non-county borough councils
	162	Urban district councils
	160	Rural district councils
5,000 to 10,000	38	Non-county borough councils
	129	Urban district councils
	82	Rural district councils
1,000 to 5,000	44	Non-county borough councils
	104	Urban district councils
	39	Rural district councils
Below 1,000	1	Non-county borough council
	4	Urban district councils

(Source: Registrar General's Population Estimates for mid-1964.)

C.R.R.—7*

habitants, Westmorland only 66,950. The Welsh counties vary from
Glamorganshire with more than three-quarters of a million to Radnor-
shire with less than 20,000. Even if we omit the extremes there are
large differences of population in the middle ranges.

We find a similar situation among the county boroughs. Birmingham has a population of well over a million, Liverpool nearly three-
quarters of a million, while Canterbury has slightly over thirty
thousand, Dudley below sixty-five thousand, Gloucester seventy
thousand. The non-county boroughs range from towns like Swindon,
Cambridge and Poole, all approaching the hundred thousand mark, or
Rhondda which has just exceeded it, to tiny places with less than two
thousand souls like Bishops Castle in Shropshire, Eye in Suffolk or
Appleby in Westmorland. The urban districts range from Basildon
with a population of 103,000 to Saxmundham with only 1,500; from
Thurrock with 117,150 to Lynton with 1,680. Similar anomalies occur
among the rural districts, which include in their ranks Chesterfield
with a population of 104,130 at one end of the scale and Easington
with 1,460 at the other.

There are similar disparities of territorial size. There are very large
administrative counties like Devon (1,649,401 acres) and quite small
ones such as the Holland Division of Lincolnshire (267,847 acres).
Among the non-county boroughs we find Keighley with 23,640 acres
and Woodstock with only 157 acres. Much the same applies to the
urban and rural districts.

TABLE III: AREAS OF COUNCILS IN ACRES

Territorial Size	Number and Type of Local Authorities
Below 1,000 acres	11 Non-county borough councils 40 Urban district councils
1,000–1,999 acres	43 Non-county borough councils 87 Urban district councils
2,000–2,999 acres	1 County borough council 43 Non-county borough councils 80 Urban district councils 2 Rural district councils
3,000–4,999 acres	11 County borough councils 73 Non-county borough councils 143 Urban district councils 2 Rural district councils
5,000–9,999 acres	41 County borough councils 83 Non-county borough councils 128 Urban district councils 5 Rural district councils

10,000–14,999 acres	13 County borough councils
	10 Non-county borough councils
	23 Urban district councils
	5 Rural district councils
15,000–19,999 acres	7 County borough councils
	5 Non-county borough councils
	21 Urban district councils
	9 Rural district councils
20,000–29,999 acres	6 County borough councils
	5 Non-county borough councils
	4 Urban district councils
	38 Rural district councils
30,000 plus acres	3 County borough councils
	2 Urban district councils
	405 Rural district councils

(Excluding County Councils and the GLC Area.) (Source: *Municipal Year Book*, 1965.)

We would not expect to find even approximate uniformity of size among the local authorities in each category, but such vast inequalities as these show that the municipal structure is utterly irrational. There must be a maximum and a minimum size of local authority for the effective and efficient performance of any specified group of functions; and whatever these may be, many existing authorities surely do not fall within them.

In short, a large proportion of local councils are not able to perform with tolerable efficiency and economy the functions they may reasonably be expected to discharge. Thus a county council should have not less than half-a-million population if it is to provide services at a satisfactory standard; but forty counties are below this figure and only eighteen are above it. For a county district the figure of 60,000 has been repeatedly laid down as the minimum population for giving a district council the right to have functions delegated to it by the county council covering a wide range of services, such as education, health, welfare and planning control. Yet in 1964 only thirty-two districts, or one in twenty-six, reached this level.

Turning to county boroughs, the statutory figure which is 'presumed' to be sufficient 'to support the discharge of the functions of a county borough council' is 100,000. This figure is of doubtful validity. It merely crystallizes the outcome of the lengthy negotiations carried out between local authority associations over several years, and which involved a great deal of horse trading among vested interests. I am inclined to believe that a minimum figure of 200,000 is more realistic today than 100,000; and even this should not apply to the conurbations, in which much larger towns should be most-purpose rather than all-purpose authorities. The new London Boroughs have an average population of 250,000 and only four of them are below 200,000. The Home Office favour a population of not less than 200,000 mainly in order to be able to attract and retain staff of high quality; and for police purposes the population should not be less than 250,000.

The most important phenomenon of our time which has affected local government is that modern methods of transport have greatly increased the area of daily movement and enable large numbers of people to work in one area and live in another. The great cities draw their workpeople of all classes from housing estates, dormitory towns, and suburban, rural or semi-rural areas outside their boundaries. These people have to be provided with many services by the city in which they work, but most of them pay rates only to the council of the area in which they live.

The Attitude of Local Authorities to Municipal Reform 1942–3

On the wider question of municipal reform, local authorities are also partly to blame for the present position. They have taken far too narrow a view of the situation and been far too occupied with the sectional interests of particular classes of local authority. The larger threat to local government as a whole has been almost overlooked.

During 1942 and 1943 each of the associations issued a report dealing with the problems of areas and organization. There was general agreement among them that the existing organization of local government had a few defects and that the war-time system of Regional Commissioners must be abolished. Beyond this there was little or no agreement. The associations put forward widely differing proposals as to the kind of structure which is desirable, the proper distribution of powers and functions among authorities, the methods of creating urban and rural areas, the provision to be made for large-scale planning and administration, the number of tiers of authorities, the relations between the tiers and the optimum sizes of authorities.

The Proposals of Four Associations of Local Authorities 1953

After the dissolution of the Local Government Boundary Commission the Association of Municipal Corporations, the County Councils Association, and the associations representing urban districts and rural districts decided to confer together to see if they could agree upon a scheme of local government reform for submission to the

Government. In May 1952 the Association of Municipal Corporations withdrew from these discussions and the National Association of Parish Councils was invited to participate in them. In March 1953 a report was issued containing the proposals and recommendations agreed by the representatives of the County Councils Association, the Urban District Councils Association, the Rural District Councils Association, and the National Association of Parish Councils.

The joint report of the four associations consisted of a short introductory statement followed by an appendix containing the recommendations. We were surprised to learn from the former that members of both Houses of Parliament are 'intensely interested in the reorganization of local government'. This good news had indeed been kept secret for an unduly long time. An even more astonishing remark was that 'the existing framework of local government has proved to be not only satisfactory but also so flexible as to be capable of modification and evolution without the necessity of any alteration of structure. The proposals are therefore based upon the existing types of local authorities.' Would that these observations were true! For in that event local government would not be in the parlous state in which it now finds itself.

Plain Speaking by Mr Crossman

Mr Crossman, in an address to the Association of Municipal Corporations at their Torquay Conference in September 1965, spoke more plainly than any Minister of Housing and Local Government had ever done before about the present state of local government. He began by saying that the once friendly though indifferent attitude of the public towards local government had given way to one of resentful disillusionment. The basic cause of this distrust is that 'the whole structure of local government is out of date, that our county boroughs and county councils as at present organized are archaic institutions, whose size and structure make them increasingly ill-adapted to fulfilling the immensely important functions with which they are charged. The greatest obstacle, in fact, which prevents efficient councils from retaining public confidence is the obsolete constitutional framework within which they have to operate.' He warned councillors and officials that they would have to accept the unpleasant truth that drastic reforms could not be indefinitely postponed without the danger of a breakdown.

Mr Crossman went on to say that effective planning is impossible at present owing to the cold war between local authorities, their under-sized areas, and the impossibility of providing enough qualified planners to meet the needs of 150 local planning authorities. Water supply and water resources, the police forces, transport and traffic regulation, all present problems which cannot be solved within the existing framework of local government.

The Local Government Commission, said the Minister, is prevented by its terms of reference from producing the reorganization of local government that we so desperately need. He deplored the appallingly slow and time-wasting procedures laid down by the 1958 Act, and the way in which they have been deliberately exploited in order to frustrate change. Nonetheless, he thought the Commission could still do useful work and he intended to allow it to continue, although he had been tempted to replace it by a new Commission with clear instructions about the changes at which it should aim. The obstacle to such a course is that there are at present no 'accepted principles of reorganization; no established doctrine according to which a Commission could proceed to reshape the areas and the functions of local government so as to enable it to do its job in modern terms and to regain the public confidence that has been lost'. He therefore believed it would be necessary to appoint first a 'powerful and impartial committee' to work out a general policy on which the Commission's terms of reference and directives could be based. This policy would emerge from an authoritative analysis of the two main problems: namely the relation of size to function, and the relation of local democracy to efficiency. The work of this hypothetical committee, he postulated, would be of such overwhelming validity that 'its analysis would be accepted as established doctrine by both sides in the conflict'.

These were brave and challenging words; and they must have been highly unpalatable to the participants in the conference. But Mr Crossman is doomed to severe disappointment if he imagines that the local authority associations, which are defence organizations of the most pronounced type, would accept any analysis by any committee he or anyone else might appoint, if its recommendations threatened the interests or the existence of their members.

Fundamental reform is in any case likely to be effected not by speeches at conferences, but by clear thinking at Ministerial and Departmental level, and above all by political drive and legislative and administrative follow-up. The only action indicated by Mr Crossman in his Torquay speech was the appointment of a Committee to tell him what he is to tell another Commission to do. This is scarcely likely to produce the rapid action which he rightly desires.

Furthermore, if the powers and procedures of the present Local Government Commission are inadequate to solve the larger problems which confront local government – as they certainly are – it is surely wrong to allow it to continue, since its proceedings take up an immense amount of time and energy on the part of councillors, aldermen, and the chief officers of local authorities – not to mention the members and staff of the Commission itself. Shortly after Mr Crossman's speech, the Commission announced it would itself suspend operations.

While, therefore, we may applaud the substance of the Minister's speech and the candour which inspired it, the wisdom of making such an onslaught in the absence of a clear policy of reform with which to back it up, is less evident. It is, however, refreshing to have some plain words from a responsible Minister in place of the deadly soothing syrup to which we have been accustomed for so long.

The Redcliffe-Maud Commission's Report

From Report of the Royal Commission on Local Government in England 1966–69, Vol. I, *Report*. Cmnd. 4040, 1969, pp. 109–17.

The main body of the Commission proposed the division of England, outside the Greater London area, into 61 areas. In 58 of these there would be a single local authority with executive powers, called a 'unitary' authority, and in the other three areas the local government functions would be shared by a metropolitan authority for the whole area and a number of metropolitan district authorities. Yet the Commission accepted that there was a need for provincial councils to deal with the economic strategy, land use and investment framework and to settle the planning and development policies of the operational authorities. The following extract explains how the Commission saw the detailed arrangements for these provincial councils.

MAKING THE PROVINCIAL PLAN

412. The main function of each provincial council will be to make and keep continually up-to-date a strategic plan for the future development of its province. This plan will settle the framework and order of priorities within which unitary and metropolitan authorities will work out their own planning policies and major investment programmes. It must bear realistic relationship to resources likely to be available at different times and must be drawn up in the closest collaboration with the unitary and metropolitan authorities and with central government. In preparing the plan, the provincial council should concentrate on issues that concern more than one authority or are important for the province as a whole. Key elements in the plan will be the changing distribution of population, migration to and from a province, the location of major new growth points, the large-scale movement of people from one unitary or metropolitan area into another, the broad divisions of the province into urbanised, agricultural and recreational areas, major industrial developments with their implications for employment, housing and transport, the provincial pattern of road and rail communications, the siting of airports, the future of seaports, and the siting of new universities and of cultural and sporting facilities serving a wide area.

413. The plan will not be a static set-piece but will consist of an evolving series of objectives and policies. The provincial situation can change rapidly. Massive spontaneous growth can occur in some areas

because economic development, technological advance, the discovery of new resources, an altered pattern of trade, or social trends, give these areas a marked advantage over others. Elsewhere, established industries can decline, causing serious unemployment and poor prospects for the young and calling for reconsideration of the whole future of a wide area. A provincial council must be able to detect such changes early on, discuss with central government and the main authorities what policies and action are necessary, and make whatever alterations are required in its strategy.

414. Provincial plans will need approval by the Minister. Once approved, they should be binding on main authorities, who will have to comply with their provisions. Structure plans made by unitary and metropolitan authorities for their areas will also need Ministerial approval. As provincial and structure plans should together compose an integrated pattern for the whole of each province, structure plans should not be submitted for Ministerial approval until the provincial council has examined them for their consistency with each other and with the provincial plan. This will allow provincial councils to exercise an appropriate degree of influence over the planning policies of individual authorities. A provincial council will thus be able to prevent, for example, the gradual coalescence of built-up areas for which separate authorities are responsible and which the provincial plan approved by the Minister keeps apart; to ensure that structure plans devote a proper proportion of land to agricultural, recreational and other rural uses, in accordance with the general needs of the province as a whole; and to see that land required in one authority's area to solve another authority's problems is allocated for that purpose. Where neighbouring authorities' problems are closely related, the provincial council should be able to set up a committee, in conjunction with the authorities concerned, to deal with those planning questions that require to be considered as a whole. This could happen, for example, in the case of the Southampton and Portsmouth areas, where we have concluded that there should be two separate unitary authorities (chapter VII) but recognise the likelihood of developments which will need common consideration over both areas. Where planning problems overlap a provincial boundary, the provincial councils and main authorities concerned will of course have to ensure that appropriate provision is made on each side of the boundary.

415. We believe that, after full discussion of the issues, the provincial council will normally be able to settle its strategy in agreement with the main authorities, though where any main authority remains unable to accept provisions in the provincial plan it should be able to

approach the Minister direct and seek to persuade him that the plan should be changed. Co-operation will be much more likely in the new system than it has been in the past. When every authority is responsible for a continuous area and has room in which to manoeuvre – even if it is not able to satisfy all its land needs within its own territory – the boundary questions which have done so much to bedevil planning and prevent co-operation between authorities will largely disappear. Moreover, all unitary and metropolitan authorities will possess the full range of planning, transportation and development powers and will be able to discuss their problems on an equal footing. Later in this chapter we explain why we consider that the provincial council, as the forum where the strategic framework for the operational responsibilities of the main authorities is decided, should be rooted in local government and elected by the main authorities. This organic link between the two levels will itself foster co-operation between main authorities and between them and the provincial council.

DEVELOPMENT

416. Provincial councils will not normally undertake development. The main authorities will be the development authorities in the new local government system; and we do not propose that provincial councils should, for example, be responsible for such schemes as are needed to build houses in one area for people from another. Nor do we suggest that they should take over the building of roads from the Ministry of Transport's road construction units or become responsible in place of development corporations for building new towns.

417. A provincial council must, however, have a reserve power to undertake development if such action ever becomes necessary to give effect to the provincial plan. This power is essential to deal with what we expect will be the very rare case where a main authority refuses to carry out development necessary for the success of the provincial plan, as finally approved by the Minister.

418. A possibility that should be kept open is that a provincial council might occasionally handle a large project intended to be of benefit to a whole province or to a number of authorities within it. A barrage and an opera house are contrasting examples.

OTHER PROVINCIAL FUNCTIONS

419. In chapter VIII we referred to the part that provincial councils have to play in further education. At present, regional advisory councils for further education help to decide the siting of new developments but their role is purely advisory, decisions being made by the Department of Education and Science. In future, the provincial coun-

cil, acting in consultation with the main authorities and the universities, will be well placed to assess provincial priorities in further education, and to settle which existing centres should be expanded and where new ones should be placed. The council should seek the advice of the Department of Education and Science on individual proposals, and should act in accordance with the Department's policies both on further education generally and on particular aspects of it.

420. The provincial council should not, however, assume operational responsibility for further education. Some witnesses argued that it should have such responsibility, especially for advanced further education, but we cannot agree. The unitary authorities and metropolitan districts are capable of administering advanced further education and no gain outweighing the disadvantages of divided responsibility would result from giving this part of the service to provincial councils.

421. There will of course be some educational institutions that not every main authority will provide. Some authorities will have to make facilities available for the inhabitants of areas other than their own. Local authorities are already accustomed to this kind of co-operation. It should continue in the new system – and will be easier when there are fewer authorities, each responsible for a continuous area, and when provincial councils, representative of the main authorities, settle the pattern of provision in agreement with them.

422. The provincial council should exercise a broad planning function in the specialist education of handicapped and other children, where provision in a limited number of carefully selected centres will meet the needs of the province as a whole, and also in those personal social services where problems, and provision for dealing with them, ought to be considered over a wide area. For example, the White Paper 'Children in Trouble' proposed joint committees of local authorities to plan the development of the child care service over large areas. This task should become the responsibility of the provincial councils. With their establishment the need for joint committees will disappear.

423. In conjunction with the main authorities, provincial councils should draw up a policy for the planned development of cultural and recreational services throughout each province; and they should take over the work of the present regional arts and sports councils. Main authorities, when promoting the arts and opportunities for recreation in their own areas, should do so within the framework of the provincial policy. The planned development of tourism should be another

provincial function, again to be exercised in co-operation with the main authorities.

424. In general, the ability of provincial councils to consider problems on a large scale and over wide areas will make less likely the establishment of nominated *ad hoc* bodies for special public purposes and so reduce the danger that has threatened local government with erosion whenever the effective provision of some service has appeared to call for a unit larger than the existing local authorities.

PROVINCIAL COUNCILS AND CENTRAL GOVERNMENT

425. An important part of provincial councils' work will be to make sure that central government is fully aware of provincial needs and aspirations, and acts in full knowledge of the effect on the provinces that its policies and decisions will have. The questions involved will be debated in representative provincial bodies; in consequence there will be a livelier awareness in both local and central government of the issues at stake and a better informed atmosphere for decision-making.

426. Central government, provincial councils and main authorities will have to work in close collaboration if their economic, social and development policies are to be harmonised. As an integral part of such co-operation, government departments will need to have provincial offices, in close touch with the problems and opinions both of provincial councils and of main authorities, and able to ensure that, for their part, councils and authorities understand the issues that face central government. This continuing dialogue will be essential in establishing the right relationship between central and local government.

427. Provincial councils will of course be able to assume responsibility for many matters that now engage the attention of central departments, such as the co-ordination of statistical and economic information, surveys in search of the best places for large scale public investment, and the knitting together of local authorities' planning proposals into a coherent pattern.

FINANCE

428. Provincial councils will not be heavy spenders. Their costs will be mainly administrative and should be met by precepting on the main authorities.

429. A provincial council should, however, have power to give financial aid to projects which will be of benefit to an area wider than that of any single authority. The power should be used sparingly but it will

set schemes going which are essential for the development of a province's economic, artistic or recreational resources and might otherwise hang fire. It will also enable the council, by deciding which schemes are most urgently needed, to see that those which will bring the greatest good to the province move ahead first. The cost of such assistance should also be met by precepting on the main authorities.

430. We do not recommend that a provincial council should have a general power to equalise the resources of the main units in its province. There will be considerable variation between their resources. But the greatest differences will be between authorities in different provinces. In any system of local government, subventions from central funds will be necessary to bring the resources available to poorer areas, in any part of the country, nearer to the level of the richer. Only on a national scale can justice be done between them.

431. Arrangements for the provincial council to consider and comment on main authorities' investment proposals are described in Chapter XIII (on finance).

AREAS OF PROVINCES

432. A province should cover an area of the country where there are major issues that ought to be considered together. Its various parts should be economically and geographically linked; and its work will be made easier if there exists among its inhabitants a sense of provincial identity, rooted in history, economic traditions or geographic facts. Our investigations suggested that the present eight economic planning regions not only provide areas of suitable size for the functions of provincial councils but also roughly reflect such sense of provincial identity as exists in various parts of England. The present regions differ greatly in population and the extent of territory they cover; and their boundaries are sometimes arbitrary, closely resembling those of the regions into which England was divided for civil defence during the second world war. But they provide an appropriate model for the provinces. Apart from the advantage of building the new provincial level of government on areas where people have already grown accustomed to working together, we believe that the economic and geographical composition of the country falls broadly into the pattern of the eight economic planning regions.

433. The proposed provinces, therefore, depart from boundaries of the present regions only where there would be clear advantage in their doing so. One of the biggest differences is that the northern economic planning region becomes the North-Eastern province, Cumberland

and Westmorland joining the North-Western province and most of the North Riding forming part of the Yorkshire province. Another is the inclusion in the South-Eastern province of most of Northampton-shire, now in the east midlands economic planning region. There are several other instances where provinces diverge from economic planning regions. In each case examination convinced us that the change would help to associate areas which have common problems in one province.

434. In the south-east, so much of the work of the provincial council will be concerned with pressures exerted on the province by the problems of Greater London that the only sensible arrangement is for Greater London to be part of it, as it is now part of the south east economic planning region.

ELECTION AND COMPOSITION

436. Successive governments have recognised the existence of econo-mic and physical planning problems that ought to be handled on a provincial scale. These problems are beyond the compass of individual local authorities and will continue to be so in any new local govern-ment system. But they are of vital importance to local government and their solution almost always depends on action which only local authorities can take. At present local government plays little part in dealing with them.

437. Regional economic planning councils have done their best to fill the gap between central and local government. Their reports have analysed the problems in their regions and proposed policies and action. But their primary function is to advise central government; they have no executive powers; all their members are nominated by central government; and the staff who serve them are drawn from the regional offices of government departments. The councils' member-ship includes local authority councillors and officials but they are nominated as individuals and not as representatives of their auth-orities. When provincial councils are established as part of the structure of local government, there will no longer be a place for regional economic planning councils.

438. Provincial councils must be rooted in the main local authorities and must have powers and staff of their own. They must be elected, not nominated, bodies. Their decisions must be complied with by elected local authorities; and nominated bodies by their nature do not have the organic relationship with the electorate or with local government which would make this a workable arrangement.

439. The terms of reference of the Commission on the Constitution, as approved by Your Majesty and announced by the Prime Minister

on 11th February 1969[1], suggest the possibility that what we have called provinces may enjoy a greater measure of self-government in future. If there were a substantial devolution of central government functions to provincial councils or if they became directly responsible for the operation of major local government services – and especially if both of these things happened – it would be logical to envisage provincial councils as becoming largely composed of directly elected representatives. We do not believe, however, that the province is the right area for the operation of local government services. The new main authorities are specifically designed for that purpose. Whether provincial councils should be called upon to assume functions now concentrated in an overworked system of central government must be left to the Commission on the Constitution to consider.

440. The purposes for which we think that a provincial council is essential as part of the total structure of local government will be best served by a body elected by the main authorities. The council's chief task will be to create a broad strategic framework for the exercise of main authorities' operational responsibilities. Its members, therefore, should be drawn from these authorities, thus establishing an organic link between the strategic and operational levels of local government. There should also be provision for co-option of members from outside local government to bring experience from other walks of life to bear on the problems of the province.

441. A provincial council should be as small as is consistent with adequate representation of all main authorities. We considered whether all main authorities should elect the same number of members to a provincial council. But to do this would ignore differences in the size of authorities and in the extent to which their problems will require consideration by the provincial council. The Doncaster unit, for example, with a population of 284,000 should not elect the same number of members to the Yorkshire provincial council as the Sheffield and South Yorkshire unit with a population of over 1,000,000. Nor on the other hand should main authorities be represented directly in proportion to size. A provincial council should not contain such a

---

[1] 'To examine the present functions of the central legislature and government in relation to the several countries, nations and regions of the United Kingdom:

To consider, having regard to developments in local government organization and in the administrative and other relationships between the various parts of the United Kingdom and to the interests of the prosperity and good government of our people under the Crown, whether any changes are desirable in those functions or otherwise in present constitutional and economic relationships:

To consider, also, whether any changes are desirable in the constitutional and economic relationships between the United Kingdom and the Channel Islands and the Isle of Man.' Hansard, Written Answers, Col. 290, 11 February, 1969.

majority from the larger authorities that the smaller would feel swamped.

442. If each unitary or metropolitan area has two members for the first 250,000 of its total population and one further member for each additional 250,000 – or part of 250,000 – councils will not, we think, be too big for the transaction of business, will contain adequate representation of all main authorities and will reflect the size of the larger authorities without permitting them to dominate. . . Leaving aside the south-east, the number of indirectly elected members of a provincial council would range from 14 in East Anglia to 41 in the North-West.

443. In the South-East, where there are more main authorities than in any other province, application of the same formula as elsewhere produces 61 members, with Greater London representatives to be added. We do not think it would be right to adopt a different principle in the South-East from the rest of the country but, to prevent the size of the council from becoming unwieldy, we suggest that there should be a limit of 20 on the number of representatives from Greater London. This would still give Greater London four times as many representatives as any other area in the province.

444. The representatives of the metropolitan areas on provincial councils should be drawn from both metropolitan authorities and metropolitan districts – and in Greater London from both the Greater London Council and the London boroughs. We make no proposal on how the number of metropolitan members should be divided between the two levels in each area but both levels must be represented.

445. The chance of serving on a provincial council will, we hope, be an added inducement to men of ability to stand for election to a main authority. As members of a main authority they will guide the affairs of a body with operational responsibility for the main local government services over a wide area. If they are chosen for service on a provincial council too, they will serve an area wider still, settling the framework of its future and co-operating with central government in major issues of economic and planning policy.

446. But provincial councils should not consist only of members chosen by local authorities. Regional economic planning councils will cease to exist but there is value in the present practice of bringing people together from several walks of regional life who can contribute from their varied experience to the formulation of a regional policy, and this practice should be continued. It should therefore be obligatory on the indirectly elected members of each provincial council to

co-opt additional members to the council from outside local government.

447. We do not seek to prescribe the background of co-opted members. The capacity of particular persons to make a contribution which will strengthen the authority of the province as a new element in English public life should be the chief consideration. But provincial councils should be expected to draw co-opted members from industry (private and nationalised), commerce, the trade unions, universities and the professions.

448. Co-opted members should have full voting rights. But a provincial council should contain a substantial majority of indirectly elected members, owing their place on the provincial council to the fact that they were first elected to a main authority by popular vote. The advantages of outside experience would be combined with a clear democratic majority if co-opted members never constituted less than 20% or more than 25% of the total membership of a provincial council. This would mean, in comparison with the figures for indirectly elected members in paragraph 442 above, that the total size of provincial councils apart from the South-East, could vary from 18 to 55, and that in the North-West the two metropolitan areas of Merseyside and Selnec would not together possess a majority of seats on the provincial council. The total number of members on the South-East provincial council might be as high as 108, but the province's population is 17 millions, nearly 40% of the total for all England.

449. The members co-opted to the provincial council should not be the only members from outside local government to be involved in provincial councils' work. Matters considered at provincial level will not always require the attention of the whole provincial council. By virtue of their interests and experience, some members are bound to be more qualified than others for dealing with certain questions. Further education and the social services, for example, are likely to be subjects for which committees of the provincial council will be established while the council retains final responsibility. Such committees should consist not only of provincial council members who have a special concern for education and the social services but also of other persons who are neither indirectly elected nor co-opted members of the council but who are particularly qualified to contribute to the planned development of these functions. There should be the same width of choice in recruiting able and experienced people from outside council membership for service on any other committees set up by the council to deal, say, with particular aspects of economic development or with cultural and recreational services.

450. For certain purposes provincial councils may wish to set up panels rather than committees. Such panels need not include a majority of provincial councillors. Some of the members might be specially qualified officers of main authorities.

STAFF

451. Provincial councils must have their own staff, in their direct employment. There will be clear advantage in seconding officers from both central departments and main authorities for tours of duty with provincial councils: such practice will give the seconded officers valuable experience and help to weld the different levels of government together. But a provincial council must have its own permanent officials whose primary loyalties are to the province and whose careers depend on their performance in the council's service.

452. As we recommend for main authorities, each provincial council should have an officer who is the recognised head of its staff. Integration at official level will be essential if advice to the council on policy is to be based on a provincial view of affairs and not on a number of disparate studies of particular problems. Responsibility for this should be clearly borne by a single officer at the head of the council's paid service. This will be an appointment of crucial importance. The person selected should be chosen strictly on the grounds of his general experience and ability, not because of any particular professional background.

453. The work at provincial level will not call for large staffs. Provincial councils will need highly qualified officers with all relevant techniques of analysis and data processing at their disposal. But they should be relatively few in number and should build on the work done by the staffs of main authorities.

454. Whenever appropriate, provincial councils should make use of the services of consultants and staff on short-term contracts. The placing of contracts with universities for the study of economic, social, physical planning and other questions should also be a normal feature of their arrangements.

Mr Senior's Dissent

From Report of the Royal Commission on Local Government in England 1966–1969, Vol. II, *Memorandum of Dissent by Mr D. Senior*, Cmnd. 4040–1, 1969, pp. 19–21, 47–8, 49–51, 83, 91, 134–5 and 136–45.

These extracts give Mr Senior's criticism of the proposals of his colleagues in so far as they depend on the necessity for provincial councils in addition to the so-called 'unitary' authorities. Then come the brief details of Mr Senior's own scheme for a two-tier system of local authorities, and finally his discussion of two alternative schemes for provincial authorities according to the extent of devolution from the central government. Even here Mr Senior's views are limited to the extent that he assumes that devolution will be in the fields of economic and strategic planning; he has less sympathy with regionalist demands arising from other causes.

WHAT KIND OF PROVINCE?

75. A provincial council is needed to do those necessary things that can be done only at the provincial level and only by a body which represents the interests of the province as a whole. I take issue with my colleagues in this context only in so far as they rely on the provincial council also to make good the inherent incapacity of most of their unitary authorities to do those still more necessary things that can best be done by directly elected local authorities of city-region scale.

76. My colleagues do not admit that most of their main authorities would be deficient in this cardinal respect. On the contrary, they claim that all of them have coherent areas designed to match the way of life of a mobile society, make good units for planning and transportation and give them the space they need to assess and tackle their problems. But these protestations are belied by their admission that land may have to be acquired in one authority's area to solve another authority's problems, and that even one of their metropolitan authorities may have to build houses for people from its area inside another authority's boundaries.

77. No such problem would arise if each planning and development authority covered the whole of the region from which people could commute to its regional centre more conveniently than to any other, for no such authority could ever have the slightest need, right or inclination to consider rehousing any of the people displaced by urban renewal beyond potential commuting range of its regional centre. Any large-scale developments (such as the Leyland/Chorley scheme)

beyond these limits, and therefore in another regional authority's area, might incidentally help to ease its problem, but would otherwise be none of its business; it would not be an 'overspill' operation but part of the shaping and strengthening of another city region, and as such would be the concern only of the provincial council and of the regional authority in whose area it took place – apart, of course, from central government itself. But my colleagues have proposed such authorities only in some of the areas where the population living within commuting range of a regional centre happens to be below the million mark, and for Merseyside and Selnec. (In the West Midlands they have thrown away much of the advantage of a two-level structure by drawing a boundary so tight, except to the north, as to leave virtually no room for choice in the siting of any major developments beyond the green belt.) Elsewhere the structural planning problems are not comprehended or soluble within the areas of the authorities they propose.

78. A provincial council could make up for the deficiencies of these authorities only by itself taking over the making *and implementation* of their structure plans. In so doing, however, it would relegate the 'unitary' authority to the status of a 'metropolitan district'. This is the dilemma that accounts for the vagueness of what my colleagues say about the powers of the provincial council.

79. Would it, or would it not, have effective power to undertake development? By this I do not mean could it build an occasional barrage or opera house; I mean would it have the power, the staff and the money to carry out a major town expansion for which its strategy provided but which the unitary authority for the area concerned was unwilling to accept?

80. This is the issue on which the whole nature, status and structural significance of the provincial council depend. If it were to have this power – and the resources to use it – reality would be given to all the other planning powers with which my colleagues say it should be endowed. But it would then become an operational planning and development *authority*, and as such would have to be directly elected. It could then properly assume responsibility for functions transferred from central government, or for any new function needing to be discharged on a scale larger than that of the 'unitary' authorities. But the unitary principle itself would be blown sky-high.

81. If, on the other hand, the provincial councils were either not to have this power or not to have the resources to use it, all the other powers of positive decision-making and of negative control over

development with which my colleagues would ostensibly endow them would prove an empty sham, masking but not effectually making good the incapacity of most of the unitary authorities to deal with the structural planning and development problems that are regional in scale. In most of the areas where this is going to be local government's most important and exacting task over the rest of this century, the job would simply not be done – unless central government did it in local government's default.

82. I am unable to divine exactly where my colleagues collectively stand on this, the most crucial of all the issues before us. They seem content that the provincial council should take over whenever the provision of some service appears to call for a unit larger than most of their new authorities, on the tacit assumptions that this is a bridge we can cross when we come to it, and that meanwhile we can defer to a comfortably indefinite future any need to face the implications of crossing it. But under my colleagues' proposed pattern the structural planning and development functions would from the outset call for a unit larger than those of the new authorities in most of the areas where the jobs needing to be done in these fields are of particularly urgent importance. This is not a question of what might happen at some time in the future: it is a matter of how the immediately present and desperately pressing challenge of massive growth and change is to be met. It lies at the very heart of the job we were commissioned to do.

196. The city region is by definition of the right scale for the organisation of all the functions of local government that are necessarily associated with 'structural' planning. By this I mean the planning of the functional relationships, in terms of location, scale and phasing, between the main elements in the physical context of a motorised society's activities – its homes, workplaces, shopping and service centres and recreation areas and the communications between them. It forms a virtually self-contained employment pool: almost everybody who lives in it works in it, and almost everybody who works in it lives in it. It is also a virtually self-contained retail market: what its people spend outside their own locality or district centre is almost all spent in its regional centre. Its transport system is virtually self-contained, apart from national rail routes and inter-city road services. A diagram of its traffic flows shows a dense tangle towards its centre, dominated by radial commuting bands, all thinning out towards the 'traffic watersheds' between it and neighbouring city regions.

204. The city region owes its existence to the geographical scope of those activities of a motorised society which also create the main problems with which local government must deal in the 'environ

mental' field. There is thus an automatic identity between the areal requirements of this complex of statutory functions and the geographic scope of a social entity on which a level of local democracy can viably be based. What may be the population of a local government unit based on such an entity is immaterial, functionally speaking, provided only that its resources are adequate to employ the necessary staff.

205. But there is no *automatic* identity between the geographic scale of this or any other social entity and the functional requirements of the personal services, because some of these requirements are related not to area but to caseload. This is by no means to say that in the personal-service field the acreage of a local government unit, or its coherence in terms of social geography, does not matter: far from it. The functional *effectiveness* (as well as the democratic vitality) of a personal-service unit depends on how easily its citizens can reach its headquarters and on how closely its chief officers can keep in touch with what is happening on the ground and in other departments.

206. What this means is not that the distance between the furthest corner of the unit and its administrative centre should be kept within a predetermined mileage, but that its administrative centre should be in the same place as the shops and offices with which nearly every citizen is likely at some time to have occasion to deal. As our Community Attitudes Survey disclosed, people living near the town hall value their easy access to it; if they live further away, they don't much care how far it is *from their homes;* but I have no doubt a very positive response would have been obtained if they had been asked whether, if it must be far away, they wanted it within half a mile of the shops in which they buy their shoes, suits and bedroom suites.

207. For functional *effectiveness*, then, the personal-service unit should be based on a strongly influential shopping centre, and its boundary should be drawn to include everybody who will find that shopping centre more conveniently accessible by public transport than any other comparable centre. But the town district so defined is very variable in population size in different parts of the country, and for functional *efficiency* – the economical provision of a high professional standard of service – it may be found desirable that the unit's population should come within a certain size range

208. If so, in those sparsely populated parts of the country where the social entity at city-region level is inordinately extensive and at town-district level inadequately populated, it will be necessary to define personal-service units within the desirable population range primarily

by reference to the relative accessibility of the most influential in a group of shopping centres. Such units will be the most convenient that respect for the requirements of functional efficiency will allow, but they will not fully satisfy the requirements of local democracy, since each will contain minor town districts whose inhabitants have no common interest, except at city-region level, with the people who normally shop in the selected district centre.

DEFINING THE REGIONAL UNIT

209. No such difficulty can arise at city-region level, where the areal requirements of functional efficiency, functional effectiveness and community representation must necessarily coincide, since they are all determined by the same facts of motorised life. Nevertheless there are parts of the country where the boundaries so determined are not easy to identify, because the part played by a city region in the lives of its inhabitants tends to diminish in relative importance with increasing distance from the regional centre. At the margin between adjoining city regions, therefore, there is usually a 'zone of indifference', of varying width, inhabited by people who find access to either regional centre equally convenient (or inconvient) and may use both for different purposes.

210. The idea of the city region was originally conceived for academic purposes – to enable the facts of motor-age life at the 'city' level to be meaningfully described, analysed and compared – and for these purposes it is not always necessary to define a boundary. If it is, the academic may define it on whatever basis is most relevant to the particular aspect he wishes to study – for example, he might choose the five-per-cent commuting limit and ignore the interstitial areas left over. But nothing can be left over when one is using the city-region concept as a basis for the definition of local government units. Each unit must have a common boundary with the next.

211. This presents no difficulty where strong regional centres are no more than about fifty miles apart, as is the case throughout by far the greater part of England. Here the journey-to-work information recorded in the Census, traffic-flow studies for development plans, social surveys (where they have been made) and durable-goods retail marketing surveys enable one to identify within narrow limits the 'watersheds' between spheres of regional influence. It does not matter for this purpose what may be the level of commuting (for example) at the watershed: all that matters is that it should be the same in both directions. But where regional centres are so far apart that the level of commuting to one sinks to zero before any commuting to the other is

encountered, mapped traffic flows thin out to hair-lines, durable goods are bought by mail order and nobody ever goes to the theatre, the city region has no determinate boundary. Yet for local government purposes a boundary must be drawn.

212. To suggest that this invalidates the city-region concept as a basis for the definition of local government units for planning and develop-ment purposes seems to me unreasonable. Social entities that play a dominant and ever-increasing part in the lives of well over ninety per cent of the population, even in the more sparsely populated provinces, are not rendered 'unreal' by the fact that a few thousand upland farmers would be hard put to it to decide which of two such entities they predominantly belonged to. Indeed, it might well be argued that this degree of indeterminacy is to be welcomed as an advantage. If there is a 'zone of indifference' between two city regions, it cannot much matter for regional purposes where in that zone one draws the boundary; one can therefore give precedence to the much more definite lines of demarcation between the regions' peripheral town districts without risk of creating any functional difficulties for the regional planning and development authorities, or of doing any violence to their representative integrity. In practice, however, one usually finds that a natural boundary is clearly indicated within the zone of indifference by a physical watershed (like the Pennine ridge between Cumbria and Northumbria), or by some psychological barrier to free association.

A Two-level System

350. The conclusion seems to me inescapable. If one refrains from prematurely plumping for an ill-founded theoretical determinant and approaches our problem by way of an analysis of the functional requirements of local government's main jobs in relation to the facts of social geography and the demands of local democracy, one finds that all service needs are met by one or the other, or both, of the levels of authority at which the main 'environmental' and personal-service functions should in any case be organised. The general correspondence of these two basic groups of purposes with the way our mobile society organises itself in city-region and town-district units extends right across the functional board and even to the demands of the human element in the membership and internal organisation of local authori-ties.

351. A two-level local government structure based on these social entities might have, in the first instance, a number of regional units

ranging from 27 (if the London Metropolitan Region had a single regional authority and the Leeds/York, Southampton/Bournemouth, Plymouth/Exeter and Cambridge/Peterborough groupings were preferred) to the 35 indicated on Fig. 7 and Maps 7–9, with the possibility of three more (based on Lancaster, Shrewsbury and Swindon) being hived off in due course. . . .

352. Detailed study of the same areas in relation to the functional needs of the personal services and associated functions identifies some 150 district units. Of these over 130 are coherent town districts, each based on a centre which effectively serves the whole of the area included with it. Each of the others is made up of two or three small town districts which have some interests in common, but which individually lack the resources to sustain fully efficient personal services. In nearly all of these cases, planned or spontaneous growth of population is expected to increase the relative importance of the most influential centre and make it in due course an effective focus of community life of the whole of the unit.

353. Just over half of these units will have populations in the range 140,000–260,000 by 1981. Another third will have between 260,000 and 450,000 inhabitants. One-tenth will have over 450,000 and the remaining half-dozen between 90,000 and 140,000. In four cases the unit identified by analysis of personal-service requirements in relation to socio-geographic realities is identical with the city-region unit required for the 'environmental' complex of functions. In the other cases the city regions (in the 35-unit version illustrated) contain from two to twelve district units each. Accordingly I recommend that the new structure of local government should comprise two levels of authority for the exercise of statutory functions everywhere except in the monocentric areas based on Leicester, Lincoln, Peterborough and Cambridge; these should have unitary authorities for all statutory purposes. . . .

Relations with Central Government

453. The flexibility inherent in a properly articulated two-level structure makes it unnecessary for any part of any of local government's statutory functions to be discharged at any other level. All the district units can and should be of such a scale that every free-standing former borough that is too large to be appropriate for, or content with, the quite different role of a common council is itself a district centre. Similarly, each regional unit can and should cover the whole of the area within which all the problems involved in the discharge of its

present and possible future statutory duties are comprehended and properly soluble, given the degree of co-operation between neighbouring units which no regional authority will have any built-in disposition to withhold. This complete provision for the proper performance of local government's statutory functions enables the remaining requirements of a viable system of local democracy to be met by equally self-contained forms of organisation, designed specifically and exclusively for quite different purposes, both at grass-roots level and at a level intermediate between central and local government.

454. The need for an intermediate or provincial level of governmental activity arises from the existence of problems which cannot be comprehended (and therefore cannot be solved) except by bodies operating at that level – problems which stand in the way of the proper discharge by both central and local government of their respective responsibilities. I therefore agree with my colleagues that some kind of provincial organisation is necessary to bridge the gap – to take a synoptic view of the combined effects of departmental policies over as wide an area as possible, to bring local needs and aspirations to bear on decisions that have to be made nationally but cannot rationally be made from Whitehall, and to give local planning authorities a long-term strategic context for structural plan-making. But I cannot agree that this organisation must necessarily, or even should preferably, be an integral part of local government. The bridge must be built from both sides, and in such a way that the two halves meet in the middle.

455. When we began our deliberations – and for a long time thereafter – central government gave no sign of being alive to the need for such a bridge. In these circumstances we were tempted to try to design one that could be built wholly from the local government side; and this, it seems to me, is what my colleagues have persisted in trying to do. The result is the kind of bridge that (in the unlikely event of its being built) would collapse if it were not enormously strengthened. If it is intended to be enormously strengthened, the specification for the permanent structure should be stated in the first place, and its implications faced.

456. In the absence of any hint of bridge-building activity from the central government side, the proper course for us was to ensure that our proposed new structure of local government did not leave too wide a gap, to incorporate in that structure the form of abutment that would best fit the needs of local government, and to draw attention to the need for a bridge without expressing any view as to how the other end of it should be designed. It would then have been reasonable to hope that central government would see what was required of it.

457. At a late stage, however, the situation was changed by the announcement that a Commission on the Constitution was to be set up,
with terms of reference that seemed to me to call for a reappraisal of
this part of our task. It now appeared that central government was
conscious of the need for the sort of bridge that would afford a
serviceable platform for undepartmentalised decision-making at the
provincial level as well as a means of two-way communication between
itself and local government. There was no longer any point in our
trying to get the whole thing built from the local government side.

466. Whitehall's approach is based on the premise that it is not possible for central government to abdicate its responsibility for the
country's economic well-being; nor, in a country that is economically
so close-knit as ours, can central government discharge this responsibility by handing over large areas of economic decision-making to
politically powerful provincial authorities (or to a federal consortium
of such authorities), at least two of which will always be controlled by
the political party which is in opposition at Westminster.

467. The role of central government in this sphere has become
increasingly positive in the course of this century. In Edwardian times
it was just a matter of 'holding the ring': the government prescribed a
legal context for economic decision-making by other agencies and
dealt as best it could by fiscal means with the national consequences
of their independent action. Between the wars the emphasis began to
shift to a purposeful management of the national economy, but only
through measures applied uniformly to the country as a whole. After
the last war it was accepted that the purposes of economic management
should include the maintenance of a high and stable level of employment. But the structure of our economy was such that it was found
impossible to mop up unemployment by expansionist policies affecting
the country as a whole without overheating parts of it to the point of
upsetting the balance of payments. And when the commitment to full
employment was extended to cover the promotion of a faster rate of
economic growth, even industrially selective measures came up against
the uneven *geographical* distribution of under-used and fully-
stretched resources. Central government found it could not discharge
its new commitment without deliberately discriminating between one
part of the country and another in the distribution of growth-promot-
ing capital investment in the infrastructure of both economic and social
development.

468. Given the limited resources available at any time for capital
investment, and the still stricter limitation on the proportion of these
resources which in a mixed economy can be pre-empted by the public

sector, central government cannot promote public investment in one part of the country without restraining it in another. Moreover, in so far as it devotes national funds to this purpose, it is giving the inhabitants of one area the benfit of taxation levied on other areas. The only justification for so doing is that it is only by enabling the industrially declining areas to make fuller and more productive use of their resources that central government can bring about a maintainable increase in the rate of growth of the national economy to the benefit of all. But this justification is valid only if central government sees to it that the resources it channels into a hard-hit 'region' are not dissipated in 'fair shares', but used only where and how they will do the most good, on the projects with the highest potential for self- sustaining and ramifying growth, regardless of greater social needs elsewhere.

469. The selection of such growth areas and projects demands a thorough knowledge of conditions in the 'region' concerned. It is not a job that can be adequately done from Whitehall. Still less can it be done through a departmentalised machine for the transmission of control over investment resources from Ministers preoccupied with their particular functions to equally single-minded local government officers, with no attempt to consider the priorities or mutual repercussions among the functional programmes except at Cabinet level, in relation to the interests of the country at large, and at council chamber level, in relation to the interests of individual local authority areas. It calls for decision-making at an intermediate level by an agency that is effectively responsible for the general economic wellbeing of a large area, capable of assessing the needs and potentialities of that area, and fully informed of the possible impact on it of the policies of central government, nationalised industries, local authorities and other major investing agencies, public and private.

470. These conditions are not met by a regional economic planning board whose members are responsible to their departmental chiefs in Whitehall rather than to a chairman who is himself the servant of a department with no executive powers. Such a body can usefully help its respective masters to make better-informed functional decisions and can iron out the little local nonsenses that arise when the local application of one departmental policy conflicts with that of another. But it cannot ensure, for example, that a motorway programme takes as much account of the development it will generate as of existing traffic flows, or that the location of a new university is regarded as a vital element in the up-grading of a regional centre no less than as an exercise in the correlation of A-level results with the seasonal demand for lodgings.

471. What *central* government means by 'regional planning', then, is primarily the correction of economic imbalance *between* one 'region' and another; and it is only with reluctance that central government is reconciling itself to the fact that this purpose – crucial to its central function in the economic field – necessarily involves the making of investment decisions *within* 'regions' on a territorial as well as a functional basis. What *local* government means by 'regional planning', on the other hand, is primarily the expression of national policies in terms of a comprehensive long-term strategy for economic and physical development *within* each provincial-scale 'region', in the context of which local planning authorities can work out meaningful structure plans for their own areas.

472. Such a strategy cannot be a fixed framework dictated by higher authority; it must take account of, among other things, the local needs and aspirations for which the local planners want to provide. But neither can it be formed by piecing together locally initiated structure plans. As at all other interchanges between two levels in the planning process, there must be a circulatory evolution of ideas: strategic concepts must be tested out at the structural planning level and firmed up in the light of the feed-back. But it is essential that the strategy should be conceived with the interests of the wider area as a whole in mind, that it should itself be validated by central government as an acceptable basis for national investment decision-making, and that the agency responsible for it should be able to get its positive provisions implemented.

473. It is evident that, in spite of their different approaches to 'regional planning', what both central and local government need to have done in this field is one and the same job, calling for a new kind of provincial agency. But that agency could take either of two quite different forms, with the choice between them depending ultimately on how much power central government would or should be willing to transfer to local government in order to keep itself free from territorial responsibilities at a sub-national level.

PROVINCIAL COUNCILS

474. The form of provincial organisation that I advocate is based on two assumptions. The first is that the boundaries of the new local authorities responsible for the making and implementation of structural development plans will be so drawn that each unit contains the whole of its centre's potential commuting hinterland and service area. It follows that it will never be necessary, or even desirable, for any such authority to look beyond its own boundaries for space to rehouse

people displaced by slum clearance or road building, or dispersing themselves of their own accord but continuing to work in or near the centre. There will, however, be a need for an organisation that can help the poorer and less populous development authorities to build new towns and cities planned to strengthen their unit centres, to serve as growth points for the ultimate benefit of wider areas, and to further a national policy for housing the increase in our rapidly growing population in such a way as to put the widest possible range of opportunities within easy reach of all.

475. The second assumption is that central government will so organise itself that, having determined the national priorities for capital investment, it can implement that part of its programme which concerns local government through agencies designed to take a comprehensive view of the whole process of development over wide areas and authorised to take some account of the differing priorities of local government.

476. How this part of the bridge between central and local government should be built is, of course, a question that falls outside our terms of reference; and even if it did not, I could not pretend to be competent to answer it. On the other hand, I find it impossible to make clear how the bridge should serve as a platform for combined operations without at least illustrating the *kind* of organisation that is needed. What follows is, therefore, purely hypothetical.

477. Let it be supposed that a Minister of Regional Development with a small central staff has been made responsible for keeping the capital expenditure of local government within the limits set by a national investment programme (based in part on works programmes put up by the regional authorities) which allows an unallocated margin of (say) five per cent over the combined total of the agreed departmental programmes. Let it also be supposed that this Minister has under him a Minister of State (with a more numerous staff) in each of five English provinces, responsible for vetting local development authorities' rolling programmes, incorporating them in a provincial investment programme for submission to Whitehall, and in due course for authorising capital expenditure up to the total amount allocated to his province, with discretion to allocate part of the five per cent margin to any development authority which, having dealt with its share of the departmental minimum programmes, can make good use of it.

478. Let it be further supposed that each Minister of State is authorised to set up, jointly with any regional authority in his province whose centre is selected as a growth point, a regional development

corporation on the lines of a new town development corporation, but having an operational area coterminous with that of the regional authority. And let it finally be supposed that each Minister of State also has at his command a provincial road construction unit and a provincial or national organisation for the design and execution of such exceptionally large and specialised engineering and building projects as barrage schemes, major airports, universities and teaching hospitals, which are of importance to the economic and social development of the province as a whole.

479. For the purposes of this strictly hypothetical exercise I need not, and therefore must not, specify which functions of what existing government departments would be most conveniently transferred to such a Ministry – with two exceptions. It would clearly have to be the Ministry responsible for the approval of local authorities' structural development plans, and it would equally clearly have to be responsible for the location of employment. Under any such system the central government's responsibility for correcting 'economic imbalance' between provinces by inducing the movement of employment from one province to another would be discharged solely by such means as a *provincially* selective employment tax and by loans, grants and allowances for industrial development available only in specified parts of the country. The issue of industrial development certificates and office building permits (if still in use) would be left wholly to the discretion of the province-based Ministers of State, except in cases of unquestionably national importance.

480. I repeat that the foregoing is a purely illustrative sketch of what central government's end of the bridge might look like from the local government side. There may well be better ways of building it from central government's point of view, and they would serve the needs of local government no less well provided only that they brought the middle of the bridge to the same general position. But I must emphasise that the whole system of planning, structural as well as strategic, will be stultified if control of the location of employment continues to be exercised by a functionally blinkered central department with no territorial responsibility. If no arrangements are made whereby it can be exercised on behalf of central government by provincial agencies with a synoptic view of their areas' social and economic needs, it should be transferred direct to the regional planning authorities.

481. Given these two assumptions, a clear role emerges for a provincial council. Its most important task would be to resolve the long-term planning problems presented at provincial level by demographic

projections, technological innovations, economic trends and the functional investment programmes of government departments, nationalised industries and other agencies – problems which cannot be comprehended at any other level – and thereby to enable local authorities to produce soundly based structural development plans with real meaning and capacity to bear on development. Confidentially briefed by the Minister of State on national policies from the formative stage, and by the nationalised industries and major private enterprises on their manpower and land requirements, it would formulate the objectives of a provincial strategy. Its research and planning staff would work out alternative 'broad-brush' models for the realisation of these objectives, taking account of committed developments and of the medium-term proposals of the local planning authorities. Having considered these options in the light of studies of their local implications, the provincial council would submit its strategic plan to the Ministry of Regional Development, where it would be reconciled with other provincial plans. The resulting national strategy would be used as a basis for the approval of local authorities' structure plans.

482. There could not, however, be any formal statutory approval of the provincial plan itself, since its content would necessarily be flexible and its specific projects would be subject to objection and inquiry when they came to be more precisely expressed in statutory structure plans. (Any notion that a long-term strategic plan at the provincial scale – or, indeed, any other kind of plan – might be given the force of law is absurd. The only effective sanction a plan can have, or needs, is the power of the responsible authority to implement its proposals.) The planning process, at this as at other levels, would of course be continuous, and the plan would be periodically republished as changes in conditions and objectives gradually shifted the balance of advantage between long-term options.

483. Among other important functions which cannot be discharged except at a provincial level and by a provincially-rooted council are:

1. to advise the central government on the implications, for the well-being of the people of the province, of developing government policies and intended legislation before they reach a stage at which rethinking becomes too difficult.

2. to assist the Minister of State in preparing and revising the provincial contribution to a medium-term (four or five years) national plan for the promotion of economic growth, in formulating his medium-term programme of capital investment and in exercising his control over the location of employment.

3. to monitor the progress of the provincial economy and exert a managerial influence on it by drawing attention to the mutual repercussions of the current policies and short-term programmes of all major public and private employers and providers of services, and seeking to promote concerted action among them consistent with the objectives of the provincial strategy.

4. to help local authorities to interpret the significance for them of the provincial strategy, participating with them in joint studies of any special inter-authority problems and promoting co-operation among them.

5. to provide a forum of confrontation between the differing priorities of local and central government and between public and private enterprise in all matters affecting the social and economic well-being of the province as a whole.

484. In carrying out these duties a provincial council would not have any need to intervene (except by way of providing specialist help on request) in the internal structural planning of any regional unit, or detract in any way from the regional authority's responsibility for putting up (and carrying out when approved) the works programme for which it would be the executive authority. The provincial council would not even be required to resolve inconsistencies between the structural plans of adjoining regional authorities. Constituted as I propose, with boundaries running through areas of minimal development pressure and with no built-in conflicts of interest, the regional authorities would have no difficulty in sorting out for themselves such common problems as the alignment of inter-city highways. It is important also that the local planning authorities should submit their statutory structure plans direct to the Ministry of Regional Development for approval, and not to the provincial council. The Minister's statutory responsibility must be clear-cut.

485. A provincial strategic plan is needed because of the interlocking character of the problems – spatial, social and economic – that arise at the provincial scale and can be comprehended and resolved only by an agency looking at the province as a whole. To represent the provincial plan as the meeting-point of national economic planning and local physical planning is fundamentally to misconceive the nature of the planning process, and any structural arrangements based on that misconception are doomed to futility. National, provincial (strategic), regional (structural) and local (design) plans must all have, in varying proportions, an economic content, a physical content and a social content.

C.R.R.—8*

486. Pending the creation of the kind of machinery I have postulated for the devolution of central government decision-making to province-based Ministers of State, provincial councils could nevertheless function on the lines I have proposed, dealing directly with the departmental Ministers concerned. But in order to avoid being virtually ignored as mere territorial pressure groups, they would have to get together to thrash out inter-provincial priorities within a realistic assessment of the national resources available for investment in provincial-scale projects.

487. In the light of the functions and the relationships with other agencies outlined above, the basis on which a provincial council should be constituted is clear. (i) It need not and should not itself have executive powers. (ii) It should represent the interests of the province as such, and not only the interests of the local authorities within the province; but a majority of its members should be members of regional councils. (iii) Its members must have access to confidential information about the intentions of central government, and must therefore be appointed by the responsible Minister and bound to secrecy. (iv) It should not be a large body (between twenty and thirty members would be appropriate), but it should be encouraged to co-opt 'non-political' people to its specialist committees and study groups. (v) It should have its own independent chief officer, secretariat and planning and research staff, adequate in number and calibre for their limited but important and exacting tasks.

488. Thus the provincial council would not be in any sense an *authority* – a level of decision-making government. Its members, though for the most part nominated by the regional authorities, should be appointed on their individual merits as 'good provincialists'. The Minister should be free to appoint not only academics, business men, trade unionists and professional people but also suitable members of regional councils who have not been nominated by them.

489. The fact that such a provincial council would be non-elective and non-executive should not be misunderstood as implying that it would be weak. Indeed, given the kind of *province-based* executive complement I have postulated, I am convinced that it would be a great deal more influential than an indirectly elected council with the assortment of executive and advisory duties proposed by my colleagues. The present regional economic planning councils are ineffective not because they are 'only advisory', but because central government has failed to complement them with machinery for the exercise of its own executive powers in the same territorial dimension – or to give them adequate planning staffs. A province-based Minister of State and his staff would

become, as even the English members of the Scottish Development Department do, more provincial-minded than the provincials themselves; they would soon be treating the advice of their provincial council with more respect than Ministers treat that of Members of Parliament.

490. An indirectly elected body, especially at this level, would have several serious disadvantages. Its members would inevitably regard themselves as answerable to their electors (the members of the constituent councils) and therefore could not have the necessary confidential relationship with central government. (The leaders of local authority associations are not privy to the central government's 'undocumented thinking', as even the present regional economic planning councils are.) Again, the majority party among the members of an indirectly elected council would seek first to assure itself of solid political control, and would therefore co-opt loyal party pensioners and defeated candidates, rather than the paragons predicated in my colleagues' report. If their party were in opposition at Westminster, as would always be the case in at least two provinces, a co-operative relationship between central government and provincial councils in respect of controversial departmental policies would be impossible to maintain.

491. Even more important is the objection that an indirectly elected provincial council, precisely because it would be 'rooted in local government' (and only in local government), would be disqualified from dealing with a great many of the problems that need to be tackled at provincial level. Any province-based arm of central government would then have to deal separately with private interests, nationalised industries and other non-political institutions, and would therefore be obliged to rely more on its own judgment and less on the advice of the provincial council in deciding what action by central government would best serve the interests of the province as a whole.

492. As to the number and boundaries of the areas with which the provincial councils should deal, I cannot share my colleagues' view that the 'regions' originally worked out for civil defence purposes, and adopted with modifications by the Department of Economic Affairs for the purpose of correcting inter-regional economic imbalance, are also by some happy chance the areas which reflect such sense of provincial identity as exists. Still less can I accept them as the areas into which the economic and geographical composition of the country may be said to fall. These two criteria are in any case incompatible, for the second would require the South-West province to include South Wales, the Midlands to include Central Wales, and the North West to

include North Wales. Given the two-level structure of local government I propose, there would be no justification for regarding the disproportionately light-weight and decreasingly self-contained North-East, East Midland and East Anglia areas as provinces. What the North-East faces today will confront Yorkshire tomorrow; the fall-out from the exploding metropolis already covers East Anglia; the Birmingham/Coventry and Nottingham/Leicester areas have closer ties with each other than the former with Hereford (which the Severn Bridge has brought nearer to Bristol) or the latter with Lincoln (which might well be included in the South-East province). I think the five provinces indicated on my maps represent areas which are more likely than my colleagues' eight to need comprehensive strategic planning over the decades ahead. They are certainly more suitable in scale for decentralised decision-making by central government.

THE 'SUB-PROVINCIAL' ALTERNATIVE

493. At the end of the first section of this chapter I said that the real need for comprehensive planning and action at a level intermediate between local and national government could be met in either of two ways, depending on how much power central government was prepared to transfer to local government in order to avoid having to co-ordinate its policies anywhere below Cabinet level. In the last section I have described the kind of provincial council (and postulated a complementary arm of central government) which I think would best meet the need, assuming that central government does not continue to shirk the obligation to add a provincial dimension to its decision-making – an obligation which seems to me implicit in its assumption of responsibility for the healthy growth of the national economy. I now turn to the other possible way of meeting the need, based on the assumption that central government would rather transfer to local government the power to make the necessary decisions at this level – including the location of industrial and office employment, the routing of regional motorways, the selection of sites for new regional cities, the determination of development policies for ports and airports, poly-technics, universities and teaching hospitals, and the settlement of all intra-provincial public investment priorities. This alternative would have major repercussions on the organisation of local government itself.

494. In the first place, an agency exercising such powers would un-questionably have to be directly elected. It would therefore have to be based on units with some claim to community of interest and socio-geographic coherence. It would also have to take the place of my regional authorities, since there could not be room for two directly

elected authorities with functions of the same general kind at such narrowly separated levels.

495. Both of these necessities point to the 'large-city-region' or 'sub-provincial' scale of organisation to which I referred in Chapter II of this Part. This is in some parts of the country equivalent, though nowhere identical in area, to the scale on which the smaller and more coherent D.E.A. 'regions' have been established, but quite different from that of the larger ones, which cannot pretend to the degree of unity required to support democratic institutions.

496. This scale would be large enough to enable each unit (if suitably constituted) to deal with both strategic and structural planning problems, provided there were established a national planning agency comprising representatives of all the units and of the appropriate government departments to thrash out such problems as the routing of motorways, the priorities among barrage schemes and the bulk supply of water. Each individual unit would be capable of tackling other aspects of strategic planning, and every other function that might conceivably be entrusted to it, but would be needlessly large and remote for all existing local government functions except higher education.

497. Over much more than half the country, it would be possible to form 'large-city-region' authorities that would not be too unreal as organs of representative government by amalgamating strong-centred with relatively weak-centred adjoining city regions as follows:

Plymouth with Exeter
Bristol with Gloucester
Southampton with Bournemouth
Birmingham with Coventry and Stoke
Nottingham with Leicester
Sheffield with Hull ⎫
Leeds with York   ⎬ (perhaps united)
Newcastle with Teesside
Preston with Carlisle
Norwich with Ipswich

498. Elsewhere, however, 'sub-provincial' units would have to be formed by combining neighbouring regions with centres of similar strength though with some community of interest:

Peterborough with Cambridge and Lincoln
Oxford with Northampton
Manchester with Liverpool

499. There remain the Brighton and Ashford regions, which could make a somewhat elongated unit with at least some things in common; and the London Metropolitan Region, into which they might otherwise be absorbed.

500. A possible, but less satisfactory, variant would be to unite Lincoln with Nottingham and Leicester, and Cambridge and Peterborough with Norwich and Ipswich. Another would be to unite the Preston region with the Manchester and Liverpool regions; but this is no improvement as far as the Carlisle region is concerned. It is an unblinkable fact of geography that the amalgamation of Cumbria with any other English region would make an absurdly hollow-centred unit.

501. These twelve to fifteen 'sub-provincial' authorities would discharge all the functions I have assigned to city-regional authorities as well as whatever powers were ceded by central government. The district authorities would have the same areas and functions as in the city-region pattern; its four unitary authorities would become district authorities. The common councils would be unaffected.

5

The Prospects —
Change or Decay?

Neither the main report from the Royal Commission on Local Government, nor the memorandum from Mr Senior, put forward proposals for effective regional institutions. The provincial councils proposed in the main report were akin to joint boards of the operating authorities in their manner of creation and legal constitution, but in practice they would exhibit the characteristics of joint committees, destined to impotency by the lack of a will of their own, because of the denial to them of directly elected members, and by the absence of a capability of action owing to their lack of operational powers. Mr Senior confused the issue by describing his relatively small units as 'city regions', but he defined them by a very narrow concept of the factors which determine such an organism. His resort to motorised transport as the basic determinant ignored many other relevant factors in social and economic life. His resulting scheme as a whole left the problem of large-area services completely untouched and so he, too, finished up favouring an emaciated form of provincial advisory body. To be fair, he did of course recognise that different arrangements would be required if the government should endow regional bodies with executive powers, but to Mr Senior this was very much a second-best solution.

This Commission, then, made no effective contribution to the progress of regionalism. In fact its proposals, were they to be enacted, would create a great stumbling block to further regional developments, since the new unitary or other operating authorities which would be established would be more powerful pressure groups against further advance to regional government than our present local authorities could ever hope to be. So the crucial question still remains. It is whether a fully-fledged system of regional government is likely to emerge in the forseeable future. By this is meant a series of multi-purpose authorities, each backed by a representative assembly formed by a direct and popular franchise, and with full executive powers in their own fields. It is a question of rationalising our system of government as a whole, to make it easier for the citizen to find his way about it; to bring into more effective democratic control a wide range of existing regional authorities at present managed by nominated or appointed boards; and to provide a more efficient area of operation for many of the public activities which can best be done at the regional, rather than the central or local, level. There is no sign of such a development yet.

The real issues of controversy arise in the political not the administrative field. As the experience of the last fifty years shows, there is no great obstacle to the creation of administrative units on a regional basis, only to giving them a political direction. It is really a struggle over political influence and the manner in which it is exercised, as a result of which operational efficiency and democratic responsiveness take the hindmost.

The idea of a regional political activity is opposed by the national politicians who resort to arguments about the necessity of maintaining control over the national economy, and who emphasize the national interest in such activities as education, housing, highways and planning. Granted the value of these laudable objectives, there is nevertheless a large amount of decision taking which can be done at the regional level without disturbing the essential unity of national policies. There is too much of a tendency to see devolution as a vertical division between functions rather than, as it should be, a horizontal sharing of responsibilities within a function according to the extent of the influence of the different kinds of decisions. It should be possible to think in terms of a regional strategy within a national policy for a wide range of public activities; this is what devolution really means in the modern state.

On the other hand, the local councillors attack the idea of a regional political system on the grounds that its representatives would be 'remote' from the people, that it would not be a very democratic system. This implies that democracy is to be measured in spatial or numerical relationships, and that the smaller the ratio of representative to acres or number of electors represented, the more democratic the system will be. This is not so. Democracy is basically the ability of the people, via their representatives, to influence what a public authority does. That influence is primarily determined by the quality of the representation and by the organization by which it is brought to bear on the officials. These two factors are so overwhelming in their effects that considerations of size of territory or number of people represented are of only minor relevance.

What is important, and what we do not now enjoy, is effective political direction and control over the many activities carried on at the regional level. This range of activity is likely to increase rather than diminish in the future. No system of nomination or ministerial selection of persons 'representative' of the social and economic life of the region, no method of appointment of some of their number by local councillors, is an adequate substitute for a body of directly elected representatives. None of these existing devices secure adequate accountability. They simply cannot because the only device which can be used by the people to determine the continuance in office of their so-called representatives, the ballot box, is missing. In no other way can those who make the decisions and give direction to the officials be made to defend in public the policies and actions they operate, and the financial consequences of what they do.

The creation of the Commission on the Constitution has kept the regional issue alive. It does at least mean that the arguments *for* regional politics will be aired; hitherto, the arguments against have made all the running. There is another prospect, too. It is that the initiative will at last be taken from those who are primarily concerned with the reform of local government. Few of them have been as perceptive as G. D. H. Cole, whose early views are still worth reading. Even those journals which are concerned to lead opinion, can often be led themselves. Radical views such as those expressed by *The Economist* have been outnumbered by staid conservative ones such as those expressed in *The Times*. As will be seen from the earlier chapters, the arguments for regional authorities come out more frequently in the learned journals.

Finally, what is the reaction of the local government interests to the Commission on the Constitution? Judging from their views, it is clear that most of the local authority associations are still fighting for the retention of local authorities, albeit in reconstituted areas, as the main, if not the only, form of subordinate government. Why do they wish to adhere to institutions so obviously outmoded?

The answer lies in men: in the men and women who form the large army of elected councillors in the existing mass of local authorities. They, for the most part, form the motivating force in the local authority associations, which are as much associations of councillors as of authorities. Larger authorities, regional authorities, will inevitably call forth new systems of organization and new methods of management. The Committee on the Management of Local Government which reported in 1966, demonstrated that modern techniques of management and organization, and a more democratic role for the elected representative, would require fewer councillors than now exist.

A fully-fledged system of regional government would undoubtedly carry the process still further.

It is, of course, against the interests of contemporary councillors, from the standpoint of their power and glory, for them to support the case for regional government. (Amongst paid officials opinion is much more varied. Though some see the advent of larger authorities as detrimental to their own personal interests, there is undoubtedly a recognition that larger authorities can provide wider career prospects and a more effective structure of employment.) Nevertheless, the evidence in favour of a regional government is strong if what we seek is a system of government which promotes, rather than hinders, the best use of resources and which gives value for money in terms of the manpower and resources withdrawn from private use. New authorities with new forms of organization will undoubtedly change the role of the councillor. The true role of the councillor, in addition to his representative function, is to determine priorities, to appraise the action of officials, and to establish and monitor systems of control and progress. It is a sad fact that too many of them can only measure their role, and democracy, by the number of opportunities they have to say 'yes', or 'no', to the spending of fifty pounds. That is the mark of the small man, indeed.

It would be a great loss to our future well-being, in both the material and spiritual senses, if an efficient and responsive system of government were to be sacrificed to the continued office holding of a large army of minor politicians making minor decisions. Therein lies the danger of rule by small men, and on that we can do no better than to echo the concluding words of John Stuart Mill's essay *On Liberty*:

'A government cannot have too much of the kind of activity which does not impede, but aids and stimulates, individual exertion and development. The mischief begins when, instead of calling forth the activity and powers of individuals and bodies, it substitutes its own activity for theirs; when, instead of informing, advising, and, upon occasion, denouncing, it makes them work in fetters, or bids them stand aside and does their work instead of them. The worth of a State, in the long run, is the worth of the individuals composing it; and a State which postpones the interests of *their* mental expansion and elevation to a little more of administrative skill, or that semblance of it which practice gives, in the details of business; a State which dwarfs its men, in order that they may be more docile instruments in its hands even for beneficial purposes – will find that with small men no great thing can really be accomplished; and that the perfection of machinery to which it has sacrificed everything will in the end avail it nothing, for want of the vital power which, in order that the machine might work more smoothly, it has preferred to banish'.[1]

[1] John Stuart Mill, *On Liberty*, Blackwell, Oxford, 1948, p. 104.

Expanding Local Government

From G. D. H. Cole, The Future of Local Government, Cassell, London, 1921, pp. 36–43.

The importance of this work lies in its recognition of the necessity of a regional scale of organization. In this extract, the initiative for regionalism is clearly seen as stemming from local government rather than parliamentary devolution; but Cole is much less parochial in his arguments than most contemporary reformers of local government. His later work, *Local and Regional Government,* continues the argument but is mainly concerned with expounding Cole's rather complex regional apparatus.

Regional Administration *versus* 'Devolution'

Throughout the preceding chapters I have stated the case for regional organization mainly in terms of Local Government, and have represented it as involving an extension of the scope and functions of the local authorities rather than as a scheme of parliamentary devolution. It carries with it, no doubt, a devolution of the work of Parliament, and this is an essential feature of any regionalist scheme, and one of its strongest recommendations. But it is fatal to the whole idea of regional organization that it should be treated as a proposal for the multiplication of Parliaments, instead of as one for the expansion of Local Government. For the methods and forms which are required in the regional bodies whose constitution is suggested are those not of the 'Mother of Parliaments,' but, far more nearly, of the Borough Councils which administer our great urban centres to-day.

There is, therefore, nothing positive in common between the proposals put forward in this book and the suggestion that subordinate Parliaments should be set up for England, Scotland and Wales. The doing of this, whether or not it is desirable, would not affect the case for regional organization. There is indeed common to the two proposals the negative argument based on the present congestion of Parliament; but it is clear enough that, even if it made this congestion slightly less, parliamentary devolution could in fact do little to remove it. The impossible burden of administrative supervision, and of dealing with all the internal legislation required by the various interests and Departments, would still remain upon the subordinate Parliaments; and before long the position would become again as bad as it is now. I am not concerned to argue the question whether, on national grounds, 'Home Rule' for Scotland, Wales and England is, or is not, necessary to national self-expression; but the proposal for regional organization must be clearly distinguished from this quite different question.

It is very unfortunate that the two have, so far, been continually confused. It is perhaps inevitable that a Committee appointed by Parliament should be quite unable to escape from the point of view of the parliamentary politician, as the recent House of Commons Committee on Devolution clearly was; but there is no such excuse for those who have not the misfortune to be members of Parliament. The Devolution Committee appears merely to have dismissed, without any attempt to examine it, the proposal to establish areas of government on a 'provincial' or regional basis. They were only considering the establishment of more Parliaments; and any proposal to set up a dozen or more 'Parliaments' is manifestly absurd.

We have to escape from the parliamentary obsession in order to tackle the vital problems of government and administration in any constructive way. Mr. F. W. Jowett's name has, indeed, become closely connected with a proposal that the methods of conducting parliamentary business should be remodelled largely on the basis of the existing procedure of local authorities. His projected 'Committee System' for Parliament, which has little or nothing in common with the Committee Systems already in operation in certain foreign legislatures, is in essence an adaptation of the procedure of the Bradford City Council to the business of the House of Commons. As a proposed reform of present parliamentary methods there is a very great deal to be said in its favour; but in facing the problem of regional administration we shall be well advised to have nothing to do with 'Parliaments,' however modified, and to build openly and completely on the basis of Local Government methods and procedure.

The whole problem, indeed, is in its essence administrative rather than legislative. I am well aware that, in practice, it is increasingly difficult to draw any clear line between administration and legislation; and, given the proper reorganization of the structure of government, there is no reason why such a line should be clearly drawn. But there is a broad distinction which it is necessary here to keep in mind. Whenever the nationalization of any industry or service is suggested, it is always pointed out that the machinery of Parliament is extraordinarily unsuitable for the administration, or even for the effective supervision, of such nationalized services, both because the politician has no expert knowledge of or concern in them, and because, under the conditions of General Elections and parliamentary business, no real popular control can be exercised, or mandate secured, on matters which are not, in any reasonable sense of the word, political.

Now, the work of the present local authorities is very largely administrative, and has been developed principally with a view to the administration and supervision of services. This is the case even where the local authority has not taken any steps in the direction of what is known as 'Municipal Socialism'; for every authority has to concern itself with the administration and supervision of 'non-trading' services, such as those concerned with public health, if not also of 'trading' services. I do not pretend to believe that the machinery of the local authorities is suitable for the control of industrial administration; for, as a Guild Socialist, I hold that the responsibility for this ought to be placed upon the workers organized as producers rather than as consumers; but I do believe that, so far as the machinery of any 'consumers' body can be fitted for it, that of the local authorities is so fitted, and that, while neither they nor any other body of consumers will conduct the administration of industry in the coming Society, they can and will play an important part in supervision and in the ultimate control of industries and services jointly with the organized producers. This point I have discussed in other books, and it is to some extent dealt with in later chapters of this book; but, whatever conclusion may be reached with regard to it, the contention that Local Government machinery is far better adapted than national State machinery for dealing with the control and supervision of industries and public services is in no wise affected. 'Politics,' if such a thing need exist, may be the province of 'political' bodies: industrial and service administration plainly demands the care of a very different form of organization.

I shall, therefore, continue throughout this book to treat the problem of regionalization as essentially a problem of Local Government, whatever sacrifice of dignity confirmed parliamentarians may consider such a method of treatment to involve. For I, at least, take a very different view of the respective dignities of Parliament and of the local authorities from that of the ordinary advocate of parliamentary institutions. Local Government to-day is indeed vitiated, like Parliament, by that fundamental cause of human ills – the capitalist system; but with the abolition of capitalism Local Government is capable of demonstrating at once the essential sanity of the principles on which it is based, whereas the victory of economic democracy may well serve only to show up further the final futility of Parliament as an instrument of government and administration.

The problem, then, which we shall have to face in the next chapter is not how far the present area of the State can be divided by the creation of subordinate legislatures, but how far the local authorities can be integrated over wider areas. I do not mean that the function of the integrated regional authorities which I am proposing will not be to some extent legislative: undoubtedly it will be. But if we start from the legislative end we shall get all our proportions wrong. We must tackle the problem first from the standpoint of administration, and only thereafter proceed to consider how far the creation of these wider administrative bodies involves, or makes desirable, the direct devolution of legislative power. All administration carries with it in some degree a power of legislation in detail: the degree of legislative devolution that is desirable, and also the whole form to be assumed by the legislative power in the future, will be far more easily considered when we have dealt more fully with the administrative problem.

We have, then, next to consider in more detail what we mean when we speak of 'regional organization' – a phrase which has been used so far almost without explanation. Certain indications have, indeed, already been given, and certain distinguishing marks of the 'Region' exhibited. We have seen, for example, that it is of the essence of the Region that it should embrace both urban and rural areas, and should be not, like the present local authorities, either a town or a country authority, but necessarily both. We have seen that it must possess a certain homogeneity, both economic and social; but we have not attempted to define wherein the necessary conditions of this homogeneity are to be found.

The constitution of regional bodies has been advocated by persons of very diverse temperaments and scientific equipments, and different advocates have laid very varying stresses on the distinct factors which have to be taken into account. The pure geographer, for example, will draw – and has drawn – one regional map of England, where the economic geographer will draw – and has drawn – a different one. The expert in language and dialect would draw yet another, and the transport expert another again. Indeed, there is hardly a form of scientific knowledge or expert concern that might not be made the basis of a different regional map. In France, where Regionalism has a far longer and more controversial history than in this country, numerous rival maps have actually been drawn. Historians with royalist sympathies have proposed the restoration of the pre-revolutionary Provinces of the Kingdom of France; Socialists have drawn maps based mainly on economic considerations; another school has based almost its whole case on the building up of each regional area around a definite and clearly indicated capital city.

I do not profess, in the suggestions which follow, to base my case on any one predominant principle, least of all that of geography. Geographical features, it appears to me, are only important for regional organization in so far as they are actually reflected, or are likely to be reflected, in other factors. Geography obviously determines, to a great extent, the location of industry; but it is the present and probably future location of industry, and not the geographical feature itself, that, when military considerations are absent, is important from the standpoint of government and administration. Geographical features have also a powerful effect on language, customs, and social feeling on the one hand, and on transport and methods of communication on the other; but the geographical causes are important for government only if they manifest themselves, or are likely to manifest themselves, in these and other social and economic results. In some of the regional schemes which have been put forward, and particularly in one proposed about three years ago by a committee of geographers called upon to advise the Government, it appears to me that far too much importance in the drawing of boundaries was attached to pure geography. Mr Fawcett, whose draft regional schemes are the best considered that have yet been produced, is primarily an economic geographer, and is not nearly so prone to such mistakes.

But, while the map of each expert will differ according to his particular expertise, I believe it would be found, if a dozen committees, consisting each of a single kind of experts, were set to draw a dozen regional maps of England, that there would be a strong resemblance among all their plans. They might look very different, because they would all place their actual boundaries at rather different points; but the 'heart' of the Region is, after all, of more importance than the precise point at which its boundaries are drawn, and I believe that the 'hearts' would, in the majority of cases, be the same, however much the apparent shape and conformation of the proposed Regions might vary. This contention is, of course, not susceptible of definite proof unless the actual experiment is made; but a good deal of evidence in support of it can be produced by an examination of the actual regional areas of administration which have been adopted for a wide variety of purposes by Government Departments, Trade Unions, and all manner of voluntary bodies.

For the Region is not a new thing, nor need we begin in the dark the drawing of the regional map of Great Britain. Not only have many theoretical plans been produced: regional areas of administration exist already for an immense number of different purposes.

It does not, of course, follow, merely because an arrangement of areas has been found, in the existing circumstances, convenient for a particular purpose, that it would be convenient for all, or that it is regarded, even by those who have adopted it, as in itself the best possible arrangement for their immediate purposes. It is often necessary to adapt one arrangement of areas to another, even if this involves a sacrifice of real suitability. For example, the areas of the Housing Commissioners follow, everywhere except in the Metropolitan district, the boundaries of the Administrative Counties; for since the County Councils are important housing authorities, it is manifest that each County must fall entirely within the jurisdiction of a single Housing Commissioner. But it does not follow that the existing County areas afford in themselves the best possible boundaries for housing and town-planning purposes.

Similarly, there may be good reasons for a greater sub-division of areas in the administration of some functions than of others, and plainly a scheme based on the recognition of, say, thirty Regions cannot bear a close resemblance to one which allows for only ten or a dozen. But, even where such variations occur, it may be possible to trace the working of a common principle, and the minuter areas may be found, on examination, to be, in the main, actual sub-divisions of the larger.

Radical Progress: *The Economist*
From The Economist, 18th May, 1963.

The Economist has often campaigned for structural reform in government, and this is one of a number of articles on this theme. These views were expressed six years before the Royal Commisssion on Local Government published its report; more than two year before Mr Crossman spoke his mind to the Association of Municipal. Corporations – yet reaction remained the order of the day.

Federal Britain's New Frontiers
Nobody really believes in Britain's present local democracy: it should be scrapped and replaced with a viable organisation by regions

Local government in Britain is a godsend to the temperamentally disgruntled. If roads are unmade, school meals ill-served, planning decisions muffed, policemen insolent, rents high, 'the council' gets the blame. The most monstrous errors of Whitehall are errors of principle. They can never attract a personalised fury like that which greets the council dustman's misdemeanours in refuse collection. This year, local government has been at the centre of three whopping political rows, over teachers' pay, London government and rating revision But in last week's council elections a mere 40-odd per cent of the voters bothered to go to the polls: and the psephologists have established, in exhaustive detail, that a straight projection from local election results can show how the nation would vote at a general election. Local elections are a rite in which the more politically involved part of the population goes through motions of voting, unaffected by truly local issues, in accordance with national preconceptions.

Britain, from the urban district of Saint Just to the district of Tongue and Farr (via, perhaps, the Soke of Peterborough and the two Machynlleths, urban and rural) is a network of superimposed and elected local bodies. Their origins may lie in the petulant gift of a medieval autocrat, or the tired decision of a Victorian committeeman: once in being, each authority acquires a pseudo-historical dignity, participation in which is the only reward of its members. Even that local government unit created for the most brutally rational of nineteenth-century reasons – the London County Council – has acquired a corps of passionate defenders now that the brutal rationale of a new age demands that it be replaced.

There is a certain logic about local government boundaries: but it is a logic that splits towns from the countryside in which they are set, that has no bearing on the demands of economic necessity, of historical growth, of spreading communications, of urban sprawl, of booming population. Green belts and national parks spread through the domains of several authorities, needing each an *ad hoc*, hence administratively expensive, body for their supervision: conurbations lack even this much co-ordination. The most adventurous, coherent and successful experiment in regional development, economic and humane, has been the creation of the new towns: but when a new town is planted on the countryside, responsibility for its early development is vested in a corporation directly responsible to Whitehall.

There exists, of course, machinery for reviewing the extent of local authorities' responsibilities. The local government commissions for each of the four kingdoms keep a watching brief on the map. The English boundary commission had to be supplemented by a Royal Commission on London, and even this high-powered body funked the question of what to do with the City whose population of 5,000 lies at the centre of London city. In five 'special review areas' – the intensely populated city-regions of Tyneside, West Yorkshire, South-east Lancashire, Merseyside and the West Midlands – the local government commission can unify the cities; but they remain cut off from the countryside around. In rural areas, the commission's recommendations do tend towards the creation of larger, thus fewer, local government areas (its timid report on East Anglia is examined on page 666). But the commission has no power to change the basic conception of boundaries, which is to draw lines separating urban from rural areas, to perpetuate the pattern of the county borough as an independent authority divorced from its rural setting. The one really drastic official proposal for reform, by the post-war Local Government Boundary Commission in 1948, was dropped like a hot brick by subsequent governments. Local government remains too diverse, too locally particularist, and too hard to adapt to change.

What we shall consider now is an entirely new pattern of policies under which each region of the country would be able to realise its full potential as a contributor to the wealth and happiness of each Briton. The operative word is each *region*: the county, or the city, is too small a unit when populations are counted by the hundred thousand, and motorway mileages push up (so much too slowly) into the hundreds. The planner may spend hours with an atlas: each map will, in its own way, mislead. Physical features are no longer obstacles to travel (the English Channel itself awaits a mere technical decision between tunnel and bridge until its days as an obstacle are numbered). The administrative map is a clutter of historic anomalies. The most important map is that which shows how the population of this island is spread, with cruel inequality, across its surface; it is for those people – not for sectional interests like shipbuilders or miners or Welshmen – that the new regions must be laid out.

The first need, then, is to offer to each block of population the space that it needs for expansion, economic and domestic. The profile of the land – not imposing barriers, but marking out the windy and inhospitable open spaces that offer recreation but no rest – is the first ally. To each great lump of population can be assigned a less populous, but potentially habitable, space for expansion: between the new regions the frontiers can be drawn across the least habitable ground. From the mouth of the Mersey down to the Staffordshire potteries, only a narrow greyish green belt divides the great cities; here the industrial concentration up from what used to be the terminus of western trade, and the historical burden of the cotton industry's development, must be forcefully countered.

This, it is proposed, will be done by opening up to the dignified capital of Liverpool the underdeveloped wastes of north Wales (via an easily constructed road-and-rail link obliterating the obstacles of the Mersey and Dee estuaries). Manchester, in turn, gets the land running north to the Lake District mountains. The siting of these two provincial capitals on the edge of their provinces must give them an incentive to develop and expand into the neglected regions whose resistance to change, in an elected regional assembly, can be quelled by the massed votes from the cities. Elsewhere, provincial capitals select themselves at the heart of viable regions. Britain, then, it can be envisaged, might have sixteen regional assemblies, and a national parliament whose members, freed of the constant pressure to bring up pettifogging constituency points, would have the time and the opportunity to think about national policy. The national government would continue to levy by far the greater proportion of taxes (although a regional income tax, sales tax, or whatever, might be raised by the provinces); the tune on education and the social services would evidently continue to be called from the centre, where the money comes from, but with ample room for diversity and experiment. (Northern Ireland, which already has a large nominal autonomy on social questions, rarely deviates from the national norm since it depends for money on the Whitehall treasury.)

The most important economic job of the 'federal' parliament, on the domestic side, would at first be its responsibility for the national trunk road network. The chief purpose of this network would be to counteract the excessive economic importance conferred on London in the last century by the railways. Next in importance would come its

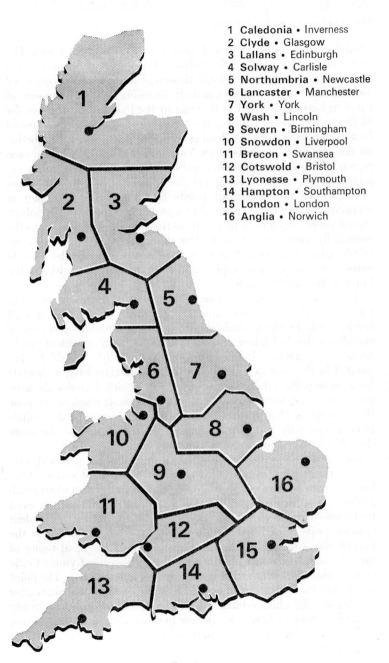

1 Caledonia • Inverness
2 Clyde • Glasgow
3 Lallans • Edinburgh
4 Solway • Carlisle
5 Northumbria • Newcastle
6 Lancaster • Manchester
7 York • York
8 Wash • Lincoln
9 Severn • Birmingham
10 Snowdon • Liverpool
11 Brecon • Swansea
12 Cotswold • Bristol
13 Lyonesse • Plymouth
14 Hampton • Southampton
15 London • London
16 Anglia • Norwich

FIG. 4.

administration of the National Economic Equalisation Fund. The map shows how Carlisle in Solway, Plymouth in Lyonesse and Inverness in Caledonia would rule those regions that, in over-congested Britain, are sorely underpopulated: financing the development of these regions – a project like that run by the Palermo government for Sicily, backed by the funds of the *Cassa per il Mezzogiorno* – should be a main function of the federal government (in its seat of Elizabetha, on the now open moors between York and Harrogate?). Within each region, the provincial government would be empowered – even enjoined, at the risk of being penalised under the equalisation tax principle – to choose growth points that would (for example) in Snowdon attract people away from congested Liverpool, and in Solway attract people (including people from the congested regions) into the potentially rich Carlisle area. The differential tax – preferably on employment, but possibly a sales tax – would naturally be used to encourage a dispersal of employment from the congested cities of the London–Birmingham belt.

With seats of effective regional government in sixteen parts of the island, the preponderance – and the number – of the central civil service could be vastly diminished: meanwhile a middle-class core of spenders – the legislators and civil servants, with attendant stock-brokers, managers, administrators, even journalists – could be implanted in the provincial capital, which would thus have a clientele for a metropolitan-style pattern of services (which includes the arts, now so sadly neglected outside London) in tolerable reach of everyone in the country. That this has not happened in American state capitals is no reason why it might not happen in the far smaller, far more densely populated provinces of Britain.

One serious objection to these stargazing, but really practical, proposals will remain, even when the tradition-bound objections have been overridden. In a couple of dozen years from the start of regionalisation, the provinces may develop passionate local loyalties, even traditions, of their own. One can picture, in the future, the violent Geordie protests of Northumbria at a treaty seeming to favour the French above their kinsfolk, the Danes; or hear the nasal twang of Snowdonian delegations pleading for their Hibernian-Cymric Celtic culture. But every innovation in time ossifies into tradition. The point now is that local government as it is, less than one hundred years after the Act of 1888 which established it in recognisable form, has already ossified to a point where it is a danger to economic growth – and even, by bringing it into disrespect, to democracy.

Conservatism: *The Times*

From Ronald Butt, 'A Basis for Reform', *The Times*, 12th June, 1969.

In its leading article *The Times* made a brief reference to
regionalism 'in the sense of having from five to a dozen directly
elected regional authorities in England with wide powers' and
concluded: 'The question now stands over for consideration by the
Crowther commission, and nothing this commission has done or
omitted prejudices the outcome.' With that judgment we can
hardly concur. On the other side of the centre-fold in the same issue
of this newspaper Mr Butt's views were presented. These certainly
do not leave the issue unprejudiced; but Mr Butt is also author of
'The Power of Parliament' and no doubt he is as much concerned
to protect it against attacks from the regionalists as well as from
the encroaching power of Whitehall and Downing Street.

Those who find the Radcliffe-Maud plan inadequately radical will
almost certainly prefer a period of masterly inactivity in the hope that
Lord Crowther's constitutional commission may produce a more
revolutionary regional plan out of which a reformed structure of local
government could be fashioned.

Yet even if it had wished to do so, the Radcliffe-Maud commission
would not have been justified in advocating any thorough-going
scheme of regionalization since, to be effective, this would inevitably
demand a devolution of powers from the central Parliament which it
was not open to the inquiry on local government to recommend under
its terms of reference. In any case, regional devolution is not, I think,
the answer to Britain's problems in the twentieth century.

Until recently, it has been the lamentable fact that anyone in Britain
who sought success made straight for London and, within our social
structure, it has never been fashionable to live anywhere else – except
the country. This may be changing as a result of new industrial areas,
new universities, and the dispersal of what may be loosely called the
"new graduate" population. But I do not think that in a country the
size of Britain there is any need or logical basis for the installation of
regional authorities that can compete for government with the centre.

. . . The historical strength of England has always been the power of
the central authority and I do not think it would be either sensible or
feasible to retreat far from that tradition now. Eventually it may be
politically necessary to establish separate Parliaments for Scotland and

Wales, on the Ulster model. This would impose some degree of financial autonomy and self provision on Scotland and Wales, and if these countries did not succeed in being effectively self-supporting they would have to be seen to be receiving open subsidy. If that is what Wales and Scotland want – that is what they want. But it is no justification for anything like a full regional system in the United Kingdom as a whole.

The Radcliffe-Maud commission, therefore, is right to make the proposed regional councils dependent on the main operational bodies below them for their membership and on the sanction of the central government to ensure the implementation of their plans by the main operational units of local government.

Editor's note: Small things sometimes loom large: the name of the Royal Commission's chairman was used no less than eight times in this short article, and was wrongly spelt on each occasion. One cannot help but feel that Mr Butt was less concerned to understand the problems of local government reform and regionalism than to protect the power and status of the central Parliament.

Status Quo: County Councils Association

From County Councils Association, *Royal Commission on Local Government in England – Memorandum of Views on the Report of the Commission*, London, 1969, p. 12.

This memorandum records the reaction of the County Councils Association to the Royal Commission's proposals. The following extract comes from that part of the memorandum which suggests modifications to the Commission's scheme.

It is the view of the Association that there should not be an intermediate level of government between central government and the main local authorities. They agree, however, that there is need for a formal method of consultation, with a view to co-ordination of planning in the wider sense, between the main local authorities grouped over regional or provincial areas and between these groups of authorities and central government. This consultation would be concerned with national policies that affect local authorities and also with the co-ordination of the actions of local authorities when undertaking their statutory functions, particularly in planning matters, insofar as they may affect one another. The creation of provincial councils for this purpose would be supported by the Association who would accept a limited amount of co-option on to the Council from interests outside local and central government although it is their view that these councils should be made up predominantly of representatives of the local authorities. Provincial councils should not have executive statutory functions and should be advisory only but it would appear to be necessary for them to have a small planning staff, to advise them on problems in the planning and economic planning field.

The Association entirely reserve their position as to the devolution of any central government functions to provincial councils until they have considered the wider matters which lie within the terms of reference of the Commission on the Constitution (the Crowther Commission).

Moderate Progress: Association of Municipal Corporations

From Association of Municipal Corporations, *Reorganisation of Local Government in England*, London, November 1970, pp. 1–4 and 6.

The Association of Municipal Corporations has consistently argued that the reform of local government should result in the great bulk of services being left in the hands of local authorities. In its comments in November 1969 on the proposals of the Royal Commission on Local Government it grudgingly accepted the principles of reform advocated by the Royal Commission, but thought that the number of provinces proposed was too few, the areas of some of them too great, and that many of the proposed unitary areas of local authorities were too large. In a further paper, a year later, the Association appears to move slightly further along the road towards regional authorities with its proposal for a 'dual system of provinces and most-purpose authorities'. Following the line of the earlier comments the Association has suggested 13 provinces and 132 most-purpose authorities, compared with the Royal Commission's 8 provinces and 61 main areas, but in allocating functions the Association gives rather more to the provinces than the Royal Commission proposed. Nevertheless, this apparent move towards regionalism is somewhat deceptive for, like the Royal Commission, the Association does not envisage the direct election by the populace of the members of the provincial councils. This, and other elements of primacy accorded to the local authorities, is the crucial weakness in the scheme. The following extracts explain the Association's proposals relating to the constitution and powers of the provincial councils which it proposed.

THE GENERAL APPROACH

1. Since the announcement of the appointment in 1966 of the Royal Commission on Local Government in England the Association has not departed from its traditional preference for the all-purpose form of local government wherever this can be achieved, but, recognising that for certain purposes, few in number and usually limited in scope, a wider area of planning or administration may be required, has consistently advocated a dual system of provinces and most-purpose authorities. This system was proposed in the Association's written evidence to the Royal Commission, supported and amplified in the oral evidence of its representatives and has been endorsed in its comments on the Royal Commission's report and on the last Govern-

ment's White Paper: 'Local Government Reform in England' (Cmnd. 4276). Following discussion at a Special Meeting of the Association on 12th March, 1970, meetings of member corporations have been held in various parts of the country to discuss in greater detail how the dual system recommended by the Association could be applied locally in all parts of England. Consideration of the results of these meetings has led the Reorganisation of Local Government Sub-Committee and the General Purposes Committee to prepare this general paper, which elaborates the functions appropriate for provincial councils, discusses how far the requirements of these functions would be likely to affect the number and size of provinces, and consequentially will bear, along with the needs of the functions remaining for the main local authorities, on the number and size of the latter.

2. The Association believes that only by the adoption of such a dual system in any local government reorganisation will democratic control continue to have meaning. It is of as much importance now as it has always been that the emphasis in any tiered system of local authorities should be at the level closest to the people. Only by so concentrating the responsibilities of elected members and at the lower level giving them effective oversight of the major services of vital personal significance to the community, can the public identify satisfactorily with the local authority and use the electoral process for the purpose for which it was designed.

THE PROVINCE AND THE PROVINCIAL COUNCIL

3. The size and number of provinces will best be determined by the functions to be entrusted to provincial councils, qualified by consideration of extent, cohesiveness and manageability in the sense of size of council needed to secure adequate representation of all the constituent areas, and in the determination of precise boundaries by socio-economic factors. It is on account of these qualifying considerations that the areas of the present eight economic planning regions, adopted with only small variations by the Redcliffe-Maud Commission, are not all appropriate for adoption as provinces of the kind the Association has envisaged. Some may, with minor adjustments be suitable but others require more radical adjustment even though this may mean, particularly in an area like South-East England, close and continuous inter-provincial collaboration and co-operation. The all-important requirements are that the provincial councils should be able to assume responsibility for those local government functions which are too wide-ranging to be undertaken by any existing local authorities and that they should be capable of receiving responsibilities devolved upon them from central government.

4. The first main function of the provincial councils must be to undertake the strategic planning for each province, settling the framework and priorities within which the main local authorities will plan their policies and major investment programmes. Responsibility for the strategic planning of the province will involve:

(1) town and country planning, i.e. the preparation of the overall master plan in broad outline (mainly in the form of written statements rather than maps or plans),

(2) the determination of the main highway network,

(3) traffic and transportation planning,

(4) overspill housing, where the function will be strictly confined to planning but not building or management,

(5) the co-ordination of refuse disposal, and

(6) unless more extensive powers of allocation are devolved by central government, the co-ordination, in association with the local authorities in the province, of capital programmes to ensure that the programmes collectively reflect strategic planning policy.

5. In relation to several of these matters standing conferences of local planning authorities were established, some many years ago, by the spontaneous action of the constituent bodies to facilitate the study of common problems and consultation on matters of common concern. Following the establishment in 1964 and 1965 of regional economic planning councils to provide machinery for assessing the economic potential of each region, for assisting in the formulation of regional plans within the framework of the national plan and for advising on their implementation and on the regional implications of national and economic policies, the standing conferences were further developed to maintain a dialogue with the new economic planning councils where the matters with which these bodies sought to deal had implications in relation to physical planning. It would be feasible and sensible for the provincial councils to supersede the standing conferences and to absorb such work as they and the regional economic planning councils may have endeavoured to undertake in relation to the distribution of population, migration, location of growth points, with their resulting implications for employment, housing and transport, provincial patterns of road and rail communications, and the siting of airports and of cultural and sporting facilities to serve the various parts of the regions.

6. Experience has shown that the standing conferences have not been particularly successful in their relations with the economic planning

councils and the economic planning councils themselves lack acceptability because of their nature as appointed bodies. The effectiveness of the standing conferences is impaired by several factors. Foremost among these is probably their lack of professional and technical staff able to devote their time to the work with which the conferences have sought to concern themselves, aggravated by an inadequacy of supporting administrative staffs to organise the work of the conferences and to bring together the results of the studies undertaken on their behalf. This work is, moreover, made more difficult by the consensual character of the conferences: they have no powers other than those given to them with the agreement of all the constituent bodies and are accordingly unable to require the production of information by constituent bodies or their active co-operation in investigation and research. Additionally the membership of the standing conferences is not drawn from all the local authorities in the area having statutory responsibility for the provision of the services sought to be planned. They would not, therefore, be able to take over the work of the regional economic planning councils and so long as two separate bodies of this kind exist, side by side, divergencies of objective and of the means to attain objectives will persist.

7. The Association's analysis of the position is supported by the recent report of the South East Joint Planning Team, *Strategic Plan for the South East*, which frankly states the present limitations and difficulties. The provincial councils proposed by the Association would be ideally placed to undertake the work envisaged by the Team, furthermore, the failure to reconcile economic planning and land use planning would be largely remedied by combining in the provincial councils the roles of the existing bodies now separately concerned with each. This would also provide what is at present lacking, namely, a regional machinery for co-ordinating sub-regional studies.

8. All these considerations point to the conclusion that provincial councils need to have appropriate professional staff under their own control and powers to secure the implementation of planning strategy.

11. The provincial council would be responsible also for the strategic planning of functions incapable of being discharged by any existing local authority, acting on its own, for which purpose it has already been necessary to try to make special co-ordinating arrangements. These include the oversight of:

(7) the local authority sector of higher education,

(8) the distribution of special schools,

(9) the provision of adequate accommodation for children in care,

(10) the development of major cultural and recreational services, and

(11) the development of tourism generally and especially in those places where several local authorities are concerned.

12. The problems of the local authority sector of higher education have already made it necessary for local education authorities to try to find the means of more collective involvement. The allocation of national resources for higher education depends upon an unsatisfactory relationship at the present time between the Department of Education and Science at the one end and individual local education authorities at the other. The regional advisory councils that have been brought into being have a relationship with the Department in connection, especially, with the approval of courses in establishments of further education but the concerned local authority Associations have already agreed that it is necessary for local government, through the Associations, to develop a central Joint Committee through which the totality of the local authority interest can be more effectively expressed and pursued. To do this satisfactorily the Joint Committee will need to make use of the regional advisory councils or something approximating to them if the planning of the local authority higher education provision by individual authorities is to be reasonably controlled and at the same time adequately inter-related. The existence of provincial councils would enable the function of the regional advisory councils, which is essentially one of educational planning, to be brought into close relationship to the other overall strategic considerations which will operate at this level.

13. The need for accommodation in special schools varies considerably from one authority to another and it is likely for many years to be necessary for authorities to co-operate with each other in providing it. The function of the provincial council would be to ensure as far as possible that the requirements of the province as a whole are met by provision within the province, not by becoming a providing authority itself but by securing that where economy, efficiency and convenience are served by one authority providing a special school to meet the needs of others, the accommodation is planned and made available accordingly, appropriate inter-authority payments for use being made in the customary way. In planning the provision of community homes for children in care, the provincial council would be taking over the responsibilities of the regional planning committees for which provision was made in the Children and Young Persons Act 1969. This is a statutory recognition of the need for bodies covering a larger area of the country than any existing local authority

and of the inability of existing authorities on their own to undertake planning on a broad enough scale.

14. Regional organisations for the encouragement of the arts, for the support of orchestras and for museums co-operation have been developed since the war. They operate unevenly over the country and the extent of local authority co-operation and support varies considerably. Regional sports councils were established in 1966 to plan requirements for sport and recreation in relation to other aspects of regional planning and to advise the Government through the Sports Council of the problems, pressures and priorities in each region. Provincial councils would provide a better basis for many aspects of the work undertaken by these bodies and they could be used to provide a link with local government at the regional level, without necessarily interfering with the direct and often close relationships which can exist between the regional bodies and individual local authorities.

15. In addition to the functions referred to above, it is suggested that provincial councils should provide:

(12) the regional tier for the health services, or, if these are to be separated from local government, the local government body to be linked with any regional body which may be established for the health services and which should cover a co-terminous area.

Furthermore the provincial council could undertake such executive functions as are required in connection with:

(13) ambulances, unless and until separated from local government with the health services,

(14) the fire service,

(15) the police and

(16) the bulk supply of water.

16. The services referred to at 15 (13), (14) and (15) are stand-to services which need to be deployed over wide areas. The police service is already organised on an ad hoc basis and some existing police forces cover areas which include more than one of the proposed unitary authorities of the Redcliffe-Maud Commission and of the last Government's White Paper. The Holroyd Committee on the Fire Service have expressed the view that the fire service needs to be organised in units equivalent to thirty-station brigades, and that on this basis the majority of the unitary authorities proposed by the Redcliffe-Maud Commission and adopted in the White Paper would be too small to be independent fire authorities.

17. It is arguable that the present organisation of the police service, most frequently with combined forces, and the organisation of the fire service proposed by the Holroyd Committee do not suggest the need for areas as extensive as the provinces envisaged by the Association, and that the forces and brigades which would result would be larger than any which at present exist in this country, except perhaps the Metropolitan Police and the London Fire Brigade. Objections which there might be on account of size, however, can readily be overcome by the adoption of a divisional organisation. On the credit side the existence of a force or brigade organised on a divisional basis would facilitate arrangements for deployment and reinforcement as well as provide opportunities for the improvement of communications and the standardisation of equipment. The re-arrangement of Metropolitan Police divisions to correspond to the areas of groups of London boroughs has resulted in close liaison in respect of police and local authority functions and the Holroyd Committee have suggested that the fire brigade organisation in the conurbations should be in separate commands of appropriate size for fire-fighting purposes. The Association would see these corresponding to the areas of a number of most-purpose authorities, and similar arrangements for police and fire could well apply outside the conurbations. More important than any of these, however, is the consideration that the control of these services would be in the hands of a responsible body forming an integral part of the local government structure and having multiple local government responsibilities; the alternative is to group some of the most-purpose authorities, for fire purposes particularly, and to confine any provincial function to the overall strategic planning of the service.

18. Regarding the bulk supply of water, referred to at 15 (16), it is intended that the areas of the provinces should be determined, like those of the main authorities from which they will be constituted, with regard to geographical and other considerations. It is anticipated that many of the main local authorities will be statutory water undertakers for their areas but it may well be the case that not all will possess within their own areas supplies sufficient to meet the needs of their consumers. In these circumstances, subject to any overriding physical considerations, it would appear to be convenient and desirable to use the organisation of the provincial council to obtain and distribute a supply of water in bulk to make good the deficiencies in supplies required by the main local authorities.

19. The Association envisages that the provincial council should be the normal body to undertake the planning or exercise of functions which

need to be planned or performed for areas wider than those of the main local authorities. It has been one of the weaknesses of the present system that the areas of counties have frequently been too small for purposes such as these, with the result that ad hoc bodies have been created for a variety of special purposes. While these bodies may have been technically efficient the fact that they have operated in isolation from the main functions of local government has prevented the consideration of relative priorities and the like by any body other than the central government. Inevitably this has led to an imbalance as between one function and another and in some cases to a less than satisfactory use of resources.

20. It has been suggested that the discharge of a multiplicity of responsibilities by provincial councils, the membership of which would be derived from the local authorities within the province, would be beyond the capacity of the members. Additionally, doubts have been expressed as to the practicability of staffing the provincial councils with the expertise that they will require without doing harm to the administration of the local authorities in related fields. In regard to the latter, the Association would distinguish between the expertise and specialist support required for the strategic planning functions of the province and the detailed activities to be undertaken within the broad strategy by the local authorities. As to the membership of provincial councils, it is, and the Association hopes will long remain, an important part of the responsibilities of the elected member serving in local government to relate priorities over a very wide field and in so doing to be directly concerned with the infrastructure of communities. Some areas in respect of which such responsibilities have to be exercised are already large and no suggestion has been made that elected members are inherently incompetent to continue to fulfil their traditional role. Insofar as it might be necessary for certain elected members to develop a specialist responsibility if there is still to be a democratic oversight of the development of services, there is no reason why provincial councils should not make use of panels of such specialists who would not all necessarily be members of the provincial council itself but could be drawn from the local authorities and otherwise as might be necessary.

21. Apart from these functions derived from local government or from other regional bodies, the provincial council would be in the best position to accept devolution of functions from the central government in accordance with the declared intention of the present Administration. Any such devolution would presumably be subject to the right of central government to determine any national plan or series of

social priorities, to ensure conformity of a provincial plan to the national aims and to safeguard the national economy. Subject thereto provincial councils might take over from central government the approval of the structure plans of local authorities, the allocation of the provincial shares of the national investment programme, and the exercise of controls still retained by way, for example, of approval of byelaws, default powers and the giving of directions. The extent to which the functions of inspection and advice are shared between central government and provincial councils would depend upon the nature of the service in question and the character of the inspection undertaken.

NUMBER OF PROVINCES

24. How many provinces there should be is a matter which can only be settled in the light of the decisions ultimately taken on the functions which they are to exercise and the consideration of the conurbation areas as suggested above, but to some extent the number and size of provinces and the number and size of the main local authorities are inter-related. At present there are eight economic planning regions for England, and despite the recommendations of the Redcliffe-Maud Commission, which proposed provinces broadly similar to the economic planning regions, there has been widespread support for the Association's view that several of these regions are too large. Clearly, however, if the provincial councils are to be strong bodies capable of taking over functions of central government, they cannot be too numerous.

25. The second Green Paper on the N.H.S. proposed a regional organisation related to the fourteen hospital regions and although the boundaries of these have been drawn solely with regard to hospital provision the number is within the outer limits mentioned by the Association in oral evidence to the Redcliffe-Maud Commission. At present there are forty-four police authorities in England (including the City of London and the Metropolitan Police Authority) and any further change in the number is likely to be in the direction of a reduction rather than an increase. The main question would appear to be how few police authorities is it desirable to have if the traditional link between the police and local government is to be maintained and the nationalisation of the police force avoided. As already recalled, the Holroyd Committee have proposed a substantial reduction in the number of fire authorities – about forty for the country as a whole. This in their view was the upper limit.

26. Functional requirements referred to in this paper will necessitate

areas of substantial size; and the meetings of member corporations, to which reference has earlier been made, have allowed account to be taken of the views of members and officers throughout the country. There can be no denying the feeling in local government that if certain parts of the country are to have the benefit of public investment and the development of services in the best interests of the people, greater unity of purpose is required than has so far been achieved. The Crowther Commission on the Constitution is charged by its terms of reference by implication with the identification of areas which lend themselves to a proper definition of 'region'. What the Association has found is a broad acceptance of the illustrations, based on the facts of physical geography, which were presented to the Redcliffe-Maud Commission in oral evidence.

27. In the smaller number of provinces then instanced, namely eleven, there was not in fact a great divergence, except in the South-East, from the regions recommended ultimately by the Redcliffe-Maud Commission. The Association's illustration was very much a broad brush illustration and the determination of detailed boundaries needs more study supported by expert knowledge and particularly, the Association would suggest, freedom from undue consideration of existing county boundaries. In the South of England it is suggested that the areas broadly comprising the South-West and the South-East provinces recommended by the Redcliffe-Maud Commission should be recast to make four or five provinces but much, in this area, will depend upon the view which is taken in relation to metropolitan areas to which reference has been made in paras. 22 and 23.

CONCLUSION

41. The Association believes that any reorganisation of the local government structure must, if it is to be successful, produce a simplified and clear-cut system capable of being understood by the average citizen. The proposed structure of provinces and most-purpose local authorities fully meets this requirement and also brings together town and country in a meaningful way and so as to be more likely to avoid the domination of the one by the other than is feared of other proposals. The twin aims of reform are the creation of a high degree of effectiveness and the greatest measure of democratic control compatible with efficiency and economy. If this paper appears to have concentrated on the former it is because the democratic advantages of the structure the Association has proposed are so obvious. In amplifying the case for the establishment of provincial councils with membership derived from the new most-purpose local authorities, reference has already been made to the fact that, in the

absence of any such bodies, many decisions are taken centrally – and Departmentally at that – which ought to be subject to much more local influence. The involvement of elected members at the level of provincial councils would represent a considerable democratic advance. Additionally and in conjunction with this involvement, the pattern of most-purpose authorities the Association has evolved will allow those elected for a definite community to take the decisions on the major local government matters affecting that community.

Radical Reform: Urban District Councils Association

From Urban District Councils Association, *Commission on the Constitution: Evidence of the UDCs Association*, London, April 1970, pp. 4–7.

The county and county borough councils could hope, by fighting for some increase in the number of authorities proposed by the Royal Commission on Local Government, that there could be some continuity between some of the existing councils and the new authorities. But the urban district councils could have no such hope – they were doomed to oblivion. The Urban District Councils Association had nothing to lose, therefore, in going much further along the regional road than its fellow associations.

SOME GENERAL OBSERVATIONS

6. In the post war years local government has, in part because of inadequacies of the present structure, lost functions to central government or to *ad hoc* bodies, notably the publicly maintained hospitals, gas and electricity and to some extent water supply.

7. During the same period nominated bodies have been created for specified purposes (e.g. regional economic planning councils) and local government itself has agreed to representation on regional bodies (e.g. sports councils, industrial development associations, tourist organisations).

8. The Association is strongly of opinion that as an integral part of the reorganisation of local government, this trend should be reversed. Services capable of being provided satisfactorily by local government as distinct from central government should be brought within the new local government structure at the most appropriate level. It is believed that this would require a system of district, area and provincial councils.

PROVINCIAL COUNCILS IN ENGLAND

9. In the evidence submitted to the Royal Commission on Local Government in England (referred to hereafter as the 'Maud Commission') the Association examined whether there was need for a wide-ranging authority to handle the problems thrown up by varied communities and was convinced that there ought to be a democratic unit which could influence national thought and, by interpreting the needs of a wide area, reflect to the Government and to Parliament the special requirements of that area. Such a democratic unit must cover an area larger than that of any existing local government authority.

Major traffic and transport schemes, major planning policies, public security and major recreational and cultural facilities could all be developed, thought the Association, in a unified manner over a wide area with the minimum of central control. The importance of economic problems was emphasised.

10. The Association, in its observations on the report of the Maud Commission, welcomed and supported (with reservations) that Commission's proposal for eight provincial councils based on, and arising out of the local government structure.

AREAS OF PROVINCIAL COUNCILS IN ENGLAND
11. The areas proposed by the Maud Commission for the eight provincial councils in England are broadly acceptable to the Association but boundaries need a detailed examination particularly as to their suitability for the exercise of executive functions by a provincial council. Any regional organisation of the central executive should have boundaries which coincide with the areas of provincial councils.

AN ELECTED WELSH COUNCIL
12. In the observations of the Association on the White Paper 'Local Government in Wales' (July, 1967; Cmnd. 3340), the view was expressed that the proposed Welsh Council – a nominated advisory and promotional body – had no place in the local government structure in Wales as it would serve only to delay and frustrate. On the other hand, the Association said that it would support the creation of a new Welsh Council which was democratically elected and had executive functions. References in the following paragraphs of this memorandum to 'provincial councils' are of equal relevance to a Welsh Council.

ELECTION OF PROVINCIAL COUNCILS
13. The Association is convinced that the case for democratic accountability through direct election is overwhelming, and would be opposed to any proposal for nominated provincial councils. Indeed, the argument for the transfer of functions from existing nominated bodies rests on the overriding need for greater democratic control at this level being secured by direct election.

14. In so far as co-option is concerned the Association opposes the Maud Commission's proposals. Technical skills will be available to provincial councils from their own staff but the Association sees no objection to a provincial council itself having a limited power (but not a duty) to co-opt persons of technical ability and experience to serve on committees established by the provincial council but not to serve on the council itself.

STAFFING OF PROVINCIAL COUNCILS
15. Officers serving provincial councils should be appointed by, and answerable to, that body. Civil servants at regional offices of the central government would be able to work closely with the staffs of provincial councils and there should be facilities for inter-change and secondment of staffs.

FUNCTIONS
16. Before discussing the functions believed to be appropriate to provincial councils the Association wishes to make clear its attitude towards any conflict which may arise on the allocation of functions to other levels of local government.

17. The Association advocates, and will continue to press for, the adoption of a local government structure consisting of provincial, area and district councils. There would be area councils (probably 35/40 in number) for the major services, and also district councils exercising directly those executive powers more appropriate to the district level.

18. If the study of the functions reveals that some could be exercised either at area or at provincial level then the Association believes that in such cases the functions should vest in the area council.

19. As mentioned in paragraph 9 above the Association sees the provincial councils dealing with major traffic and transport schemes, major planning policies, public security and major recreational and cultural facilities. For some of these purposes provincial councils would need to be responsible for executive action as well as for planning. In others the executive function could rest at area or district level with a reserve default power in the provincial council.

20(a). Provincial councils must be closely involved in economic planning and should therefore take over the responsibilities of the existing economic planning councils.

(b). The Association has argued for a long time that the machinery of the regional hospital boards is too remote and unresponsive to democratic influences and should, given the present system, provide for more adequate representation by elected members of local authorities. It concurs in the view of the Maud Commission that 'there can be no doubt that democratic control would be much more effectively secured by putting the (National Health) Service under the control of local authorities, directly answerable to the electorate and the citizens at large', and that in any case they 'are utterly opposed to the transfer from local government of the range of personal social services'. Inasmuch as the proposals in the Government's Green Papers on the National Health Service in England and Wales would leave the service outside the local government structure and subject to even more close central control and direction than hitherto, the Association finds them unacceptable.

(c). Responsibility for the unified National Health Service could properly be transferred to local government, but the financial implications and the levels of organisation needed to formulate general policy and secure overall coordination as distinct from the day-to-day running of the service would require detailed examination.

(d). The statutory boards for the gas and electricity industries are also too far removed from effective public participation, and the consultative councils have failed to bridge the gap between the area boards and the consumer, and to give the public any real opportunity to influence policy. There is clearly a case for making the supply and distribution of gas and electricity more responsive to the needs and wishes of the consumer by some form of integration into the local government organisation.

(e). The transfer of valuation for rating to the Inland Revenue in 1948 had the objective of greater uniformity of assessment, but there has been considerable dissatisfaction with the unevenness and anomalies thrown up by the revaluation for rating in 1963 and with the decision to abandon the 1968 revaluation because of the inability of the Inland Revenue to carry out their statutory obligation. The Association (in common with the other local authority Associations) has consistently claimed that valuation should again become a local government function. Here again, reorganisation creates the opportunity for a return at provincial level of the valuation function without any reduction in the standards of uniformity of valuation.

(f). It is for consideration also, whether the strategic economic role of provincial councils should be supplemented by the transfer from central government of responsibility for the location of industry and offices within the framework of national policies.

(g). Water supply, water conservation and river pollution which are largely the responsibility of *ad hoc* bodies, are all essentially functions capable of transfer to local government, and the Association, in its evidence to the Central Advisory Water Committee, has urged the need for those functions being integrated in any new local government structure.

(h). A provincial level of local government would create greater opportunities than hitherto for the training and organised interchange of staff.

(*i*). As proposed in the Maud Report, provincial councils should be responsible for the work at present done by the regional sports councils and regional arts associations.

(*j*). If approval is given to the recommendation of the Committee on Management of Local Government (*Volume I, p.* 81) that a procedure should be introduced for local government measures similar to that for Measures of the Church Assembly, then consideration ought to be given to the possibility of the procedure operating at provincial council level.

21. The Association emphasises that the preceding paragraph does not purport to be final in its content. It indicates some of the functions which could be the responsibility of a reorganised local government structure covering provincial councils.

Index

Index

All entries in *italics* indicate publications